Orkney and Shetland Islands

including North & Northeast Scotland

Published by
Imray, Laurie, Norie & Wilson Ltd
Wych House St Ives Cambridgeshire PE27 5BT England
☎ +44 (0)1480 462114 *Fax* +44 (0)1480 496109
Email ilnw@imray.com
www.imray.com
2016

ISBN 978 184623 579 5

British Library Cataloguing in Publication Data.
A catalogue record for this title is available from the British Library.

The last input of technical information was February 2016.

CAUTION

Whilst the publishers and author have used reasonable endeavours to ensure the accuracy of the contents of these Sailing Directions they contain selected information and thus are not definitive and do not include all known information for each and every location described, nor for all conditions of weather and tide. They are written for yachts of moderate draught and should not be used by larger craft. They should be used only as an aid to navigation in conjunction with official charts, pilots, hydrographic data and all other information, published or unpublished, available to the navigator. Skippers should not place reliance on these Sailing Directions in preference to exercising their own judgement.

The plans in these Sailing Directions are designed to support the text and should at all times be used with navigational charts.

To the extent permitted by law, the Publishers and Author do not accept liability for any loss and/or damage howsoever caused that may arise from reliance on these Sailing Directions nor for any error, omission or failure to update the information that they contain.

THIS PRODUCT IS NOT TO BE USED FOR NAVIGATION

The UK Hydrographic Office (UKHO) and its licensors make no warranties or representations, express or implied, with respect to this product. The UKHO and its licensors have not verified the information within this product or quality assured it.

CORRECTIONS AND UPDATES

These Sailing Directions may be amended at intervals by the issue of correctional supplements. These are published at www.clyde.org and www.imray.com and may be downloaded free of charge. Printed copies are also available on request from the publishers at the above address.

The publishers and author will at all times be grateful to receive corrections and information which tends to the improvement of the work.

Printed in Croatia by Zrinski

CCC Sailing Directions and Anchorages

Orkney and Shetland Islands

including North & Northeast Scotland

Edited by **Iain and Barbara MacLeod**

in collaboration with
Edward Mason, Editor, Clyde Cruising Club Sailing Directions

Imray Laurie Norie & Wilson Ltd

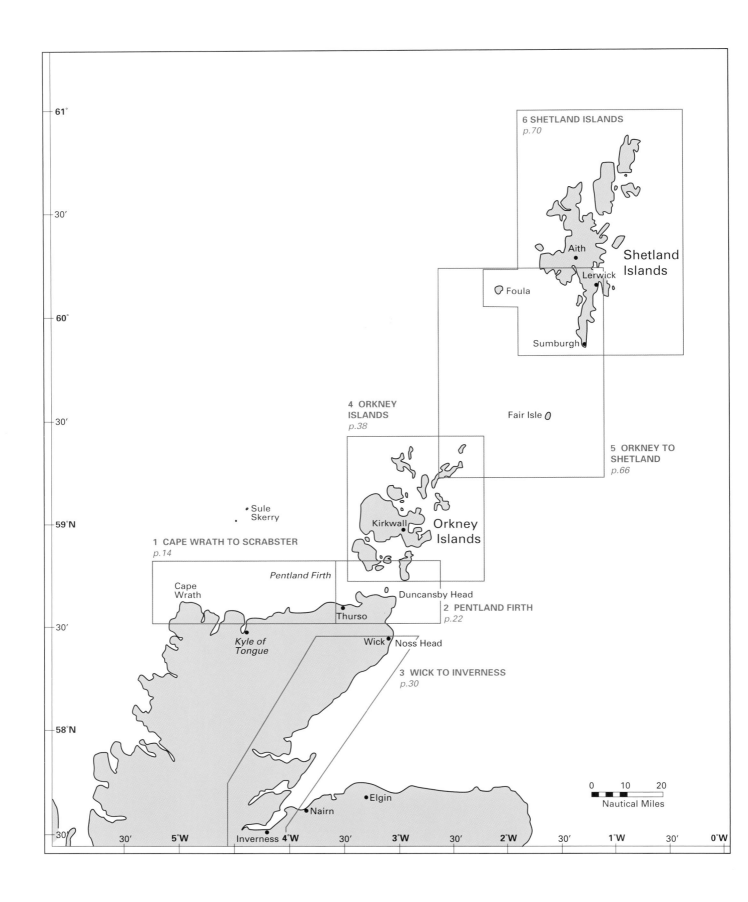

61°

30'

60°

30'

59°N

58°N

30'

30'   5°W   4°W   30'   3°W   30'   2°W   30'   1°W   30'   0°W

6 SHETLAND ISLANDS
p.70

Aith

Lerwick

Foula

Shetland
Islands

Sumburgh

**4 ORKNEY
ISLANDS**
p.38

Fair Isle

**5 ORKNEY TO
SHETLAND**
p.66

Sule
Skerry

Kirkwall   Orkney
Islands

1 CAPE WRATH TO SCRABSTER
p.14

Pentland Firth

Cape
Wrath

Duncansby Head

2 PENTLAND FIRTH
p.22

Thurso

*Kyle of
Tongue*

Wick   Noss Head

3 WICK TO INVERNESS
p.30

Elgin

0   10   20

Nautical Miles

Nairn

Inverness

Contents

Preface

It is now almost forty years since the Clyde Cruising Club published, under the hand of Godfrey Vinycomb, the Editor of the Sailing Directions throughout the 1970s, the *Shetland Sailing Directions*. This was the last of the three books that the CCC had undertaken to produce as part of the plan, formulated by the Conference of Yacht Cruising Clubs, to provide yachtsmen with sailing directions for the entire UK coastline. The three slim volumes continued to sell until stocks were exhausted and in 2003 they were thoroughly revised, updated and published in two books, by the then editor, Arthur Houston.

Since then they have been revised several times but the Club's collaboration with Imray, Laurie, Norie and Wilson in 2010 has eventually led to another complete reappraisal and updating of the content: the result is this book which includes both the Shetland and Orkney Islands as well as the Scottish north and northeast coast from Cape Wrath to Inverness. The latter is a condensed version of our previous book and includes only those harbours likely to be of interest to, and accessible by, deep-keeled yachts on passage to the Northern Isles from either the west coast or the Caledonian Canal at Inverness.

Smaller craft, and those who would like to spend more time exploring the north and northeast Scottish coast, will find that Martin Lawrence's *Yachtsman's Pilot, North and East Scotland*, also published by Imray and still available, remains the definitive guide to this coastline whilst also extending southwards to the English border. The latest edition of this was published in 2009 and Imrays have plans in hand for a replacement but no date for publication has yet been fixed.

Godfrey Vinycomb's statement in the introduction to the first edition of *Shetland*, 'the only drawback to cruising in Shetland is the time it takes to get there' is as true now as it ever was and, if possible, it is best to allow

Slow progress and a wild ride in Eynhallow Sound, Orkney. Entering from the west with 15 knots of wind against a 6 knot west-going tide. (See p.56)

Barrie Waugh

Barbara MacLeod

A variety of vessels berthed in the Albert Dock, Lerwick, Shetland

at least four weeks if both the Orkney and Shetland Islands are to be visited, assuming a start from any of Scotland's major yacht harbours. Even so, this will not give enough time to do either of these destinations justice and, unless time is no object, it would be better to plan to leave the boat for several weeks between cruises and make a season of it. With the establishment of marinas where a boat can be left safely, particularly in Orkney, it is now so much easier to do this than it was forty years ago and ferry and air services are also much improved.

Sailors familiar with the west coast of Scotland, who enjoy seeking out snug, remote anchorages, will be delighted to find that Shetland has also a large number of such places and, moreover, they are all within a small compass. Compared with the west coast, distances are small and many more places can be visited provided the urge to push on can be resisted.

Orkney, on the other hand, is different in almost every respect, apart from the friendliness of its inhabitants. From a sailor's point of view, strong tidal streams and fewer natural anchorages offering all-round protection might seem to be a drawback but if the tides are used, as they have to be, fast passages are frequently possible and the excellent local marine forecasts will ensure that a safe anchorage can always be found.

All in all, a summer spent cruising in the Northern Isles, including the easy two-day passage between Orkney and Shetland with a stop at Fair Isle, will provide the most challenging, varied and rewarding sailing to be found anywhere in Europe.

Acknowledgements

The publication of *Orkney and Shetland Islands* marks the completion of the project to transfer the publication of all the CCC's Sailing Directions to Imrays and, in the case of the west coast books, their merging with the *Yachtsman's Pilots* of Martin Lawrence. It would not have been possible for this to have been achieved within a five year time scale without some editorial assistance and I am very grateful to fellow members Iain and Barbara MacLeod, who offered to take on the considerable task of editing the two previous books into this single, expanded and updated volume. They have done it very well.

This is the first time that editing has been carried out by anyone other than the Club's Editor of Sailing Directions and now that we are in partnership with a specialist publisher, who can provide the necessary consistency and continuity, it may well be that it will set a pattern for the future, allowing more members to become involved.

Many people have provided us with information for this new edition. We would like to thank in particular:
John Hinckley, David Bowdler and Tom Rendall (Orkney); Robert Wishart, Dennis Geldard and Andrew Nisbet (Shetland); Ian Cormack (Coxswain of the Wick Lifeboat); Tony Howard and Geoff Crowley (CCC members).

Finally, nothing would have been possible without the calm competence of Elinor Cole of Imrays, who has had to cope with not only receiving copy from two editors but also disruptive interventions from myself.

Edward Mason,
Editor, *CCC Sailing Directions*
January 2016

Introduction

The areas covered by this book, the north and far northeast coasts of Scotland, the Orkney Islands and the Shetland Islands, all differ markedly in character and in the sailing experience that each offers. When, in the early 1970s, the Clyde Cruising Club (CCC) first extended their Sailing Directions to include them, they were the subject of three separate volumes, each with its own brief introductory description of the cruising pleasures and challenges that could expected. Now, with the merging of the three books into one, these general observations can be found at the beginning of each chapter and this Introduction deals only with those topics which are common to all.

Readers familiar with the CCC's other books will recognise much of the introductory material but it is indicative of the conditions that can be anticipated throughout these northern waters, especially in the Orkneys,

that a new section has been incorporated dealing specifically with tidal streams and their effect. Nowhere is this more pertinent than in the Pentland Firth which has now been given a full chapter of its own.

While careful preparation, planning and navigation are required for cruising in this area area, it can be relied upon to provide a different and rewarding sailing experience.

Emergencies

Coastguard

For all emergencies including medical emergencies the coastguard should be contacted as follows:

Shetland Coastguard For the north coast of Scotland, Orkney Isles, Shetland Isles, and the northeast coast of Scotland above 58°N (Brora), maritime rescue is coordinated by Shetland Coastguard. They listen on Channel

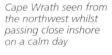

Cape Wrath seen from the northwest whilst passing close inshore on a calm day

Edward Mason

16, VHF DSC and MF DSC (but not on Medium Frequency (voice)) ☎ 01595 692976 or 999.

Aberdeen Coastguard South of 58°N Aberdeen Coastguard should be contacted ☎ 01224 592334.

Lifeboats

Lifeboats maintained and manned by the RNLI are stationed at:

Northern Scottish Mainland All-weather lifeboats: Lochinver, Thurso, Wick, Invergordon, Buckie. Inshore lifeboat at Kessock (Inverness).

Orkney All-weather lifeboats at Longhope, Stromness and Kirkwall.

Shetland All weather lifeboats at Lerwick and Aith.

Medical

In the event of requiring medical assistance the coastguard should be contacted.

Weather

Although the areas covered in these Directions have a reputation for high winds, gales are normally confined to the winter months. During the four summer months, May through to August, the mean wind strength is force 3–4 and, on average, only three gales can be expected during this period. The average air temperature is about 1° to 2° lower in the northern coasts and islands as compared with the west coast of Scotland.

Fog occurs most frequently in summer and can be experienced for approximately 3 days each month in the Northern Isles but less in the Moray Firth.

Weather forecasts

Yachtsmen tend to rely on the Maritime Safety Information (MSI) forecasts broadcast by the Maritime and Coastguard Agency (MCA).

Ronnie Robertson

Looking out over Spiggie Loch with Foula in the distance

BBC radio forecasts

Forecast	Station
Shipping	BBC Radio 4 VHF 92·4–94·6 MHz and LW 198 kHz (1500m) Broadcast at: 0048, 0520, 1201 (LW only), 1734 (LW only)
Inshore waters	BBC Radio 4 198 kHz (1500m) and VHF frequencies Broadcast at: 0053 and 0525
Landward forecasts	BBC Radio Scotland 810 kHz (370m) and VHF 92.4-94.6 MHz

Areas covered in the forecasts

Schedule	Inshore	Shipping
Shetland	Cape Wrath to Rattray Head including Orkney, Shetland	Faeroes, Fair Isle, Viking, Cromarty
Aberdeen	Cape Wrath to Rattray Head, Rattray Head to Berwick	Fair Isle, Cromarty, Forth, Forties, Tyne

Times of Maritime Safety Information broadcasts, local times

Schedule	B	C	A	C	B	C	A	C
Shetland	0110	0410	0710	1010	1310	1610	1910	2210
Aberdeen	0130	0430	0730	1030	1330	1630	1930	2230

Schedule A - Full Maritime Safety Information broadcast, including new 24 hour Inshore Forecast and 24 hour Outlook, Gale Warnings, Shipping Forecast, WZ Navigation Warnings, SUBFACTS & GUNFACTS where appropriate, 3 Day Fisherman's Forecast when and where appropriate.

Schedule B - New 24 hour Inshore Forecast and 24 hour outlook plus Gale Warnings.

Schedule C - Repetition of Inshore Forecast and Gale Warnings as per previous Schedule A or B broadcast plus new strong wind warnings.

Forecasts may be delayed or omitted during casualty working.

MSI channels and aerials

Aerial Site*	VHF *	MRCC	
		Shetland	Aberdeen
Saxavord (Unst)	23	√	
Collafirth (NW Shetland)	86	√	
Lerwick	84	√	
Fitful Head (SW Shetland)	23	√	
Wideford (nr. Kirkwall)	86	√	
Durness (E of Cape Wrath)	23	√	√
Noss Head (N of Wick)	84	√	√
Rosemarkie (57°50'N) near Tarbat Ness	86	√	√

• *For positions of aerials see plan below*

Navtex

Navtex broadcasts inshore forecasts and 24 hour outlook forecasts:

Station: Cullercoats (U), 490kHz

Inshore areas included: Cape Wrath to Rattray Head including Orkney, Shetland

UTC times: 0720, 1120, 1920, 2320

Equipment

Yachts cruising in the northern waters of the British Isles need to be more self reliant, and thus better crewed and equipped than may be necessary in more sheltered waters. The Royal Yachting Association publication *Boat Safety Handbook* provides sound standards to follow (www.rya.org.uk/shop).

Fishing equipment

Because the positions of fish farms often change they are not identified in these Directions. They are common in the Northern Isles so care is needed to avoid them by maintaining a careful lookout. Creel buoys and other fishing equipment such as mussel farms are also common hazards. If going into a bay at night to anchor, the use of a searchlight is strongly advised to identify such hazards not shown on charts.

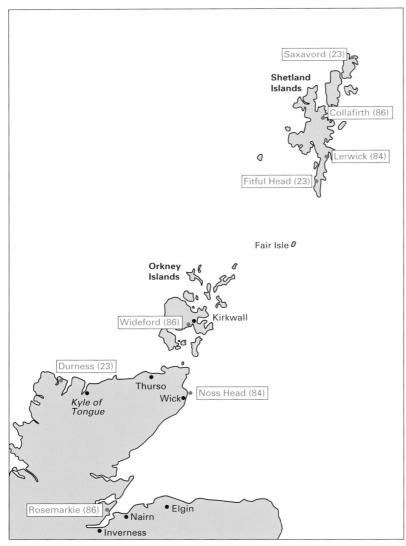

MSI AERIALS

Tidal information

Tidal constants

Constants quoted are for high tide levels and not for tidal stream times. Values quoted are average figures and may vary by half an hour or more either way.

Generally, but not invariably, Neaps (Np) are earlier and Springs (Sp) later. Constants are usually given for both local standard ports and for Dover, but the difference between tides at Dover and local ports may vary by as much as 40 minutes so that using Dover tide tables will give less accuracy than tables for local standard ports.

The tidal constants (i.e. the average difference between the time of high tide at a location and at a standard port) have been re-established for these Directions. This has been done on the basis of:

1. For constants on standard ports – from the average of the four values of time differences given in the *Admiralty Tide Tables United Kingdom and Ireland* NP201 2015.

2. For constants on Dover – from values quoted on the last page of the *Admiralty Tidal Stream Atlas Orkney and Shetland Islands* NP209 2012.

Only constants for the ports listed in the *Admiralty Tide Tables* are given in this volume.

The standard ports used in the *Admiralty Tide Tables* and in these Directions are:

- *Wick* for Orkney, the North Coast and the north part of the Northeast Coast
- *Invergordon* for the southern part of the Northeast Coast
- *Lerwick* for Shetland and Fair Isle

The values quoted for tidal constants in the previous edition of these Directions mainly used Aberdeen as the standard port.

It is best to have tide tables for the standard ports on board but if you only have the Dover tide table then the constants for the standard ports on Dover are:

Wick: +0010

Invergordon: +0014

Lerwick: −0014

Tidal heights

Heights are for rise in metres above Chart Datum, not for range except where mean levels of HW and LW are given.

Heights of tides are represented by five values:

Mean High Water Springs (MHWS)

Mean High Water Neaps (MHWN)

Mean Tide Level (MTL)

Mean Low Water Neaps, (MLWN)

Mean Low Water Springs (MLWS)

The word 'Mean' is important because, for example, Low Water Springs in any particular fortnight may be substantially higher or lower than the mean.

Only tidal heights for the ports listed in the *Admiralty Tide Tables* are given in this volume. The values quoted in these Directions were calculated by adding the differences for the port to the height for the standard port.

A simple way to assess the height of low water at a port for which data is provided is:

1. **Find the time of LW at the port** for the day in question by adding the tidal constant for the port to the time of LW at the standard port.

2. **Calculate the mean tidal range at Dover** for that day (i.e. subtract the height of HW from that of LW from values in the tide table for Dover).

3. **Establish the nature of the tide in relation to springs and neaps.** Compare the mean tidal range for the day at Dover with the following ranges:

Mean range (m)
LAT*	2·0
MLWN	3·2
MHWS	6·0
HAT**	7·0

*   *Lowest Astronomical Tide*
** *Highest Astronomical Tide*

For example if the mean tidal range at Dover is 3·4m then low tide will be just above MLWN.

4. **Estimate the height of the tide above chart datum** on that day from the values in the table in the Directions.

For example if the port was Kirkwall the tidal heights are:

MHWS	MHWN	MTL	MLWN	MLWS
3·4	2·7	2·1	1·6	0·8

Therefore an estimate of the height of the tide above chart datum at low water at the port would be 1·7m (i.e. just above MLWN = 1·6m.)

More accurate predictions of tidal heights than from the tables in these Directions may be obtained using methods described in the *Admiralty Tidal Atlas* or in an Almanac such as *Reeds*.

Software for tidal predictions is also available for computers, iPads and phones. As for all electronic sources it is strongly recommended that a paper version of the tide tables is also kept on board e.g. the CCC *Yearbook* gives a table of the tidal heights at Dover.

Tidal streams

Rates of tidal streams are given in knots (kn). Standard ports for the tidal stream constants in these *Directions* are:

- *Ullapool:* for Cape Wrath to Kyle of Tongue
- *Aberdeen:* for Orkney and the Northeast Coast
- *Lerwick:* for Fair Isle and Shetland

Tidal stream information can be found:

1. in the *Admiralty Tidal Stream Atlas Orkney and Shetland Islands* NP209 (Essential to have on board) and the unpublished Admiralty tidal stream diagrams for the Westray and Stronsay Firths, reproduced on pp.142–144

2. from tables for the tide diamonds on Admiralty charts

3. from the *Admiralty Sailing Directions North Coast of Scotland Pilot* NP52 2012.

The values for tidal stream times quoted in this volume are those that are available in the *Admiralty Sailing Directions*.

Working the tides

If not considered in the passage plan, the tidal streams in the Northern Isles can cause much difficulty and be dangerous. If you work them, the tides can be a boon. They can give you speedy and relatively calm passages: calm, because they can overpower wind generated waves. This section gives advice about how to work them. To many, making use of the tides is a major positive feature of cruising in the Northern Isles.

Directions of the tidal streams

The flood tide runs eastwards in east-west oriented channels and southwards in north-south channels. However the time of high tide and the turn of the tidal stream can be out of phase. In these Directions the stream direction is identified in relation to its direction and not to whether it is ebbing or flooding.

That the tidal flow rate at springs can be more than twice than at neaps needs to be taken into account.

Roosts

A main danger is broken water. *The Dictionary of the Scots Language* has the following definition:

ROUST, n. Also roost, rust; rost; roast. A turbulent stretch of sea caused by a strong current in a restricted passage or by the meeting of conflicting currents, specif. in the seas between Sh. and Ork. between the Atlantic Ocean and the North Sea.

There is usually white water at a roost but just because there is no white water does not mean that there can be no problems with turbulence.

The word 'overfall' is used in other CCC *Sailing Directions* but the local term 'roost' (using the local spelling) is also used in this volume.

Reasons for a roost to form include rapid changes in the profile of the sea bottom and waves against tide. For example the water depth in the Pentland Firth increases quickly to the west of the line from Tor Ness on Hoy and west of St John's Point on the Scottish mainland. On the west-going tide this causes a roost to form right across the Firth known as the 'Merry Men of Mey'.

Roosts are best avoided unless you have local knowledge about them.

Waves

Waves can be generated by local winds or can be swell coming in from the North Sea or more commonly from the Atlantic. The fetch for a westerly wind on the west coast of the

Gutcher Bay, Shetland

Chris Downer - Geograph

Northern Isles goes all the way to Canada so big swells can come in from the west.

Local wind waves can die out quite quickly after the wind pipes down but swell is likely to be more persistent.

Waves against tide

While roosts can form in calm weather they become much more dangerous when opposed by swell or local waves. Wind against tide can make the going difficult even with no roost and with relatively light winds. Under such conditions waves tend to be steeper and shorter in length making progress against them difficult especially for small boats. So a roost with a strong wind against a spring tide is likely to be a major hazard – not worth risking.

On a longer passage it may not be possible to avoid going to windward against a tide but it is often possible to get away from the main tidal stream as described below.

Passage planning to work the tides

Identify the times of HW Dover for the day in question and the timings of the tidal streams in the line of the passage to be planned.

Where the tide is going to be strong, plan to have it with you for as long as possible. If you are sailing in a channel, keep to mid-channel to get the best lift from the tide.

If you need to work your way against the tide, keep close to the shore if you can. Go in to bays (watching out for hazards such as shallows, rocks, fish farms, lobster buoys, etc.) to get a slacker stream or often an eddy that will give you lift against the direction of the main stream.

Look out for eddies; they can help you if you work them or hinder you if you neglect them.

Notes on sailing directions and plans

Plans

Symbols used on the plans are illustrated on the front cover flap and on page 13.

The plans given in this guide are compiled from a number of sources but are mainly based on British Admiralty charts with the permission of the Hydrographer for the Navy. They are intended as an illustrated guide to the text and should not be used for navigation.

Generally the conventions used on Admiralty charts have been followed so that these Directions may be used with them.

All plans are drawn with North at the top except where stated. All depths are in metres. None of the plans are to a recognised scale and the drawn scale should be used to estimate distances. They only provide information relevant to the size of craft for which these Directions are written.

Bearings and distances

The bearings given in these Sailing Directions both in text and on the plans are always from seaward and always refer to True North.

Distances are given in nautical miles and cables (10ths of a nautical mile); distances of less than a cable are generally expressed in metres.

Depths and heights

These are given in metres to correspond with the current Admiralty charts. Depths are related to the current chart datum which is generally lower than that on older charts. This datum, the lowest astronomical tide (LAT) is the lowest level to which the surface of the sea is expected to fall owing to astronomical causes. If high barometric pressure and/or strong offshore winds coincide with a low spring tide, the water may fall below this level, in which case there will be less depth than shown on the chart, or sketch plan.

Heights are given as the clear height above the highest astronomical tide (HAT) which is higher than the previously quoted MHWS used on older charts and previous editions of the *Sailing Directions*.

LD means Least Depth.

Place names

In some cases the popular name for a place, or its spelling, differs from that on Admiralty charts. The latter is normally given. For guidance on local names and terms relating to the topography etc. in Orkney see p.142.

Lights

The position and characteristics of lights are shown on the plans. **They are not listed in the text as in previous editions.**

Light characteristics are as used on Admiralty charts.

F	fixed
Fl	flashing
Gp Fl or Fl( )	Group flashing
Occ or Oc	Occulting at regular intervals
Iso	Isophase - equal duration of light and eclipse
Q or Qk Fl	Quick Flashing - about 60 flashes per minute
VQ or V Qk Fl	Very Quick Flashing - about 120 flashes per minute
s or sec	time in seconds to exhibit one complete sequence
M	maximum distance in sea miles at which a light can be seen when visibility is 10 miles (taking account of the earth's curvature)
m	elevation of light source above HW in metres

Colours of lights, buoys and beacons (lights are white if not stated) are:

B   black
Bu   blue
G   green
R   red
V   violet
W   white
Y   yellow

Sectors and arcs of visibility and the alignment of direction lights and leading lights, are given in the text and on the plans as seen by an observer from seaward. All bearings are relative to True North.

Changes, corrections and supplements

Despite appearances, things do change. Buoys, lights, piers, pontoons and many shoreside facilities slowly evolve. Readers are asked to bear this in mind and to make sure that they have the latest amendments issued at intervals on the CCC and Imray websites, and also to report any discrepancies, or even uncertainties, which may be further investigated by other readers.

This is greatly appreciated not only by the Club and publishers, but also by the Hydrographic Office to whom any relevant information is forwarded.

Shetland Bus Memorial, Scalloway

Edward Mason

Charts and maps

Charts

These Directions contain many plans but they are not intended as a substitute for Admiralty charts. Although many of the plans in this book are of a larger scale than the charts and include more detail, they cover only small areas and it is essential to have a comprehensive set of charts at both small and large scales. A list of current charts for the area covered by these Directions is given in the Appendix (p.138). For passage-making, Imray's charts C23 and C68, at a scale of around 1:150,000, are very useful for giving an overview of the areas that they cover and provide a lot of detail.

The increasing use of chart plotters has greatly reduced the practice of plotting on paper charts. However, the limitations of the charts used as the basis of the plotter display must be recognised and due allowance made. This is acknowledged by the UKHO which has the following cautionary note on many of its charts:

'Mariners are warned that positions obtained from Global Navigation Satellite Systems such as GPS, may be more accurate than the charted detail, due to the age and quality of some of the source information. Mariners are therefore advised to exercise particular caution when navigating close to the shore or in the vicinity of dangers.'

The ability to enlarge the area of interest on a plotter display to a size much bigger than the original chart can easily lead to a false sense of security and must be guarded against. Even the latest editions of UKHO charts using information from recent surveys are unlikely to incorporate more accurate detail in the many anchorages into which a yacht may sometimes enter. If traditional bearings, transits and leading lines are available they should be used in preference to blind reliance on a plotter.

Maps

Ordnance Survey maps at 1:50,000 are well worth having on board to make up for the lack of topographical detail on current charts. For list see p.140. In places where the charts are at a small scale, the Ordnance Survey maps actually provide useful navigational detail. In some cases the OS Explorer series of maps at 1:25,000 supply essential detail where there is no Admiralty chart at an adequate scale.

Note that OS maps use a different grid of coordinates which do not even align with those of an Admiralty chart. Some GPS receivers can display OS coordinates.

Approaching North Harbour, Fair Isle

Edward Mason

Communications

VHF radiotelephones

The map on page 6 shows the locations of the main aerials used for radiotelephone communications.

Travel

The following transport services are available for the places covered by these Directions:

Mainland Scotland

Scrabster Rail and bus connections to Inverness from Thurso (short taxi ride from Scrabster); ferry to Stromness

Wick Rail and bus connection to Inverness; flights to Aberdeen

Gills Bay (W of John o' Groats) ferry to St Margaret's Hope; bus to Inverness

John o' Groats Passenger ferry to Burwick (south of South Ronaldsay) (summer only)

Orkney

Mainland Orkney Good bus service for travel on Mainland Orkney

Stromness Ferry to Scrabster

St Margaret's Hope (South Ronaldsay) Ferry to Gills Bay

Kirkwall Ferries to several Orkney Islands; ferry to Shetland; ferry to Aberdeen; flights to various locations

Houton Bay Ferry to Hoy

Shetland

Good bus service for island travel and inter-island ferries at various locations.

Sumburgh Airport: Flights to various locations

Lerwick Ferry to Aberdeen; ferry to Kirkwall

Access rights

In Scotland, since the Land Reform (Scotland) Act 2003 came into force, everyone has the statutory right of access to all land for recreational purposes, excluding hunting, shooting or fishing. These rights must be exercised responsibly and do not apply to houses and gardens, farmyards, growing crops and other commercial uses which are defined more fully in the Access Code published by Scottish National Heritage and available from tourist offices and the website: www.outdooraccess-scotland.com

Access rights apply equally to islands, despite the efforts of some owners to declare them private and forbid landing. The limitations on the access rights as stated in the paragraph above need, of course, to be observed.

Anchorages, moorings & berthing

As a heading throughout these Directions, this term covers not only locations where anchoring is possible but also mooring and berthing alongside.

These Sailing Directions aim to provide details of less familiar anchorages as well as the more popular ones. Independently minded yachtsmen will find, with the help of charts, sketch plans and experience, anchorages other than those described in this book.

Choosing an anchorage

The description 'occasional anchorage' is intended to convey that the place described is only suitable for use under certain conditions, perhaps for a brief visit ashore during daylight, or in winds from certain directions to await a change of wind or tide. In ideal conditions it might be possible for such places to be used overnight.

The description 'temporary anchorage' is used to describe an anchorage which must be used with caution even in good conditions and which would rarely ever be suitable for leaving a boat unattended or for anchoring overnight. The absence of the description 'occasional' or 'temporary' should not be taken as a recommendation that an anchorage may be used in any weather.

Some anchorages, and particularly piers and boat harbours, are only suitable for shoal-draught boats, and this should be obvious from the description; the inclusion of an anchorage does not imply that it is suitable for all yachts.

Within some anchorages there are often several suitable places to lie depending on weather conditions and the type of boat. It is not always practicable to describe them all, nor to mark each one on the plans.

Steep high ground to windward is unlikely to provide good shelter; in fresh winds there may be turbulent gusts on its lee side, or the wind may be deflected to blow from a completely different direction. Conversely, trees to windward will absorb a lot of wind and tend to improve the quality of the shelter.

Fish farms

Fish farming is a major industry throughout the Northern Isles. The temptation to anchor too close to a fish farm should be resisted.

There are two main forms: cages for 'fin fish' (usually salmon), and rows of buoys from which ropes are suspended, on which shellfish are 'grown'. These buoys may have ropes between them on, or close to, the surface.

The boundary of an area licensed for fish farming is sometimes marked by buoys, usually yellow and sometimes lit. These are often a long way from the cages, and there may or may not be moorings or other obstructions within the area marked out by the buoys. Anchor well clear of all fish farming equipment and, if in doubt, use a tripping line.

Moorings

Swinging moorings are much less common in the area covered by these Directions than on the West Coast of Scotland. The golden rules for using a mooring are to ensure that (a) you have the permission of the owner and (b) the mooring is strong enough for your boat.

Visitors' moorings

Orkney Islands Council provide visitors' moorings.

A good method to connect to a buoy that only has a ring is to use a length of nylon anchorplait which is made up with a hard eye at one end. The eye on this warp is connected to the eye on the buoy by a secure shackle. Failing this, it will be necessary to attach the rope to the ring using a fisherman's bend which will stop chafe but will be hard to undo and may even have to be cut off. The mooring warp should be fitted with a length of plastic tubing to prevent chafe at the bow roller. Care needs to be taken to ensure that the plastic tubing remains on the bow roller or fairlead. If plastic tubing is not available chaffing can be prevented by wrapping the warp with canvas or other cloth.

It is best practice to have at least two lines between the boat and the mooring.

A simple slip rope should be used only as a temporary arrangement whilst the main line is being attached or released. The practice of rafting up together on visitors' moorings is not encouraged.

Stromness Harbour looking towards Scapa Flow

David Bowdler

Marinas and yacht centres

On the Scottish mainland coast there are marinas at Scrabster, Wick and Inverness, and there is a pontoon at Helmsdale. In Orkney there are marina facilities for visiting yachts at Kirkwall, Stromness and Pierowall (Westray). In Shetland many harbours have floating pontoons that are called marinas but the facilities at them range from Lerwick that has good marina facilities to pontoons that do not have visitor berths and/or do not have sufficient depth for yachts. Details are provided in the text.

Further information can be found in *Welcome Anchorages* published annually and available free from marinas and other outlets or at www.welcome-anchorages.co.uk

For further information on the marinas etc. see Appendix p.138.

Quays, piers, jetties, slips, linkspans

These, and related structures, need some definition and description. The categories overlap and a structure identified on the chart may have fallen into disuse, or been replaced by one of a different type, or have a description well above its status. The definitions used in this book are as follows, and give some indication of what you might expect to find:

- A quay, wharf or pier is used by fishing boats and occasional coasters, and usually has at least 2 metres of water at its head at chart datum. It is often constructed of piles or open framing, or stone or concrete with vertical timber fendering, alongside which it is difficult for a small yacht to lie without a robust fender board. A pier projects from the shore, but a quay or wharf is either part of a harbour or parallel to the shore.

- Ferry terminals tend to have a linkspan for a bow-loading car ferry.

- A jetty is smaller and, for yachts, more user-friendly but often dries alongside.

- A slip, or slipway, runs down into the water, although its outer end may be above water at low tide and it may be used by a ferry to an inshore island. There is sometimes sufficient depth for a yacht to go alongside a slip for a brief visit ashore for stores.

Many of these structures are in regular use by fishermen whose livelihood depends on being able to land their produce quickly, and yachts should take care not to obstruct such use.

Principal chart symbols

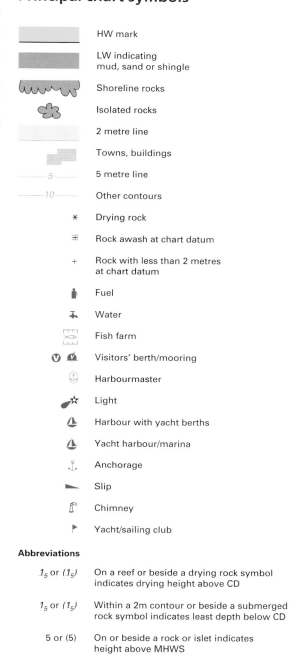

	HW mark
	LW indicating mud, sand or shingle
	Shoreline rocks
	Isolated rocks
	2 metre line
	Towns, buildings
5	5 metre line
10	Other contours
✳	Drying rock
⌗	Rock awash at chart datum
+	Rock with less than 2 metres at chart datum
	Fuel
	Water
	Fish farm
Ⓥ	Visitors' berth/mooring
	Harbourmaster
☆	Light
	Harbour with yacht berths
	Yacht harbour/marina
⚓	Anchorage
	Slip
	Chimney
	Yacht/sailing club

Abbreviations

1_5 or (1_5)	On a reef or beside a drying rock symbol indicates drying height above CD
1_5 or (1_5)	Within a 2m contour or beside a submerged rock symbol indicates least depth below CD
5 or (5)	On or beside a rock or islet indicates height above MHWS
M	Miles on land (1760 yards) Miles at sea (6080 feet)
m	Metres
c	Cable (1/10 nautical mile)
bn	Beacon

1. Cape Wrath to Scrabster

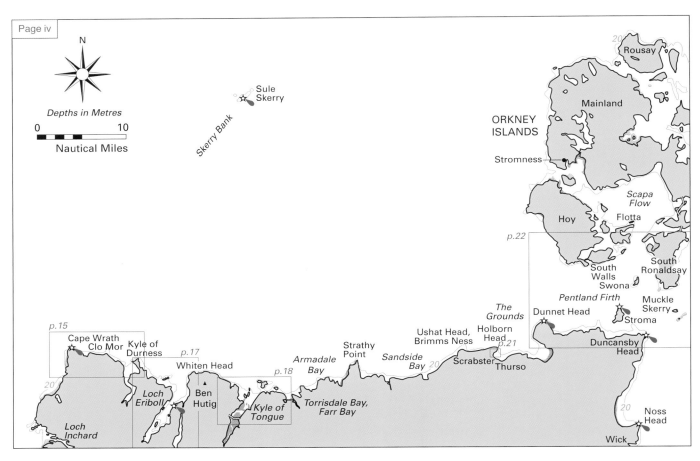

NORTH COAST

Admiralty Chart
1954, 1785, 0219

Imray Chart
C68

Ordnance Survey
9, 10

Rounding Cape Wrath

The name Cape Wrath comes from the Norse *hvarf*, a turning point. The huge cliffs of Clo Mor east of the Cape provide a magnificent bird sanctuary. In sunny weather the rock scenery on the northwest coast approaching Cape Wrath and along the north coast beyond the Cape is superb (see photograph p.4).

Great care must be taken in planning a passage round this major headland.

Tides

Between the entrance to Loch Inchard and Cape Wrath
North-going stream starts −0110 Ullapool (−0530 Dover)
South-going stream starts −0330 Ullapool (−0110 Dover)
Spring rate: 1·8kn

Close inshore southwest of Cape Wrath
A north-going eddy forms on the south-going stream. Therefore there is an almost continuous north-going stream in this area.

Between Cape Wrath and Stac Clo Kearvaig (2 miles east of Cape Wrath)
East-going stream starts −0350 Ullapool (+0415 Dover)
West-going stream starts +0235 Ullapool (−0145 Dover)
Max spring rate 3kn in both directions.

Close inshore east of Cape Wrath
A west-going eddy forms on the east-going stream. Therefore there is an almost continuous west-going stream in this area.

Between Stac Clo Kearvaig and Strathy Point (31 miles east of Cape Wrath)
East-going stream starts −0220 Ullapool (+0545 Dover)
West-going stream starts +0350 Ullapool (−0030 Dover)

Off Whiten Head and Strathy Point the spring rate can reach 3kn but the streams are weak off the bays and inlets.

The above information is for tidal streams close to the coast. For information about streams further offshore consult the *Admiralty Tidal Stream Atlas* NP209 or information on the charts.

Directions

At Cape Wrath there is a confluence of strong tides making it a very dangerous place in bad weather. It is totally exposed to the north and west and is frequently subject to very strong winds which build up a huge and dangerous sea in a very short time. Even in calm weather a large ocean swell is often present.

In light airs with no swell one can hold in quite close to the cliffs and inside Duslic Rock (a dangerous rock 7 cables northeast of the lighthouse, which almost always shows in the swell). In less benevolent conditions it is essential to keep well clear of the cape. If there is doubt about the conditions off the cape it is strongly advised to keep 3 to 5 miles off it.

Heading north and then east, it may be best to arrive at the cape at the start of the east-going tidal stream there.

If at Eilean an Roin Beag (at the entrance to Loch Inchard) there is a large irregular sea, then it will certainly get much worse approaching and rounding Cape Wrath. If, when 2 or 3 miles off the cape, white water is observed indicating turbulence from interacting eddies and breaking swell, then give Cape Wrath a wide berth.

To keep well clear of Cape Wrath head west from Loch Inchard then northwest; then steer to keep 3 to 5 miles off. If heading for Loch Eriboll or Kyle of Tongue, maintain this distance off until Cape Wrath bears approximately southwest, to seek to keep clear of the worst of the seas and tidal disturbance associated with the cape.

If the passage inshore between the cape and Duslic Rock is taken, then keep well clear of the dangerous shoal 5 cables offshore from An Garbh Eilean (30m high, grass covered, 3 cables offshore, 3¾ miles east-southeast of Cape Wrath). The summit of Ben Hutig (406m) to the southeast of Whiten Head (156m) bearing 113° and just open of Faraid Head leads northeast of An Garbh Eilean and the shoal. By keeping offshore this may also avoid an adverse tidal stream which can reach 3kn between Stac Clo Kervaig, 2 miles east of An Garbh Eilean, and Cape Wrath.

Firing Range An MOD Firing Practice Area extends up to 4¼ miles offshore east of Cape Wrath (see limits on Chart 1954) and when it is in use, red flags (at night 2FR vert lights) are shown at the east and west land limits of the range.

Before embarking on a passage through the area listen to Marine Safety Information broadcast by Stornoway CG at weather forecast times or call Stornoway CG on VHF Ch16 to confirm if there are any Gunfacts Warnings in force for the Cape Wrath Firing Practice Range. Alternatively, contact the Range directly on ☎ 0800 833 300.

Heading west and then south, the same principles of using the tides and keeping clear of Cape Wrath as described above are relevant.

Cape Wrath to Orkney

To break the journey to Orkney one can anchor at Loch Eriboll or at Talmine on the Kyle of Tongue. These are the only two places that provide good shelter for yachts. There are other places on the north coast between Cape Wrath and Scrabster that might be explored in good weather, for example: Kyle of Durness, sandy bays at Torrisdale, Farr and Armadale; Sandside Bay and Sandside Harbour.

As you approach Orkney it should be remembered that there is no sheltered anchorage on the west side of Orkney. When the west-going stream gets going, the Pentland

CAPE WRATH

Rispond Bay and harbour, Loch Eriboll

Firth, Hoy Sound, Eynhallow Sound and Westray Firth have strong tides which may be dangerous and against which it may be impossible to make headway.

For entry to the Pentland Firth see p.25
For entry to Hoy Sound see p.41
For entry to Eynhallow Sound see p.56
For entry to Westray Firth see p.58

Loch Eriboll

Admiralty Chart
2076
Imray Chart
C68
Ordnance Survey
9, 10

Lying 12½ miles east of Cape Wrath, Loch Eriboll provides a variety of anchorages which yachts use to break the passage to or from Orkney.

Tides

Tidal streams in the Loch are weak. There are strong tidal streams off Faraid Head and confused seas off Whiten Head even in good weather.

Constant –0310 Wick (–0310 Dover)

Height in metres

MHWS	MHWN	MTL	MLWN	MLWS
5·1	4·1	3·0	2·2	1·1

Directions

Whiten Head (156m) can be identified from the west by prominent white stacks known as the Sisters, that show up against the cliffs and from the north by a large cliff area of stratified white quartz.

Enter the loch between it and An Dubh Sgeir, the most northerly of the group of islands on the west side of the entrance. After rounding An Dubh Sgeir, make for the east side of Eilean Cluimhrig. On clearing this island head into the loch which narrows at White Head on the east side. This point is easily recognised by the large white patch on the rocks below the light (Fl.WR.10s) showing white over the clear water between Eilean Cluimrhig and the east shore and red to the west between the shore and the islands.

2½ miles further up, Eilean Choraidh lies in the fairway and can be passed on either hand. If using the west passage keep to mid-channel where the water is clear at a reasonable distance offshore, and continue up to the head of the loch which shoals out for about 2 cables. In southwesterly winds fierce squalls funnel down the loch.

Anchorages

Eilean Hoan Temporary anchorage can be found on the south side in 4–5m but it is subject to swell in northerly and southerly winds.

Rispond Bay is an excellent anchorage on the west shore just inside the entrance to Loch Eriboll and southwest of Eilean Cluimhrig. Anchor in the bay where the bottom is sandy in 4–5m but the swinging room may be restricted due to moorings. Good shelter in all winds except from the east. Beware of Rispond Rock (dries 0·9m) a little over a cable from Rubha na Creig' Airde, the southeast point of Rispond Bay.

Rispond Harbour at the head of the bay is privately owned and should not be used without the owner's permission. It has a sandy bottom but can only be entered at half tide and has 3·5m alongside at MHWS.

Portnancon is a convenient anchorage on the west shore opposite Ard Neackie and gives good shelter from the west and north. Anchor in 5·5m northeast of the pier but not too far into the bay as it shoals. If attaching a line to the pier, beware of visiting fishing boats.

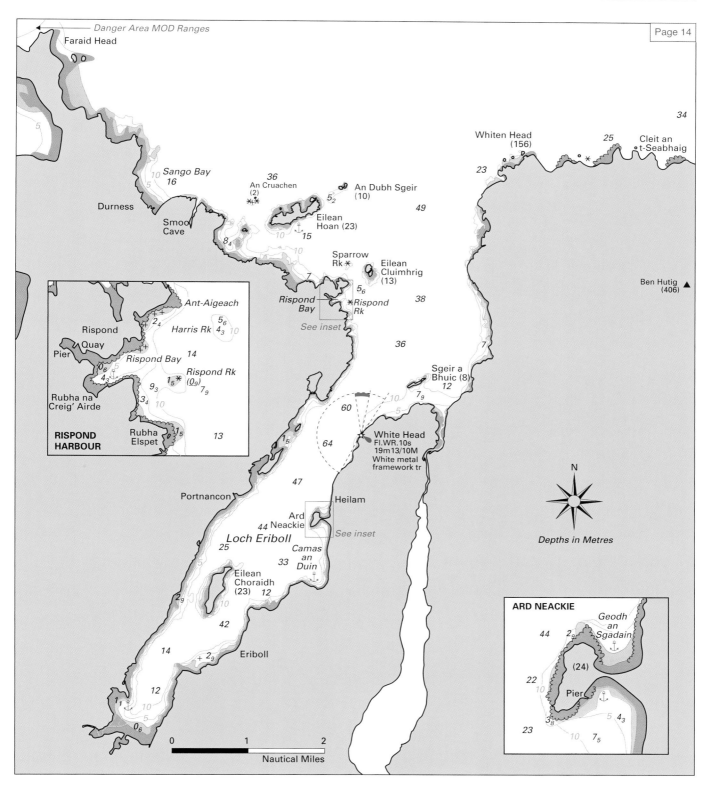

Camas an Duin is the best anchorage on the east side of the loch, well sheltered from the southwest. Anchor in 7m off the white house.

Ard Neackie is a promontory on the east side of the loch 1½ miles south southwest of White Head light. This promontory has north and south anchorages giving between them good shelter.

The main road A838 runs along the east side of the southern anchorage. The northern anchorage has a sandy beach and there are patches of weed in the southern one.

LOCH ERIBOLL

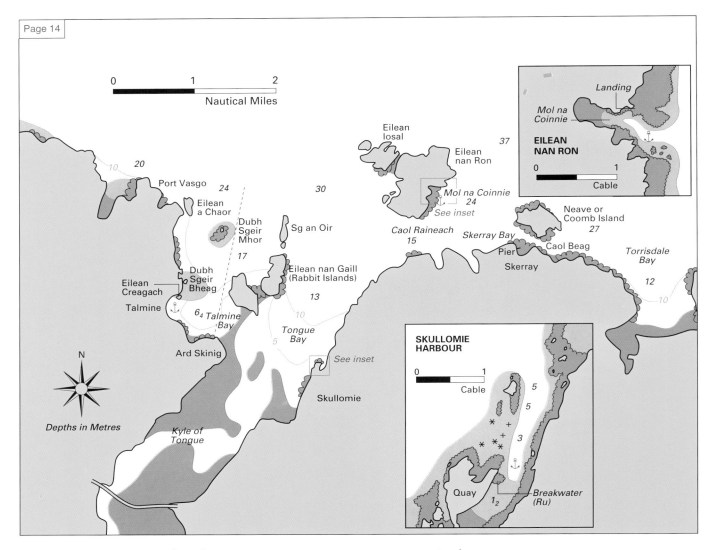

Page 14

EILEAN NAN RON

SKULLOMIE HARBOUR

Depths in Metres

Kyle of Tongue

KYLE OF TONGUE

Admiralty Chart
1954

Imray Chart
C68

Ordnance Survey
10

Kyle of Tongue

The Kyle of Tongue has a number of anchorages which give shelter, but entry during gales or strong winds from the north is not recommended.

Tides

The tidal streams are weak in the Kyle.

In Caol Raineach (between Eilean nan Ron and the Mainland)

East-going stream starts −0220 Ullapool (+0545 Dover)
West-going stream starts +0350 Ullapool (−0030 Dover)
Spring rate: 2kn in both directions

On the west-going stream dangerous turbulence can form on the south side of the narrowest part of Caol Raineach.

Directions

When approaching Talmine from the west do not turn south until the west side of the westernmost Rabbit Island closes Ard Skinid. Keep 2 cables off the west shore of that island until the point is abeam, and then steer to the south side of Eilean Creagach to anchor off Talmine, in a pleasant bay ringed with cottages.

Anchorages

Talmine gives shelter from southeast through west to the north. Anchor in 5·5m off the end of the slip. Beware of heavy mooring ground chains. Bottom sand.

Eilean nan Ron A small very small inlet, no more than 50m wide at most, Mol na Coinnie, on the southeast side of the island gives shelter from westerly and northwesterly winds. The island is uninhabited.

Rabbit Islands Shelter from west to northerly winds can be found off the beach in the bay on the south side of the largest island in 5·5m. The only approach is from Tongue Bay.

Skullomie Harbour This very small harbour on the east shore gives shelter from the east. The entrance is difficult to identify and is best done from the Rabbit Islands. Looking southeast, the harbour is directly below a house on the hillside. Anchor just outside the entrance towards the east shore and well clear of the ruined breakwater.

Supplies

Talmine Stores and Post Office which has full banking service; hotel.

Talmine harbour

Skullomie Harbour

Martin Lawrence

Torrisdale Bay

Admiralty Chart
1954

Imray Chart
C68

Ordnance Survey
10 11

Kyle of Tongue to Scrabster

Once east of Kyle of Tongue a series of sandy bays dominate the shore until Strathy Point is reached.

Strathy Point, where the mountainous scenery gives way to gentle slopes of no great height, is the meeting place of fairly strong tides and eddies, and the sea in this area off the point is usually turbulent. Keep well off. In this area there is a tendency for the weather to be more rainy to the west and more misty to the east. Strathy Point often marks the difference in local weather conditions.

From Strathy Point to Holborn Head, a distance of 15 miles, the coast is cliff-like and increasingly rock-bound. Just east of Ushat Head, Brimms Ness has a drying ledge of rock extending 2 cables north and a further submerged (8m) reef for 2 cables beyond the end of the ledge. It requires a wide berth.

Tides

Between Stac Clo Kearvaig and Strathy Point (31 miles east of the Cape Wrath)
East-going stream starts –0220 Ullapool (+0545 Dover)
West-going stream starts +0350 Ullapool (–0030 Dover)
Off Whiten Head and Strathy Point the spring rate can reach 3kn but the streams are weak off the bays and inlets.

Anchorages

Torrisdale, Farr and Armadale These sandy bays may be visited in gentle settled weather.

Sandside Bay lies 7 miles east-southeast from Strathy Point and 1½ miles west of Dounreay Nuclear Complex with its conspicuous sphere (58m).

Scrabster Harbour

Barbara MacLeod

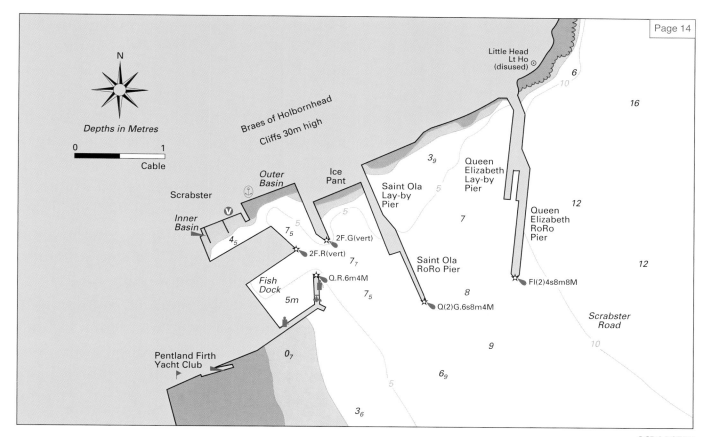

SCRABSTER

Scrabster

Scrabster is the main harbour on the north coast. The RoRo Quay on the east side of the harbour is used by the Stromness Ferry. The harbour is used as a main port for renewable energy projects.

Tides

Constant –0240 Wick (–0230 Dover)
Height in metres

MHWS	MHWN	MTL	MLWN	MLWS
5·0	4·0	2·9	2·2	1·0

Directions

The harbour can be entered in all weathers, at all states of the tide, has no bar, and offers shelter from all winds. Radio reception is poor from the west due to masking by Holborn Head.

The lights of Scrabster do not show until well round Holborn Head and are somewhat masked by the scatter effect of street and other lighting. Extreme caution should be taken so that they are not confused with the harbour lights of Thurso to the south-southeast of Thurso Bay.

Beware of floating creel lines north of the harbour entrance.

The harbourmaster at Scrabster (on duty 24hrs) is always to be contacted prior to entering the harbour. Call VHF Ch12 (or 16) or ☎01847 892779. The harbourmaster has extensive information about sea and weather conditions prevailing in the Pentland Firth and is happy to discuss.

Anchorage

The harbourmaster will give permission to enter the harbour and allocate a suitable berth. Anchoring in the harbour is prohibited except in an emergency when vessel safety is paramount.

If awaiting permission to enter the harbour, anchor off the east breakwater but well clear of the entrance to the harbour.

Pontoons are located in the Inner Harbour but are normally congested in the summer months. Depth 2m. When possible, pontoon berths will be allocated to visiting vessels, but this cannot be guaranteed.

Facilities

Minor boat and engine repairs, hotels, restaurants. Marine diesel by hose at fuel jetty. Water. Laundrette at caravan site. Laundry and shower facilities are available in the Fish Market on a 'pay as you go' basis. Keys are available from the Harbour office.

Pentland Firth Yacht Club has showers. Obtain key from duty harbourmaster in Harbour office.

Small A&E Department at Dunbar Hospital, Thurso. Main hospital is at Wick. Thurso has a rail connection to Inverness. Airport at Wick (21 miles).

There are no shops at Scrabster Harbour but there are three supermarkets in Thurso (use taxi or walk 35 minutes).

Admiralty Chart
1954, 2162, 1462
Imray Chart
C68
Ordnance Survey
11

2. Pentland Firth

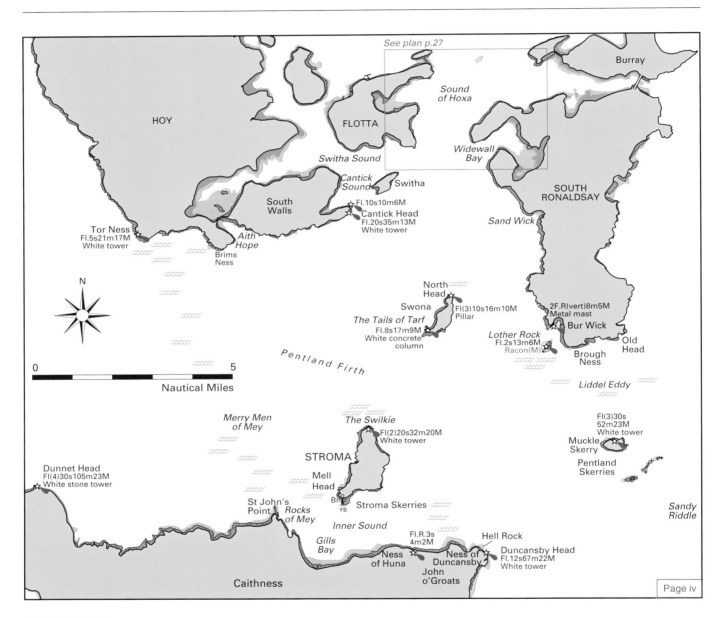

PENTLAND FIRTH

The Pentland Firth lies between Orkney and the North Coast of Scotland. Between Duncansby Head and St John's Point there are small harbours that can be explored but are only suitable for small boats or yachts that can take the ground.

Tides

The rate of the tidal stream in various parts of the Pentland Firth is higher than that experienced in almost any other part of the sea around the British Isles. Careful planning is needed for passages through and across the Firth.

The flood tide runs east in the Firth. The tidal streams throughout the whole of the Pentland Firth are complex with many eddies.

The importance of consulting the *Admiralty Tidal Stream Atlas for the Orkney and Shetland Islands*, NP209 cannot be over emphasised.

However, people who use these waters say that one should expect the unexpected. You can look at as many tide tables and streams as you want but sometimes you will be left scratching your head wondering why this or that hasn't happened or developed.

½M off Dunnet Head
During neaps, the tides in the Pentland Firth tend to run longer than shown in the tide books.
East-going stream starts +0240 Aberdeen (+0500 Dover)
West-going stream starts –0320 Aberdeen (–0100Dover)
Spring rate: 3kn

Mid-Firth 3½ miles north of Dunnet Head
East-going stream starts +0515 Aberdeen (–0450 Dover)
West-going stream starts –0010 Aberdeen (+0210 Dover)
Spring rate: 3½kn

Close to St John's Point
East-going stream starts +0420 Aberdeen (–0545 Dover)
West-going stream starts –0150 Aberdeen (+0030 Dover)
Spring rates: east-going 5½kn, west-going 7kn

3 miles north of St John's Point
East-going stream starts +0515 Aberdeen (–0450 Dover)
West-going stream starts –0100 Aberdeen (+0120 Dover)
Spring rate: 7kn

Off Tor Ness (SW Hoy)
East-going stream starts +0435 Aberdeen (–0530 Dover)
West-going stream starts –0150 Aberdeen (+0030 Dover)
Spring rate: 6–7kn

Inner Sound (between Mainland and Stroma)
East-going stream starts +0435 Aberdeen (–0530 Dover)
West-going stream starts –0150 Aberdeen (+0030 Dover)
Spring rates: East-going 5kn, West-going 8kn

Outer Sound (between Stroma and Swona)
East-going stream starts +0505 Aberdeen (–0500 Dover)
West-going stream starts –0120 Aberdeen (+0100 Dover)
Spring rates: East-going 9kn, West-going 8kn

Channel between Duncansby Head and Pentland Skerries
Southeast-going stream starts +0505 Aberdeen (–0500 Dover)
West-going stream starts –0105 Aberdeen (+0115 Dover)
Spring rates: southeast-going 9kn, west-going 8kn

Channel between Pentland Skerries and Old Head (South Ronaldsay)

East-going stream starts +0405 Aberdeen (–0600 Dover)
The Liddel Eddy starts soon after this as a southwest-going stream off the southeast of South Ronaldsay and extends to the south becoming a west-going stream.

Eventually before the true west-going stream starts the west-going Liddel Eddy extends right across the channel between Old Head and Pentland Skerries except close in to Muckle Skerry.

West-going stream starts –0229 Aberdeen (HW Dover)

Spring rate: east-going 8kn

The tidal streams in this area are complex due to the Liddel Eddy and are best understood from the *Admiralty Tidal Stream Atlas* (NP 209).

Gills Bay
Constant –0155 Wick   –0205 Dover
Heights in metres

MHWS	MHWN	MTL	MLWN	MLWS
4·2	3·5	2·7	2·0	1·0

Duncansby Head
Constant –0115 Wick   –0125 Dover
Heights in metres

MHWS	MHWN	MTL	MLWN	MLWS
3·1	2·4	–	–	–

Muckle Skerry
Constant –0025 Wick –0035 Dover

MHWS	MHWN	MTL	MLWN	MLWS
–0·9	–0·8	–	–0·4	–0·3

Tidal races

The Merry Men of Mey See information on Crossing the line of the Merry Men of Mey on p.25.

The Duncansby Race forms off Ness of Duncansby (1 mile west of Duncansby Head) mainly on the east-going stream. It extends for over 1 mile in a northwest direction and can be particularly violent at its outer end (the Boar of Duncansby).

The Swilkie Race persists almost continuously off Swilkie Point where the strong east-going and north-going tides stream through the Outer Sound meet the north-going eddies, which flow on the east and west sides of Stroma. The Swilkie can be dangerous and should be avoided even in good weather. It is most violent when the west-going stream through the Outer Sound is opposed by strong westerly winds.

Admiralty Chart
1954, 2162, 2581, 35
Imray Chart
C68
Ordnance Survey
9

Rocks of Mey off St John's Point, the southern extremity of the Merry Men of Mey

Mo - Geograph

The Tails of Tarf Race forms off the south point of Swona – in a southeasterly direction with the east-going stream, and a southwesterly direction with the west-going stream. These become violent with wind against tide and should be avoided.

At North Head of Swona a race forms to the east with the east-going stream and to the northwest with the west-going stream.

The Lother Race and Eddy that forms southwest off Lother Rock off the southwest point of South Ronaldsay during the west-going tidal stream can be violent.

Eddies

These are best understood by referring to Chart 2162 as the eddies are extensive off the east and west sides of Stroma during the main east-going and west-going tidal streams respectively. Similarly extensive eddies are experienced southeast and northwest of Swona and southeast of the Pentland Skerries. In the Pentland Firth, crossing the boundary between the main stream and an eddy can give the boat a quite violent jerk. Even large boats experience this effect.

Dangers

In calm conditions the passage through the Firth presents little danger provided due precautions are taken as described in the Passages section which follows. However the change from smooth to broken water can occur very suddenly. Any swell opposing the tide causes such severe conditions that the safety of a small vessel can be in jeopardy. The hatches and scuttles of all yachts should be secured and the safety harnesses of the crew should be properly attached before the passage is started. A number of combinations of weather and tidal conditions cause dangerous seas and if any of these conditions are present, the passage should not be undertaken. These conditions include: swell, spring tides, wind against tide, wind over Force 4 and fog,

There are also certain areas which should be treated with special care or avoided. See information on Tidal Races on p.23.

When the Merry Men of Mey Race is in full flow it forms a barrier across the Pentland Firth which should under no circumstances be attempted by small craft.

Beware of large cargo vessels in the Outer Sound and at either end of the Firth.

For local knowledge on prevailing conditions in the Firth contact the Harbourmaster at Scrabster (see p.21) or Wick (p.31).

The Merry Men of Mey
seen from St John's Point

John Dollemore-Hunt

Passages

For general guidance on working the tides see p.8.

Crossing the line of the Merry Men of Mey Race

The Merry Men of Mey is a roost (i.e. breaking seas) that forms, on the west-going tidal stream, between St John's Point on the Caithness coast and Tor Ness on Hoy. Small craft must on no account enter the dangerous breaking seas that form here. When fully established it extends the entire distance across the Firth.

The most violent part of the Merry Men of Mey is over a large sandwave field which lies approximately 3½ miles west of Stroma. In a westerly sea or swell, the entire race becomes very violent; large waves will form suddenly and come from different directions, making it difficult to anticipate what actions to take. The race forms a natural breakwater across the Firth, and even when it is at its most violent, the Firth can be crossed east of the breakers in smooth conditions.

It is very important to note that with strong west or northwest winds and/or westerly swell the conditions at the race can be unpredictable and extremely dangerous even for large craft. Small vessels are advised to remember that the west-going tidal stream emanating from the Outer Sound can be very strong; rates in excess of 10 knots can be expected and one must guard against the danger of being swept into the roost.

West-going stream As soon as the tide turns (−0150 Aberdeen, +0030 Dover) to west-going a roost forms off the Men of Mey rocks at St John's Point and initially extends west towards Dunnet Head. As the stream increases in strength, the roost extends from the bank 1½ miles northwest of St John's Point in a north-northwest direction. When the west-going tidal stream has achieved its full strength, heavy breaking seas can extend the whole way across the firth between St John's Point and Tor Ness even in fine weather.

St John's Point After about 2 hours of the west-going stream a short gap opens up between St John's Point and the breaking seas. This is used regularly by local craft but, to avoid the roost, it is necessary to hold in close to the rocks that are awash and in the absence of local knowledge it may be best to wait for the gap to open further.

At +0535 HW Dover i.e. 5 hours after the start of the stream, the southeast end of the race becomes fully detached from the Men of Mey Rocks leaving a clear passage that gradually widens north, between the rocks and the breaking seas. It is through this gap that, unless the wind is fresh or strong from the north or the northwest, it is safe for a small craft to make a west-going passage.

Approach the Rocks of Mey close in along the west shore of Gills Bay shore. If necessary anchor, just east of the Rocks, to await suitable conditions.

Tor Ness The roost at Tor Ness starts to form after about 2 hours of the west-going stream. After about 6 hours of that stream the roost there starts to decline. In fair conditions a west-going passage close to Tor Ness may be made as early as is practical at the start of the west-going stream or at the very end of the stream.

East-going stream There is broken water in the north of the line of the race in the early part of the tide but otherwise, in fair conditions, the water is clear.

Scrabster to Scapa Flow

Since the Merry Men of Mey roost does not form on the east-going tide, this passage can be straightforward in good weather.

The 'Grounds' shoal on a line between Holborn Head and Dunnet Head affords no danger in calm weather but breaks in northwest gales.

In the middle of the Firth the east-going stream starts at −0450 Dover. Note however that up to 6 cables off Dunnet Head the east-going stream starts 2½ hours earlier than this. Leave Scrabster so as be in mid-channel not earlier than the start of the east-going stream there. Seek to ensure that you have sufficient time to complete your passage to the entrance to Scapa Flow well before the west-going tide starts. Head for Hoxa Sound where the stream runs north till −0120 Dover or enter Cantick Sound.

Passage through the Inner Sound

The following dangers in the Inner Sound passage should be noted:

The Duncansby Race forms off the Ness of Duncansby (1 mile west of Duncansby Head) mainly on the east-going stream. It extends for over 1 mile in a northwest direction and can be particularly violent at its outer end (the Boar of Duncansby). At the same time as the northwest race there is broken water to the north and east of Duncansby Head which should therefore be given a wide berth to the east and to the north to clear the breaking waters.

Ness of Duncansby A clearing transit for this point is St John's Head on Dunnet Head. Do not lose Dunnet Head behind St John's Head.

Hell Rock approximately 2 cables northwest of Duncansby Head, breaks at LW.

Eddy on the east side of Stroma During the east-going streams through the Outer and Inner Sounds a north-going eddy forms off the east side of Stroma and gradually extends about 1 mile east of the island.

Stroma Skerries at the south end of Stroma: The shoal marked by the unlit Stroma Beacon extends approximately 1 cable south of the beacon.

Ness of Huna: Give this point on the Caithness shore a clear offing of 1·5 cables.

Crossing the Merry Men of Mey Race see p.25.

On a passage through the Inner Sound, a mid-channel line between Stroma and the Caithness shore should be taken. Going east with the east-going stream, the Duncansby Race should be passed to the north taking care to avoid the eddy on the east side of Stroma noted above.

Scrabster to Wick

See advice about leaving Scrabster to Scapa Flow (above). If the east-going tide is running well when Dunnet Head is reached, give it a wide berth. See sections on 'Crossing the line of the Merry Men of Mey race' and 'Passage through the Inner Sound' on p.25.

Alternatively pass 2 miles off Dunnet Head and head for the Outer Sound to pass between Stroma and Swona. Initially maintain a course closer to the south point of Swona to avoid being drawn into the Swilkie tide race which extends up to three quarters of a mile off the north point of Stroma. After passing mid-channel between Swona and Stroma alter course to southeast to keep in main tidal stream and to pass clear of the Pentland Skerries.

Wick to Scrabster

See sections on 'Passage through the Inner Sound' on p.25 and 'Crossing the line of the Merry Men of Mey Race' on p.25.

Scrabster to Stromness

This passage avoids the Firth and no trouble is likely to be experienced until entry into the Hoy Sound (see p.41). Time departure to reach the entrance to the Sound at slack water before the start of the east-going stream.

Although there are no significant dangers on the route to Rora Head (plan p.38) on Hoy from Scrabster, be aware of the last of the west-going tide in the middle of the Pentland Firth if there is a westerly swell. If there is any swell, better to wait for either the east-going stream or the full west-going stream to be on.

To Scapa Flow from the west

In good weather there is not likely to be any problem in making a passage with the east-going tide past Tor Ness, Brims Ness and the south shore of South Walls.

Scapa Flow heading to Scrabster, to the west, or to the north

See Section on 'Crossing the line of the Merry Men of Mey' on p.25.

It is recommended to arrive at Brims Ness just as the west-going stream starts. Once past Tor Ness the main tidal dangers are behind you. Note that with the last of the east-going stream in the Firth there is a west-going eddy along the south shore of South Walls.

Scrabster to Old Head (south end of South Ronalday)

Leave Scrabster as advised for Scrabster to Scapa Flow. Pass through Outer Sound nearer to Stroma than Swona. Proceed east with the Swilkie and Dunnet Head lights in line astern. This will avoid being carried on to Lother Rock if the tide is sweeping over it. When abreast of the Lother, steer to to pass at least 2 cables off Old Head to clear rocks which extend east offshore. It is essential to reach the vicinity east of Old Head not later than 4 hours before HW Dover before the strong south-going tide begins in this area and meets with the east-going stream of the Liddel eddy where there is a build up of overfalls. Care must be taken to avoid being swept on to the Pentland Skerries and the west-going Liddel eddy. For further passage to Copinsay see p.27.

Wick to Hoxa Sound or to Longhope

The tide turns northwest off Duncansby Head −0105 Aberdeen (+0115 Dover). Time departure from Wick to reach a point 2 miles east of Duncansby Head at the start of this tide. Vector a course so as not to be drawn too far to the west by the tide. After passing the Pentland Skerries the tide takes a more westerly direction and care must be taken not to be set on to Swona.

With a west wind less than Force 4 keeping clear of Swona should not be difficult. Steer to make a course for the Lother Rock, give it a good berth and vector a course to be well clear of Swona to port. If heading for Longhope give the north end of Swona a wide berth and steer for Switha Sound.

With an east wind, pass Duncansby Head as above but steer for Little Skerry. Pass close west of Muckle Skerry then proceed as for the west wind passage. If it is likely to be difficult to clear the north end of Swona, this fact must be realised early and go south of Swona giving the Tails of the Tarf roost a wide berth.

Long Hope to Wick

The east-going stream along the south coast of South Walls begins +0435 Aberdeen (−0530 Dover), and in the Outer Sound between Swona and Stroma at +0505 Aberdeen (−0500 Dover). The last of the inshore west-going stream stops in mid-firth. On passing Cantick

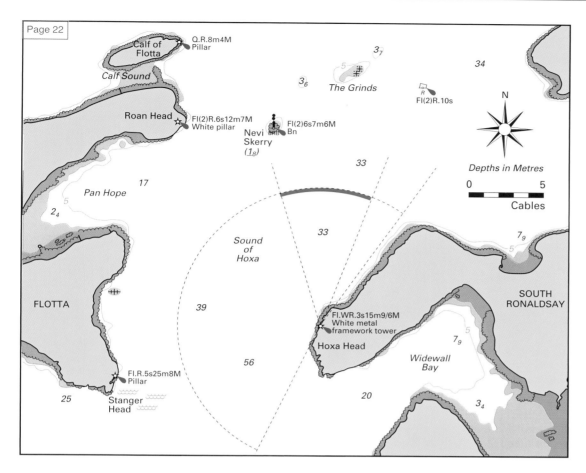

Page 22

Lighthouse heading south keep 2 cables off until the light is abeam to westward. Use the last of the inshore ebb (west-going) stream to reach Aith Hope. Wait till the main flood starts in the Outer Sound. Steer almost due south to ensure passing through the Outer Sound in mid-channel. Continue southeast to pass midway between Duncansby Head and the Pentland Skerries to avoid Duncansby Race which forms on the flood and extends 1 mile offshore.

Wick to Copinsay

Keep well clear of the 'Riddles' the shallower water that runs in a southeast direction from the Pentland Skerries. This is a meeting place for different tides and can be confused even in good weather. Avoid completely if the east-going tide and southeast winds are blowing.

The normal option for small craft is to leave Wick planning to take best advantage of the east-going tide to go south of the Riddles and then north, well off the South Ronaldsay coast so as to be in weaker tides and to avoid the south-going eddy off the east coast of South Ronaldsay.

Alternatively be off Duncansby Head at the beginning of the east-going stream (-0500 hrs Dover) or earlier and vector a course to carry you to the north of Muckle Skerry. This would help to get up to Muckle Skerry before the east

going stream develops too much, thereby having more control of the crossing. The further you can get across in the slack period, the easier your passage should be.

Once you are approximately ½ mile north of Muckle Skerry take a course due east to avoid the overfall area at South Ronaldsay before altering to the north again.

Confused seas can develop between South Ronaldsay and Muckle Skerry with wind against tide. This passage is recommended only at neap tides and in fine conditions. It is not recommended with a poor weather forecast.

Scapa Flow to Copinsay

Pass Lother Rock and Old Head at slack water +0410 Aberdeen (−0600 Dover). It is essential that this dangerous area be cleared as quickly as possible. There is a south-going stream inshore down the west coast of South Ronaldsay from Widewall Bay to Bur Wick. This should be used to reach Bur Wick at the end of the ebb. The Lother Rock should be passed on the outside though with local knowledge the inner passage can be taken. This however is liable to be cluttered with lobster creels.

The tide runs east along the south of South Ronaldsay for 2 hours only until the south-going stream starts down the southeast coast. The meeting of this stream with the eddy caused by the east-going stream forms a violent race. A small vessel making this passage must be well north off Old Head before these overfalls build up. Old Head cannot be passed close-to as rocks extend 2 cables east offshore.

The east-going stream sets towards the Lother Rock and after 4 hours of the flood it becomes extremely dangerous as the stream sets over the rocks. The flow of water is so great that there is a considerable difference in level between the two sides.

There is no north-going tide on the east coast of South Ronaldsay.

Copinsay to Wick

A south-going course east of South Ronaldsay takes advantage of the fact that the tidal stream there is either slack or runs south.

There are choices to be made for this passage.

The seaward route i.e. leaving the Pentland Skerries to starboard. Pass well (6 miles or more) to the east of the Pentland Skerries with an east-going tide to avoid west-going eddies north of them (see *Tidal Atlas* NP209) and then cross the slackening southeast-going tide to reach Wick. Leave the Riddles to the south.

The Pentland Firth route i.e. leaving the Pentland Skerries to port. This route is only recommended at neaps and in favourable weather conditions. The route relies upon the west-going Liddel Eddy between Old Head and the Lother Rock to carry one sufficiently far west before crossing the strong east-going stream in the Firth. The Liddel Eddy begins to run westward from Old Head towards Brough Ness and the Lother Rock at about +0535 Aberdeen (−0330 Dover) and it is essential to arrive off the Old Head within 15 minutes of

that time. Proceed west keeping around the 30 metre contour initially to clear the Skerries of Skaigram and then between the 30m and 20m contour until south of Brough Ness. This will ensure keeping in the inshore section of the Liddel Eddy. When Brough Ness bears northeast at a distance between 2 and 3 cables alter course to cross the main east-going stream towards Stroma to make good a course of about 240°. As soon as appropriate, aim to pass 1½ miles clear west of Muckle Skerry. To avoid the worst of the race off Duncansby Head pass approximately midway between the Pentland Skerries and Duncansby Head before making for Wick.

Stroma

Stroma Island lies 1½ miles across the Inner Sound of the Pentland Firth, off the Caithness coast midway between Duncansby Head and St John's Point. It is uninhabited and privately owned.

Tides

For information about tidal stream rates in the Inner Sound see p.23.

A strong eddy forms off the south coast of Stroma on both the ebb and the flood running contrary to the main stream with a band of quiet water inshore extending from Stroma Skerries to Scarton Point.

During the west-going streams through the Inner and Outer Sounds a north-going eddy forms off the west side of Stroma and gradually extends about 2½ miles west-northwest from the island. There is also an eddy on the east side of Stroma. See section on 'Passage through the Inner Sound' on p.23.

Stroma
Constant −0115 Wick −0105 Dover

Heights in metres

MHWS	MHWN	MTL	MLWN	MLWS
3·1	2·3	1·8	1·3	0·5

Beacon marking Stroma Skerries, Hoy in the background

Mo / Geograph

Martin Lawrence

Directions

From the east (on the west-going stream) make good a course from Duncansby Head to Scarton Point on the southeast of the island. When the strong eddy off the south coast of Stroma noted above is observed, keep to the south of it until the harbour entrance bears north or slightly east before crossing the eddy. If approaching from the west, pass east of Stroma Skerry Beacon before crossing the eddy.

Anchorage

Yachtsmen are permitted to land on Stroma provided they observe the necessary courtesies. The harbour is on the south coast at the position marked 'The Haven' on Chart 2162. Most of the harbour dries. The outer basin has a rock bottom and is subject to slight swell. Yachts are recommended to use the inner basin which has a sandy bottom. Tie up just inside the pierhead in the southeast corner.

A comfortable anchorage out of the tide may be found off the sandy beach midway between the harbour and Mell Head, the southernmost point of Stroma, in 3m on a sandy bottom with patches of weed.

Items of interest are the large Gloup Hole at the northwest, and the Swilkie overfalls off the north end of the island.

Aith Hope

This inlet lies on the north of the Pentland Firth between South Walls and Hoy, Orkney. The Ayre at the head of the inlet is an artifical causeway linking Hoy to South Walls.

Directions

The entrance between Brim's Ness and Aith Head is clear.

Anchorage

Anchor in depths of 4–11m in sand off the former Longhope Lifeboat Station. This is now an RNLI museum that is well worth a visit.

Freswick Bay

Though not in the Pentland Firth, this bay, 3½ miles south of Duncansby Head provides a useful temporary anchorage when awaiting the tide in the Pentland Firth, but it is wide open to the east. An eddy runs north round the bay for 9 hours starting +0440 Aberdeen (–0545 Dover). Anchor in 6m in sand southwest off the pier.

The drying harbour at the southern end of Stroma

3. Wick to Inverness

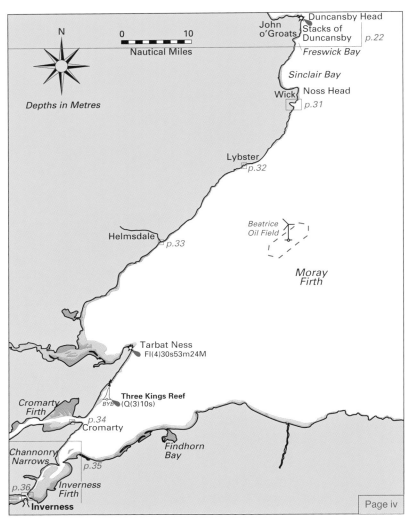

PASSAGE WICK TO INVERNESS

The purpose of this Section is to provide information for yachts making a passage along this coast. Therefore only harbours that have reasonable depths at low tide are described. There are other harbours that are worth exploring with small boats or yachts that can take the ground.

Passage Wick to Inverness Firth

On the northeast Coast from Wick to Tarbat Ness there are no isolated dangers more than 1 mile offshore other than oil rigs and wind turbines

There is shoal water close in to the northeast of Tarbat Ness.

The Three Kings Reef 3½miles north of the entrance to the Cromarty Firth is marked by an E Cardinal buoy 8 cables from the shore.

The Cromarty Bank (minimum depth 6m) that extends 1½ miles east southeast from the north entrance to the Cromarty Firth is marked by a starboard hand buoy (Fl(2).G10s) (not shown on plan).

South of the Cromarty Firth, the approach to Inverness Firth from the northeast is through the North Channel which passes between the Nativity Bank (minimum depth 2·4m) to the northwest and the much more extensive Riff Bank to the southeast, which dries at its southwestern end. The channel is marked by lit buoys which are shown on the plan on p.35. The tidal streams in this area are weak except at the Chanonry Narrows, through which the Inverness Firth is entered, and details of them can be found on p.34.

Mike Stephen Photography

Wick Marina

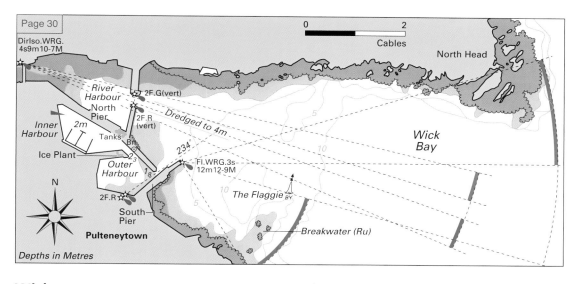

Page 30

DirIso.WRG.
4s9m10·7M

River Harbour
North Pier
Inner Harbour
2m
Tanks
Ice Plant
Outer Harbour
2F.G(vert)
2F.R (vert)
Brh
Dredged to 4m
234°
Fl.WRG.3s 12m12·9M
2F.R
South Pier
Pulteneytown
N
The Flaggie BY
Breakwater (Ru)
North Head
Wick Bay

0   2
Cables

Depths in Metres

Admiralty Chart
0115 1462-1 1942
Imray Chart
C23
Ordnance Survey
12 17 21

WICK HARBOUR APPROACH

Wick

Wick is the county town of Caithness and a traditional fishing port. It is situated 14 miles south of Duncansby Head. It is a good harbour in which to wait for the right conditions for onward cruising.

Tides

Constant Standard Port +0010 Dover
Heights in metres

MHWS	MHWN	MTL	MLWN	MLWS
3·5	2·8	2·0	1·4	0·7

Directions

The entrance to Wick harbour is dangerous in strong east winds, and heavy seas run into the harbour with winds between northeast and south.

From the north keep about 1 mile off Noss Head. The distance off is hard to judge at night. Open up Wick Bay before turning in. Rocks (dr 1·7m) extend 2 cables southeast from the North Head on the north side of the bay. On the south side a ruined breakwater 400m from the harbour entrance extends 300m north just east of the old RNLI station. The outer end is marked by an unlit N cardinal buoy (The Flaggie). The approach course for entering is 288°.

Keep well clear of the South Pier head as the turn into the Outer Harbour is very sharp. Once turned, keep close to the South Pier as the channel is narrow. The leading lights for this channel bear 234°. In east winds care must be taken to avoid being washed onto the south pier. Do not attempt entry in winds over force 4 with a swell running. If caught out, some shelter may be found in *Sinclair Bay*, north of Noss Head. Note the tide runs continuously in an easterly direction off the south shore in this bay.

Do not enter the harbour if the mast at the coastguard station on South Head (4 cables southeast from the harbour entrance) displays one black ball (at night green light). At the South Pier head a black ball or red flag indicates caution as harbour is temporarily obstructed. Pass through the Outer Harbour and enter the Inner Harbour.

Contact can be made with the harbourmaster on VHF 14, 16 or ☎01955 602030.

Marina

The Inner Harbour has a 70 berth marina with minimum depth 2·0m. Berth where directed by the harbourmaster (see above). Yachts should not enter the River Harbour.

Facilities

Stores. Water and electricity to all marina berths; toilets and showers on pier; all repair facilities; diesel; Post Office; banks; hospital; rail bus service and airport. Divers on pier do tours and equipment hire.

The entrance to the Outer Harbour at Wick

Edward Mason

Admiralty Chart
0115
Imray Chart
C23
Ordnance Survey
11

Lybster

Formerly a busy fishing port 12 miles southwest of Wick and 15 miles northeast of Helmsdale on an exposed coast, Lybster is an attractive stopping place.

Directions

Approach on 350° following the leading line of orange reflectors.

The entrance is difficult in strong east to south winds but possible in most weather. The entrance can be awkward when the wind is southwest 5/6 and the tide is low. There is currently (2015) no harbourmaster.

Beware of the rocks on the east side of the entrance and off the first pier on that side. Keep mid-channel until through the entrance and then hold close to the pier on the west side. Although narrow, (10m), the channel has a min. depth of 1·8m until past the white pierhead.

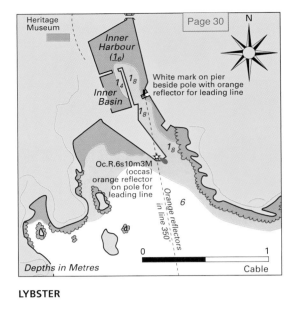

LYBSTER

Anchorage

Keel boats can lie afloat alongside the east side of the pier of the Inner Harbour (2m) and also in the Inner Basin where the depth is less but the bottom is soft mud.

Facilities

Stores in the village up a steep hill about a 1 mile walk. Water on west pier. One hotel. Boat-builder's workshop at harbour.

The Natural Heritage Museum is open April to September.

In the vicinity of Lybster there are many brochs, standing stones, chambered cairns and other antiquities, notably the Stone Rows at Mid Clyth (3 miles northeast).

Lybster Harbour, the Inner Basin

Mike Lewin-Harris

Lybster from the southeast

Martin Lawrence

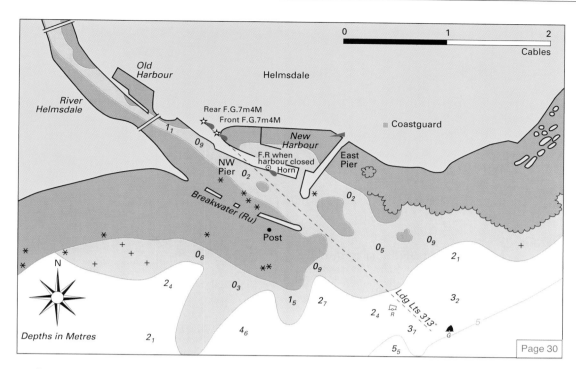

Admiralty Chart
0115, 1462-6
Imray Chart
C23
Ordnance Survey
17

HELMSDALE

Helmsdale

This village, south of Wick, is at the mouth of the River Helmsdale.

Tides

Constant +0025 Wick +0035 Dover
Heights in metres

MHWS	MHWN	MTL	MLWN	MLWS
4·0	3·1	2·2	1·5	0·6

Directions

The leading line 313° for entry to the harbour must be closely followed to avoid the dangers on either hand. Port and starboard buoys mark the channel but may be displaced by bad weather. When the river is in spate the current is strong; indeed the effect can be felt well offshore. Entry is dangerous in strong to gale force easterly weather. Contact the harbourmaster (VHF Ch 16, 12; ☎ 01431 821692) for a berth and to verify conditions for entry before entering the entrance channel.

Lights

There are two beacons (wooden posts) on a leading line bearing 313°. The beacons have F.G(occas) leading lights. A fixed red light is shown by day and by night when the harbour is closed and when it is dangerous to cross the bar of the entrance channel. This red light is exhibited from the front pole of the leading line.

Anchorage

It is not possible to anchor except offshore. The New Harbour offers good shelter and is often used by yachts on passage to and from the Orkney Isles. Although the harbour dries for one third of its area, there is a pontoon (60m in length) with minimum depth 1·3m.

The depths quoted may change due to silting or dredging. The maximum depth on entry may be 0·5m or less.

Yachts drawing up to 2m can take the bottom in soft mud. There are points for power on the pontoon.

Entry to the Old Harbour is not recommended.

Facilities

Toilets and showers, stores, water, diesel and gas. Post Office and hotels serving food.

Interest

Small golf course. Sea bird colony at Berridale 8 miles north.

Helmsdale Harbour

Admiralty Chart
1077, 0115, 1078,
1889, 0223
Imray Chart
C23
Ordnance Survey
21

Cromarty

A small harbour on the south shore of the entrance to the Cromarty Firth offering better protection from the east than others on this coast.

Tides

Entrance to Cromarty Firth
In-going stream –0605 Aberdeen (–0340 Dover)
Out-going stream –0105 Aberdeen (–0115 Dover)
Maximum spring rates: 1·5kn

Constant HW Invergordon +0100 Dover
Heights in metres

MHWS	MHWN	MTL	MLWN	MLWS
4·3	3·3	2·5	1·6	0·7

Directions

There is a port hand buoy (Fl.R.3s) at the outer entrance to the Cromarty Firth. Within the entrance to the Firth the shores are shoal, drying 2 cables offshore. Continue in mid-channel until northwest of The Ness before approaching the harbour.

The harbour offers shelter from winds from north through east to south. When entering the harbour beware of the tidal set towards the lattice bridge. There is a 50m pontoon with 2m depth at the west end decreasing towards the inner end to 1m approx.

Contact the harbourmaster ☏ 07453 695648 on arrival to obtain security code for shore access to pontoon. Berthing charges payable. With permission it may be possible to secure alongside the Nigg ferry overnight. The north quay is used by shallow draft local fishing vessels.

Visitors' moorings laid by Cromarty Boat Club southwest of the harbour are indicated on the plan. The Club boat moorings are further to the west. Should west winds make Cromarty uncomfortable, anchorage may be found north of the pier at Invergordon.

Facilities

Stores, marine diesel at ferry pier, gas, Post Office, hotel. Water and electricity available on pontoon, Cromarty Boat Club ☏ 01381 600768, *Mobile* 07591 423862, info@cromartyboatclub.org. Visitors welcome; showers available (obtain key from hotel). Ferry to Nigg.

Inverness Firth

Tides

Entrance to Inverness Firth (Chanonry)
In-going stream +0605 Aberdeen (-0400 Dover)
Out-going stream -0120 Aberdeen (+0115 Dover)
Maximum spring rates in-going 2·5kn, out-going 3·5kn
There is approximately a 1¼ hr of slack water between each tidal stream. The duration of slack water can be reduced to almost nothing by strong winds and/or outgoing flood water.

Directions

After passing through Chanonry Narrows there is a choice of channels before reaching the Kessock Bridge.

Mid Channel Route Steer 222° for the mid-channel Munlochy R.W buoy Fl.10s, then continue on same course (min. depth 2·1m) to pass the Meikle Mee G buoy Fl.G.3s close to starboard; then alter course for the middle of Kessock Bridge.

Northern Route Enter this deeper water channel by leaving the two red can buoys southwest of Chanonry Ness close to port and following the shore round, keeping between 2-3 cables off it. Note that there are many moorings off Fortrose and that between Fortrose and Munlochy Bay there can be many unlit commercial fishing buoys.

When Kilmuir Point is abeam to starboard at a distance of about 2 cables alter to 165° on the Meikle Mee G buoy to avoid extensive shallows (0·2m) known as Meikle Mee which lie 1 cable to the west and northwest of the buoy and the bank lying to the northeast of the buoy. Alter round the buoy for the bridge.

CROMARTY

Cromarty

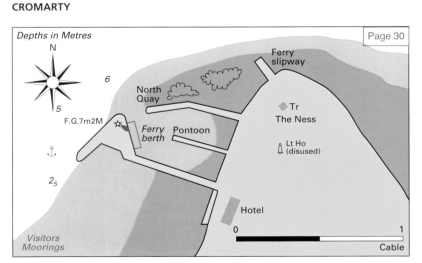

Depths in Metres

Barbara MacLeod

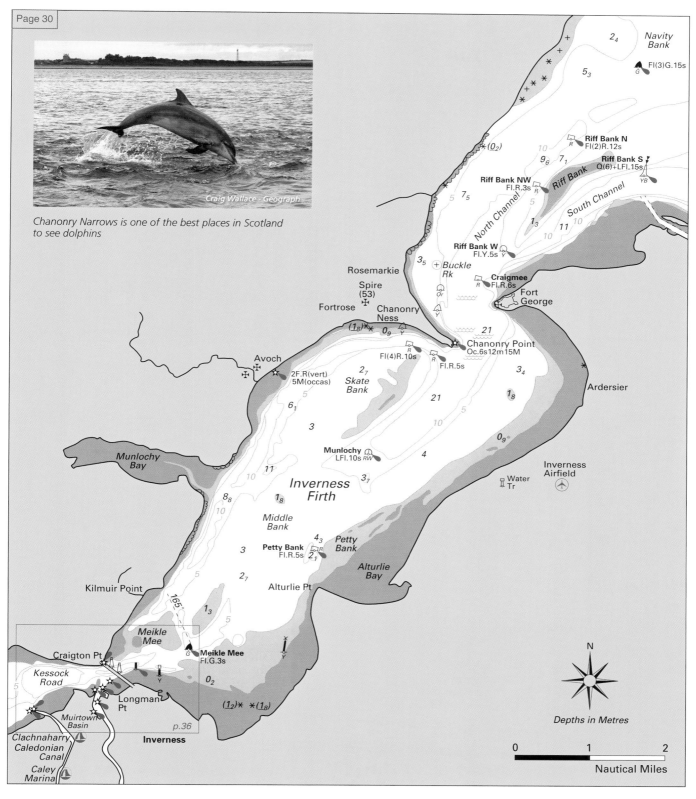

Chanonry Narrows is one of the best places in Scotland to see dolphins

Craig Wallace - Geograph

Navity Bank

2₄

5₃

Fl(3)G.15s

(0₂)

10

Riff Bank N
Fl(2)R.12s

9₆ 7₁

Riff Bank S
Q(6)+LFl.15s

Riff Bank NW
Fl.R.3s

Riff Bank

North Channel

South Channel

5 7₅

5

1₃

11 10

10

Riff Bank W
Fl.Y.5s

3₅ Buckle
Rk

Craigmee
Fl.R.6s

Or

Fort
George

Y

Rosemarkie

Spire
(53)

Fortrose

Chanonry
Ness

(1₈) 0₉

Y

21

Chanonry Point
Oc.6s12m15M

Fl(4)R.10s

Fl.R.5s

3₄

Ardersier

Avoch

2F.R(vert)
5M(occas)

2₇

Skate
Bank

5

21

1₈

6₁

3

10

5

0₉

Munlochy
Bay

Munlochy
LFl.10s RW

4

Inverness
Airfield

11

10

3₇

Inverness
Firth

Water
Tr

8₈

1₈

Middle
Bank

10

Kilmuir Point

3

Petty Bank
Fl.R.5s

4₃ Petty
Bank

2₁

5

2₇

Alturlie
Bay

165°

1₃

5

Alturlie Pt

Meikle
Mee

Craigton Pt

Meikle Mee
Fl.G.3s

Kessock
Road

0₂

5

Longman
Pt

Muirtown
Basin

(1₂) (1₈)

p.36

Inverness

Clachnaharry
Caledonian
Canal

Caley
Marina

N

Depths in Metres

0   1   2

Nautical Miles

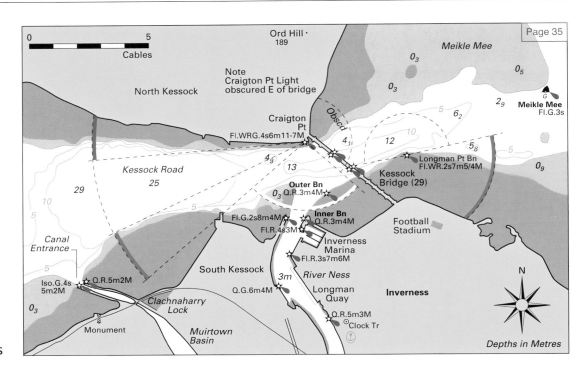

INVERNESS

Inverness Harbour

Inverness is considered to be the captial city of the Highlands of Scotland and, with its excellent communications and marina, it is an ideal place for crew changes or to leave a boat between cruises.

Admiralty Chart
1078, 1078-1
Imray Chart
C23
Ordnance Survey
21

Tides

At Kessock Narrows
In-going stream +0535 Aberdeen (-0430 Dover)
Out-going stream -0050 Aberdeen (+0130 Dover)
Maximum spring rates: in-going 4kn, out-going up to 6kn

There is 2hrs slack water before the in-going stream starts and ½hr slack water before the out-going stream starts. The duration of slack water can be reduced to almost nothing by strong winds and/or outgoing flood water when there can be violent turbulence in the narrows.

Constant 0015 Invergordon +0100 Dover
Heights in metres

MHWS	MHWN	MTL	MLWN	MLWS
4·6	3·5	2·7	1.7	0·8

Lights on Kessock Bridge

Position on bridge	Bridge	Tower
Northwest	Oc.G.6s28m5M	Q.G.3m3M
Southeast	Oc.R.6s28m5M	Q.R.3m3M

These lights are duplicated on each side of the bridge

Directions

After passing under Kessock Bridge (clearance 29·0m at MHWS, 4·7m tidal height) and intending to enter the River Ness, keep 50m off the outer porthand beacon (Q.R.) before turning into the river mouth at the inner beacon (Q.R.). A minimum dredged depth of 3m in the river channel is to be expected. Adopt a mid-channel course if heading for *Inverness Marina* which lies on the port hand just after the Fl.G.2s and Inner (Q.R.) Bn. and should be entered by holding to the starboard side of the entrance channel towards the quay. Chart 1078 for Inverness Firth and Inverness Harbour is essential.

Kessock Bridge mid-span has a Racon which marks the centre point of the bridge. Also there is a sectored light on the Longman Bn. Fl.WR.2s (stay out of the red sector) for inward bound vessels.

For vessels departing the Clachnaharry Sea Lock there is a sectored light at Craigton Point Fl.WRG.4s. Stay in the white sector until passing the old ferry slipways.

When bound for (or departing) Inverness Marina either when passing Meikle Mee Buoy or when leaving Clachnaharry Sea Lock call

Inverness Marina

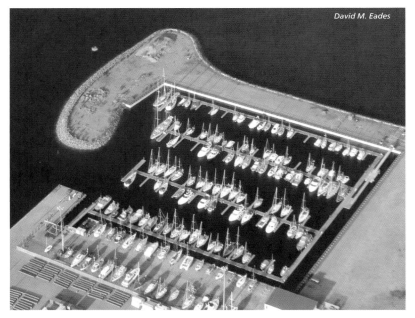

David M. Eades

Entrance to the Caledonian Canal

Scotavia Images

'Inverness Harbour' on VHF Ch 12. This alerts any commercial shipping on the move in the harbour area. Commercial shipping movements are normally from HW −2hrs to HW and occasionally at LW.

Anchorage

The new marina has 150 fully serviced berths with a minimum depth of 3m. Craft up to 22m long can be accommodated. Visitors' berths are available. Contact the Marina Office on Ch 12 or ☎ 01463 220501.

Facilities

Water and electricity on pontoons. Toilets and showers. Diesel fuel berth. 45-tonne travel hoist and masting crane. Engineering, electronic and hull repair facilities. Chandlery at Caley Marine on the west side of the Caledonian Canal (☎ 01463 236539). Gael Force Marine Equipment (☎ 01463 229400).

Caledonian Canal

The Caledonian Canal runs in a northeasterly direction from Corpach near Fort William to Clachnaharry near Inverness, a distance of 60 miles of which 38 are through Lochs Lochy, Oich and Ness, and the remainder consists of a man-made canal, which enables small craft to avoid the exposed passage round the north of Scotland.

The maximum dimensions of vessels using the canal are 45·7 x 4·1 x 10·6m (150' x 13'5" x 35'). Mast clearance is 29·0m (94') which is set by the Kessock Bridge over the Inverness Firth.

Vessels with draft >3·8m should call the Canal office (☎ 01463 725500) prior to arrival for advice.

For information about transiting the canal reference should be made to the Skipper's Guide available at www.scottishcanals/caledonianboating

Directions to Sea Lock from Inverness Harbour

If making for the canal entrance from Inverness Marina beware of the extensive shoal on the west side of the river mouth which extends 300m north northeast of the breakwater Beacon (Fl.G.2s). Many unwary yachts have been caught out on this extensive unmarked shoal by cutting the corner.

Clachnaharry Sea lock

All yachts wishing to enter the canal must call the Clachnaharry sea lock on VHF Ch 74, 16. The canal entrance is between two breakwaters. If unable to contact the sea lock keeper or if waiting for the tide, tie up to southwest breakwater or anchor north-northwest of the sea lock where the holding is good.

Clachnaharry Sea Lock operates with a minimum of approx. 1·4m of tide and within Canal operating hours. At spring tides it is closed 2 hours either side of LW. In strong northwest winds the sea lock cannot be opened.

The road and rail bridges may delay entry into *Muirtown Basin* which has *Seaport Marina* (☎ 01463 600264).

Seaport marina

Scotavia Images

4. Orkney Islands

Admiralty Chart
1239, 1954, 2249, 2250

Imray Chart
C68

Ordnance Survey
5, 6, 7

Mull Head

p.62

PAPA WESTRAY

p.64

NORTH RONALDSAY

Fl.10s43m24M

Dennis Head

Noup Head
Fl.30s79m20M

Pierowall

WESTRAY

p.59

Start Point
Fl(2)20s24m18M

SANDAY

p.52

Westray Firth

Tres Ness

p.61

p.56

EDAY

p.60

Brough Head
Fl(3)25s52m18M

ROUSAY

EGILSAY

STRONSAY

Stronsay Firth

MAINLAND

p.53

Auskerry (17)
Fl.20s34m20M

p.53

p.52

SHAPINSAY

p.40

Stromness

Kirkwall

Deer Sound

Deerness

p.42

p.44

p.44

p.51

Copinsay
Fl(5)30s79m14M

p.45

Rora Head

HOY

Scapa Flow

p.46

Rose Ness
Fl.6s24m8M

p.48

p.48

FLOTTA

SOUTH RONALDSAY

p.50

Torr Ness
Fl.5s17M

South Walls

p.47

p.43

Pentland Firth

Bur Wick

p.22

0   10

Nautical Miles

ORKNEY ISLANDS

For general information about cruising in the Northern Isles see the Introduction on p.4. The Orkney Islands provide great scope for enjoyable cruising. Care is needed with the often strong tidal streams - see p.8 and Appendix pp.142-144 for tidal stream diagrams. Using these streams to advantage and the lack of ocean swell within the archipelago both add to the enjoyment of Orkney cruising. There are lots of interesting anchorages and many fascinating ancient sites to visit. The main towns, Kirkwall and Stromness, are very attractive for a visit.

Harbours

The main harbours in Orkney are administered by Orkney Islands Council Marine Services whose head office is at Scapa, near Kirkwall. Contact with a harbourmaster is via the Scapa office, ☎ 01856 873636.

Orkney Islands Council publish a very useful *Ports Handbook for Orkney*: www.orkneyharbours.com.

Marinas

There are marinas with very good visitor facilities at Kirkwall, Stromness and Pierowall (Westray). The Orkney Marinas website at www.orkneymarinas.co.uk provides information about them. It has a section on 'Plan your trip' that gives very good advice about passages and tides written by local people. The use of this information as complementary to the passage information in these Directions is recommended.

St John's Head, Hoy

Edward Mason

Old Man of Hoy

John Albiston

Admiralty Chart
2568-1, 0035, 2249
Imray Chart
C68
Ordnance Survey
6, 7

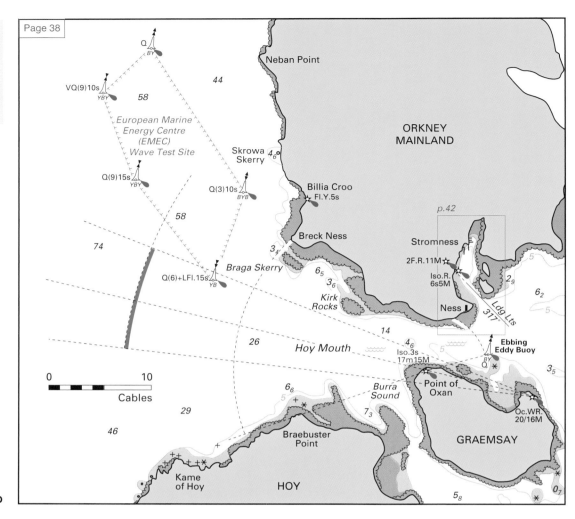

Page 38

HOY SOUND

North approach to Hoy Sound

The Mainland coast from Hoy Sound to Brough Head is rocky and generally inhospitable in most weathers. However, in calm conditions it is possible to anchor in the Bay of Skail in order to visit the outstanding World Heritage Site of Skarabrae.

Mainland west coast at Yesnaby

Inger Harston

EMEC test site

There is a wave energy test facility to the north of Hoy Sound marked by 5 cardinal buoys. Experimental devices, usually marked by yellow buoys and lights with daymarks are temporarily established in this area. The area should not be entered. Either pass west of the cardinal buoys or take an inner passage by holding west of the 20m sounding, east of the cardinal buoys. Devices marked by buoys may also be deployed between the marked area and the coast.

Information about the test site may be obtained from EMEC: www.emec.org.uk or from Notices to Mariners on the Orkney Harbours website at: www.orkneyharbours.com.

Anchorage

Bay of Skaill Temporary anchorage, in calm weather or offshore winds and when there is no swell, is possible in this bay. Keep 2 cables off the south headland of the bay before turning towards the southeast corner where a depth of 4m can be found opposite Skarabrae.

Sailing west past the Kame of Hoy

www.craigtaylormedia.co.uk

Hoy Sound

Hoy Sound is the channel between the island of Hoy and Orkney Mainland.

Tide

At the western entrance to Hoy Sound:
East-going stream starts +0310 Aberdeen (+0530 Dover)
West-going stream starts −0330 Aberdeen (−0110 Dover)

In the narrows between the north end of Graemsay and Orkney Mainland the spring rates are: east-going 4–5kn, west-going 4kn

At the southeast entrance to Hoy Sound:
Southeast-going stream starts +0320 Aberdeen (+0540 Dover)
Northwest-going stream starts −0310 Aberdeen (−0050 Dover)

The northwest-going stream is strongest (4kn springs) close to the Mainland shore and the southeast-going stream is strongest towards the Graemsay shore.

Directions

Chart 35 is strongly advised for approaches to Scapa Flow and Hoy Sound. The tidal streams in Hoy Sound are very strong (8kn) and entry should not be attempted in bad weather, nor with wind against tide, nor on the west-going tide. Accurate timing is necessary to ensure favourable wind and tidal conditions. However passage west out of Hoy Sound can be safely made at both high and low slack water.

The Graemsay leading lights give a line into the Sound (bearing 104°). When 1 mile west of the front light, alter course to make good a course between the Ness Beacon and the N Cardinal Ebbing Eddy Rocks Buoy. Note that the Ebbing Eddy Rocks are also known as the Barr Rocks.

Coming from the north, to avoid Braga Skerry and Kirk Rocks, do not turn into the Sound until the highest croft house on Graemsay is open to the south of the lower light (i.e. bearing less than 128°). In poor visibility or uncertainty concerning identification, keep on or just outside the 20m contour until Breck Ness bears northeast, then turn in to run along the 10m contour. This will keep you north of the tide race and clear of the Kirk Rocks. The approach to Stromness is marked by leading lights bearing 317° which are exhibited from small white towers within the town (see plan p.42). Keep to the buoyed channel as the shores are shoal.

It is unwise, without local knowledge, to leave Stromness on the full west-going tide. Passage west through Hoy Sound is best made about 30 minutes before the end of the west-going tide. By then the roost is much reduced and following the 10m line on the north side of Hoy Sound will lead clear of both the roost and the Kirk Rocks.

When approaching Stromness from Scapa Flow the leading lights need to be carefully identified as they are very similar to lights on the pier on the east side of Graemsay.

Buoyage

From the south approaches to Scapa Flow, up to and including Hoy Sound and irrespective of the tidal stream, buoys are laid with port hand buoys being left to port when sailing north and west.

Graemsay High lighthouse

Gerry Cannon

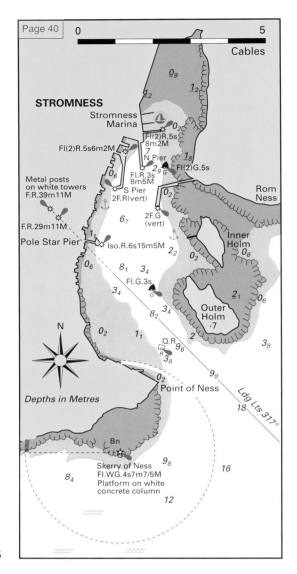

Admiralty Chart
2568, 0035, 2249
Imray Chart
C68
Ordnance Survey
7

Page 40

STROMNESS

Stromness Marina

Fl(2)R.5s6m2M

Fl(2)R.5s
8m2M

N Pier

Fl(2)G.5s

Metal posts
on white towers
F.R.39m11M

Fl.R.3s
8m5M
S Pier
2F.R(vert)

2F.G
(vert)

F.R.29m11M

Pole Star Pier

Iso.R.6s15m5M

Rom Ness

Inner Holm

Fl.G.3s

Outer Holm ·7

N

Depths in Metres

Q.R

Point of Ness

Ldg Lts 317°

Bn

Skerry of Ness
Fl.WG.4s7m7/5M
Platform on white
concrete column

STROMNESS

Stromness Harbour

Stromness is the second largest town in Orkney and a main seaport. It is a convenient port for yachts coming to and from Orkney.

Tide

Stromness −0205 Wick (−0150 Dover)

Heights in metres

MHWS	MHWN	MTL	MLWN	MLWS
3·6	2·7	2·1	1·4	0·7

Directions

Before entering the harbour area, vessels over 12m are required to report to Orkney Vessel Traffic Services (VTS) on Ch 11. Ch 14 is the working VHF channel for Stromness Harbour.

Stromness harbourmaster can be contacted via ☎ 01856 873636.

As you approach the marina in the north of the harbour, give the green starboard hand buoy (Fl(2)G) east of the RoRo ferry berth a wide berth as it marks a shallow patch coming out from Copland's Dock.

Note the large pier on the east side of the harbour (not marked on Admiralty Chart 2568 in 2015). It is not a good place to tie up due to the fendering intended for large vessels.

Anchorage

Yachts should berth at the marina which lies north of the RoRo Terminal. It has 14 visitors' berths serviced with water and electricity. Depths at pontoons (measured 2015): north pontoon 2m for all berths; south pontoon 2·3m on north side, 3·1m on south side, 2·5m at hammerhead.

Visitors' berths are on the south side of the south pontoon. Before entering or leaving the marina, yachts over 12m should contact the harbourmaster on Ch 14 to check that there are no commercial shipping movements imminent. The marina is operated by an agent who can be contacted on ☎ 07810 465825. Alternatively, anchor between South Pier and Pole Star Pier off the town and outside local moorings, or between the Inner and Outer Holms.

Facilities

All facilities are available including boatyard and laying-up. Mechanical repairs at Hamnavoe Engineering. Marine diesel, petrol, restaurants, hotels, swimming pool and showers. Showers, laundry facilities and free wifi are available in the marina. RoRo ferry from Stromness to Scrabster and air services from Kirkwall 15 miles away. Ferry service to Hoy. Excellent bus service on Orkney Mainland. Museums.

Interest

Many of the internationally important archaeological sites in Orkney can be accessed by bus from Stromness.

Stromness Harbour

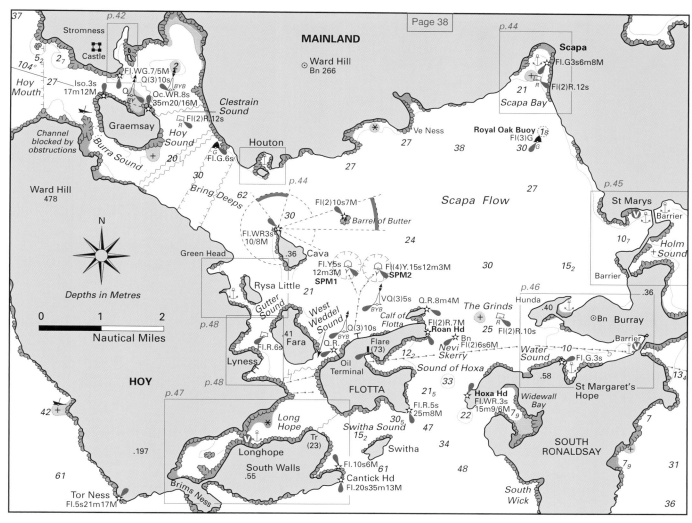

Scapa Flow

Scapa Flow is a large bay of more than 120 square km sheltered by islands. Depths generally are less than 36m and there are many good anchorages though there are large areas where anchoring is prohibited. The closing of the sounds on the east side during the Second World War by the Churchill Barriers has disturbed the tidal streams.

There is a major North Sea oil terminal on the island of Flotta.

North of Flotta and southeast of Cava are two lit towers for oil tanker mooring that have pipes for shipping oil to Flotta. The east one is decommissioned. The west one has a floating 50m pipe which needs to be given a wide berth. It is best to avoid this area.

Scapa Flow is a busy recreational diving location and there are many dive boats from March to November on the wrecks. These fly the A flag and should be given a wide berth.

Tide

The tidal flows within Scapa Flow are generally weak.

The tidal constants and heights are fairly uniform. Values for tidal constants and heights in Scapa Flow are given in the *Admiralty Tide Tables* at St Mary's and Widewall Bay:

St Mary's at north end of Churchill Barriers on Mainland Orkney south of Kirkwall
Constant –0140 Wick (–0290 Dover)

Heights in metres

MHWS	MHWN	MTL	MLWN	MLWS
3·3	2·6	2·0	1·4	0·6

Widewall Bay at northwest of South Ronaldsay
Constant –0155 Wick (–0145 Dover)

Heights in metres

MHWS	MHWN	MTL	MLWN	MLWS
3·6	2·7	2·0	1·3	0·4

Directions

Access to Scapa Flow is by Hoy Sound or from the Pentland Firth.

A careful watch must be kept for uncharted buoys, also the Barrel of Butter skerry and the Grinds shoal. Do not attempt to make a passage between Graemsay and Hoy through Burra Sound as it is partially blocked with wrecks of blockships sunk in 1939.

Beware of ferry traffic in the Sound.

For passage through the Sound of Hoxa see pp. 26 and 27.

For entry to Scapa Flow from the west via Hoy Sound see directions for Hoy Sound on p.41.

SCAPA FLOW

Admiralty Chart
0035, 2249, 2581
Imray Chart
C68
Ordnance Survey
7

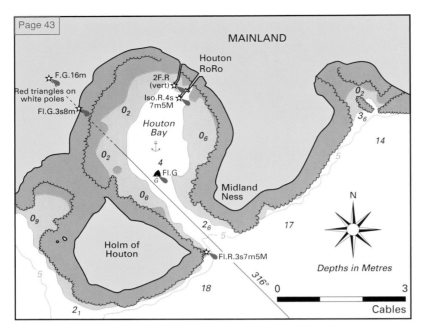

Page 43

MAINLAND

Houton RoRo

F.G.16m
Red triangles on white poles
Fl.G.3s8m

2F.R (vert)
Iso.R.4s 7m5M

Houton Bay

Midland Ness

Holm of Houton

Fl.G

Fl.R.3s7m5M

316°

Depths in Metres

N

0   Cables   3

HOUTON BAY

Admiralty Chart
0035, 2568-1

Imray Chart
C68

Ordnance Survey
7

Houton Bay

Houton Bay is a sheltered anchorage on the north of Scapa Flow about 5 miles southeast of Stromness.

Tide

The tidal stream between Holm of Houton and Cava is about 0·5kn in each direction and increases towards Hoy Sound where the maximum rate is 7kn.

Directions

The entrance is on the east side of Holm of Houton. Reefs on either side reduce the width

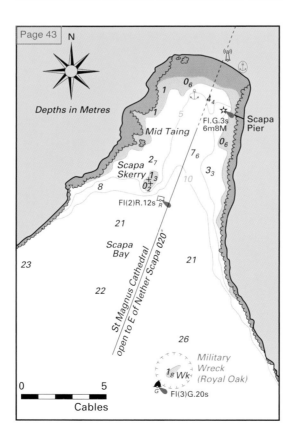

Page 43   N

Depths in Metres

Mid Taing

Scapa Skerry

Fl.G.3s 6m8M

Scapa Pier

Fl(2)R.12s

Scapa Bay

St Magnus Cathedral open to E of Nether Scapa 020°

Military Wreck (Royal Oak)

Wk

Fl(3)G.20s

0   Cables   5

SCAPA BAY

of the channel which is dredged to 3·5m for 15m each side of the leading line.

In the northeast of the bay are terminals for the Lyness RoRo ferry and the Flotta Oil Terminal passenger launches.

To the southeast of the RoRo pier there is a slip.

Anchorage

In the bay the depth is 5·5m in the centre. From there the bottom slopes steeply to the west and gradually to the east. The bottom is generally sand with some weed. Sheltered in all winds except at high water when it is exposed to the southwest.

Facilities

The RoRo ferry is met by a bus for Kirkwall.

Scapa Bay

Scapa Bay at the north of Scapa Flow is 1½ miles across the isthmus south from Kirkwall. It is an open sandy bay exposed to the south and southwest.

Directions

Keeping St Magnus Cathedral open its own length to the east of Nether Scapa (white house) and bearing 020° clears the Royal Oak wreck and Scapa Skerry 9 cables from the head of the bay. The Royal Oak Buoy should be left to starboard although there is a passage inshore. Give the west shore a very wide berth. The head of the bay dries out.

Anchorage

Anchor in 4–8m half way from Scapa Skerry to the head of the bay but keep well clear of the fairway leading to the pier as there is considerable commercial traffic, particularly the tugs which serve the tankers to and from the Oil Terminal on Flotta. Small yachts can anchor north of the pier for shelter but there is very little room because of local moored vessels. Bottom sand. There is one visitors' mooring. The pier has a depth of 3m at its outer end but is heavily used. The bay provides good anchorage unless the wind is in the south when it is subject to swell. It is an impossible anchorage in a southwest gale but in an offshore wind it is possible, with permission of the piermaster, to lie on the end or on the south side of the pier.

Facilities

The head of Scapa Bay is 1½miles from Kirkwall, the largest town in Orkney. The head office of the Orkney Islands Council Marine Services is situated at the junction of the shore road and the road leading to Kirkwall. Information on up to date availability of visitors' moorings throughout the Orkney Islands can be obtained there. (☎ 01856 873636)

St. Mary's Bay

St Mary's lies on the north side of Kirk Sound west of the Churchill Barrier. St Mary's is in the parish of Holm (pronounced 'Ham') by which name the area is known.

Tide

Tidal streams are weak due to the Barrier.

Constant - see Scapa Flow Tides.

Anchorage

Good anchorage in Bay of Ayre off the village in 2–6m keeping well clear of the barrier which is foul. Vessels may come alongside the pier and there is a slip on the east side of it. A visitors' mooring is laid in the middle of the bay.

Facilities

Post Office, shop. Active dinghy sailing club.

Interest

The Italian Chapel built by prisoners of war on Lamb Holm.

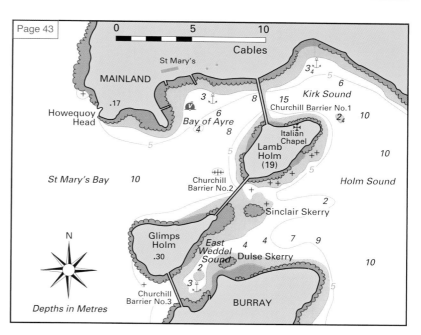

ST MARY'S BAY AND HOLM SOUND

David Hawgood / Geograph

The Italian Chapel, Lamb Holm

WATER SOUND AND
HUNDA SOUND

Admiralty Chart
0035
Imray Chart
C68
Ordnance Survey
7

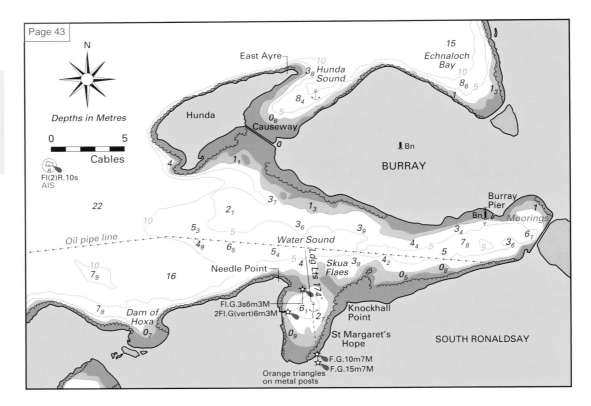

Burray Village

Burray Village is located west of the Churchill Barrier on the north shore of Water Sound.

Tide

Tidal streams are weak in Water Sound due to the Churchill Barrier.

Anchorage

Good anchorage in 2–6m just west of the Barrier. Normally there is a visitors' mooring just off the pier in summer. Keep clear of pipe line and submarine cables. Vessels can lie alongside the end of the pier. Depth 2m.

Facilities

Post Office, shop, garage, hotel. Water at head of pier.

St. Margaret's Hope

St Margaret's Hope is a small bay opening off the south side of Water Sound between Needle Point on the west and Knockhall Point on the east.

Directions

A spit of stones which dries 1·8m extends 1 cable east from Needle Point. Its end is marked with a beacon. On the east side Skua Flaes, a ridge of rocks with about 1m over it and covered with kelp, extends about 3 cables northwest. There is 2·7m in the entrance

channel. The pier, on the west side and extending 100m, has 3m at the outer end. At the head of the bay the shore is foul and dries for 1 cable.

Anchorage

Anchor south of the lifeboat mooring or berth on the north side of the pier. Beware of moorings in southeast of the bay.
Harbourmaster ☎01856 831646
Mobile 07912 063637

Facilities

Post Office with shop. Diesel at petrol station. Two hotels, café, 4-star restaurant. There is a RoRo ferry service from the pier to Gills Bay on the Scottish mainland.

Hunda Sound

Hunda Sound is on the east side of Scapa Flow and separates Hunda and Burray Islands.

Directions

Hunda Sound is entered from the northeast and is closed at the southwest end by a causeway.

Anchorage

Good anchorage in all winds. The shores are shoal close in but the middle of the sound has depths of 7–11m and good holding ground.

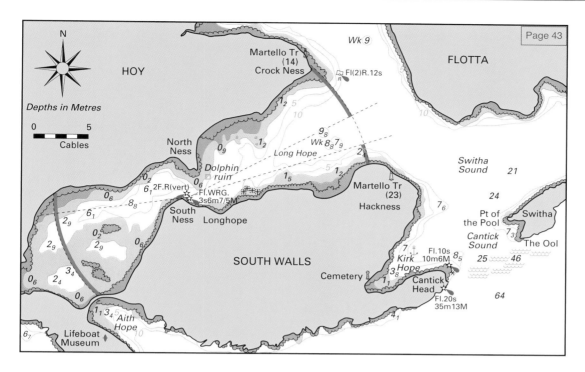

LONGHOPE,
SOUTH WALLS

Admiralty Chart
2162, 2581

Imray Chart
C68

Ordnance Survey
7

Long Hope

Long Hope is the sound between the islands of Hoy and South Walls.

Longhope village is situated at the narrows between north and South Ness on South Walls which is connected to Hoy by a causeway.

Directions

The entrance to Long Hope is recognised by the Martello towers on Crock Ness to the north and Hackness to the south. Give both shores a wide berth as they are fringed with reefs.

A shoal extends south about 2 cables from North Ness and there is a dolphin ruin (marked on Admiralty Chart as 'RU') 1 cable east-southeast of the Ness. A spit which dries 0·3m extends ½ cable north from South Ness. There is a strong tide through the narrows and this affects the approach to the pier. There is a narrow channel leading to the inner part of Long Hope. At night there is a sectored light leading to the pier. The pierhead exhibits a 2F.R(vert) light.

Anchorage

Anchor in 4 to 6m east of pier on South Ness. There is a depth of 4m at the outer end of the pier, the south side of which is used by the RoRo ferry.

A berth may be obtainable in the harbour. Care needs to be taken upon entering the harbour because of cross tides. Two visitors' moorings have been laid east of the pier. Harbourmaster ☎ 01856 791341 (at Longhope).

Facilities

RNLI station with shop. Water at pier. Toilets and showers. Hotels, Post Office, shop and garage; petrol and auto-diesel.

Longhope Harbour from the northeast

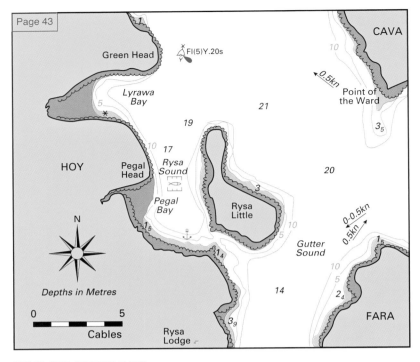

PEGAL AND LYRAWA BAYS

Admiralty Chart
0035, 2568–2
Imray Chart
C68
Ordnance Survey
7

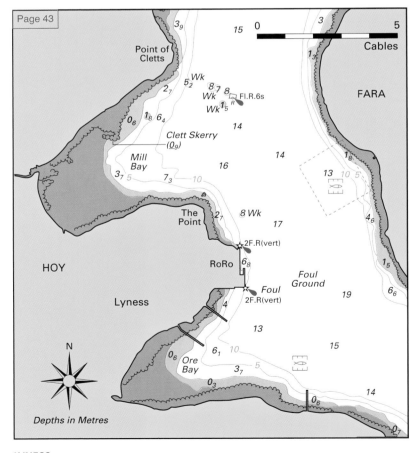

LYNESS

Pegal and Lyrawa Bays

Pegal Bay lies between Hoy and Rysa Little Island and Lyrawa Bay is north of Pegal Head.

Directions

The approach to Pegal Bay through Rysa Sound from the north is straightforward. The southeast entrance to Rysa Sound is considerably narrowed by shallow spits which extend out from each shore.

Anchorage

Pegal Bay The anchorage in the south of the bay has good holding but is subject to very fierce squalls off the Hoy hills in westerly gales. Note that the anchorage area shelves steeply.

Lyrawa Bay has good holding but is deep (9m) and exposed to east. It shoals extensively.

Lyness

An abandoned naval base on Hoy, west of Fara. It is a base for renewable energy development.

Directions

It is accessible through Gutter Sound or West Weddel Sound.

Anchorage

Anchorage in Ore Bay is not recommended due to the bottom being foul with old hawsers. Temporary alongside berths may be available on the concrete jetty on east side of Lyness peninsula but keep clear of the RoRo jetty. This provides easy access to the museum but beware of wash from passing commercial traffic. Harbourmaster ✆ 01856 791341.

Facilities

The RoRo ferry to Houton Bay on Mainland Orkney operates from here.

There is a large museum in Lyness commemorating the use of Lyness by the Royal Navy in the first and second world wars and the scuttling of the German Fleet. Well worth a visit.

Charles Tait

Lyness

David Purchase – Geograph

East Weddel Sound (pp. 45 & 51) Looking south along the barrier to the blockship and Burray.
The anchorage is off to the left in the centre of Weddel Bay

Charles Tait

Copinsay from the north

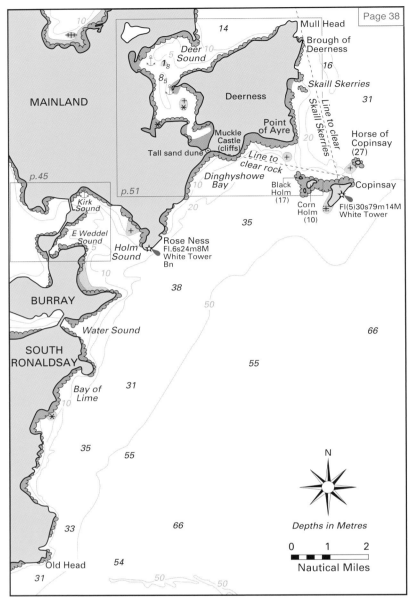

SOUTHEAST COAST, OLD HEAD TO STRONSAY FIRTH

South Ronaldsay, Copinsay in the distance

Southeast Coast

Old Head to Stronsay Firth

Tide

Between Old Head (at southeast of South Ronaldsay) and Copinsay:
The tidal stream runs dominantly southwards but is not strong. There is no N-going stream. The S-going stream tends to be weaker towards the South Ronaldsay shore.

In Copinsay Pass:
Southwest-going stream starts +0420 Aberdeen (−0455 Dover)
Southeast-going stream starts −0205 Aberdeen (+0015 Dover)
Spring rates 3kn

In Stronsay Firth between Auskerry (south of Stronsay) and Mull Head (northeast of Deerness):
Southeast-going stream starts +0450 Aberdeen (−0515 Dover)
Northwest-going stream starts −0135 Aberdeen (+0045 Dover)
Spring rates 4kn

Burray Ness at east end of Burray Island between South Ronaldsay and Mainland Orkney:
Constant +0030 Wick (+0015 Dover)

Heights in metres

MHWS	MHWN	MTL	MLWN	MLWS
3·3	2·5	1·9	1·3	0·6

Directions

Passage North If proceeding north against the tide between Old Head and Copinsay, holding towards the South Ronaldsay shore may help if the tide is contrary. Alternatively hold well out to the east.

It may be better to sail to the east of Copinsay although Copinsay Pass is negotiable with care (see below).

A race forms off Mull Head during the southeast-going tidal stream. This is particularly violent when opposed by the wind. Hold well off to even as much as 2 miles in certain weather and tide conditions to avoid steep and irregular seas. After passing Mull Head a vessel on passage to the North Islands can avoid the Stronsay Firth tide races by passing 3 miles east of a line joining Auskerry and Copinsay.

Copinsay Pass This is the channel between Copinsay and Mainland Orkney. If proceeding north, keep about two thirds of the way out between the shore of Deerness and Black Holm to avoid the rocks 5 cables southwest of Point of Ayre. Note that the tide sets northwest towards the shoals inshore. Holding a course that is south of the line between Dingieshowe, the tallest sand dune at the south end of the sandy beach (58°54·9'N 02°47'W), and the cliffs at Muckle Castle clears dangers to the north.

Copinsay to Mull Head After clearing Copinsay Pass, continue northeast until Mull Head is open off the The Brough of Deerness. The course for Mull Head then leads clear of the Skaill Skerries, which extend over 5 cables offshore, and other dangers.

Passage South The same directions in reverse apply to the passage south through the Pass. In the Pass the southwest-going stream sets towards the shoals on the southeast side of the Pass. A race forms off Mull Head and an eddy causes the stream inshore between Skaill Skerries and Mull Head to be continuously north-going. The passage through the Pass is thus of little help when southbound.

Holm Sound

Holm Sound lies between mainland Orkney and the island of Burray see plans p.45 and p.50.

Directions

When approaching Holm Sound from the east especially in poor visibility care must be taken not to mistake the apparent opening at the head of Dingieshowe Bay for the entrance to Holm Sound. The light on Rose Ness with its nearby conspicuous stone beacon with black cross topmark should help in the identification of the entrance.

East Weddel Sound

Part of Holm Sound north of Burray (see plan p.45 and photo p.49).

Directions

Take the Glimps Holm side of the Sound to avoid Dulse Skerry.

Anchorage

Excellent anchorage on the east side of the Barrier in the centre of Weddel Bay (east of the blockship) with soundings of 2–4m and a sandy bottom.

Facilities

At St Mary's 2 miles or Burray village 2 miles.

Kirk Sound

North of Holm Sound and closed on its west side by the Churchill Barrier No 1.

It was through Kirk Sound in the second world war that a U boat crept in and sank the battleship *HMS Royal Oak* just south of Scapa Bay.

Directions

On entering, note the shallow patch to northeast of Lamb Holm.

Anchorage

In the bay, close inshore, north of the east end of Lamb Holm in 3–6m.

Interest

The Italian Chapel on Lamb Holm is remarkable.

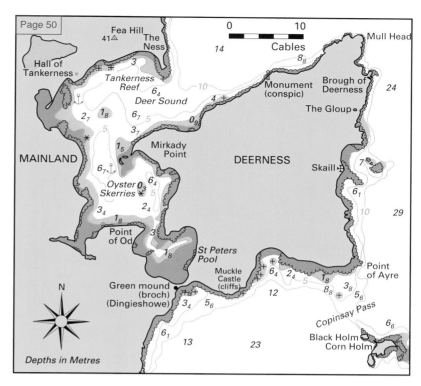

Deer Sound

Deer Sound is a sheltered harbour off the entrance to Stronsay Firth.

Tide

Deer Sound
Constant –0010 Wick (–0030 Dover)

Heights in metres

MHWS	MHWN	MTL	MLWN	MLWS
3·2	2·5	1·9	1·3	0·6

Directions

From the south and east give Mull Head a good offing - see directions for Passage Old Head to Stronsay Firth (p.50). Give both shores a good offing in Deer Sound, especially Tankerness Reef south of The Ness.

Anchorage

Give Tankerness Reef a wide berth. The Sound is reasonably free from fierce squalls. Yachts may anchor off the stone pier below the Hall of Tankerness on the northwest side of the Sound or in the Pool of Mirkady off Mirkady Point. There is insufficient water to allow lying alongside Tankerness Pier. Poor holding has been reported at the Pool of Mirkady.

St Peter's Pool is not recommended for anchoring.

Interest

The Broch of Dingieshowe, the castle at the Brough of Deerness near Mull Head and The Gloup, an archway over the sea.

Admiralty Chart
2162, 2250

Imray Chart
C68

Ordnance Survey
6, 7

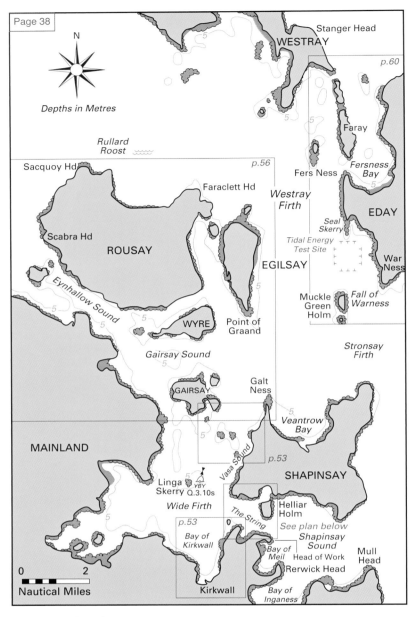

Page 38

N

Depths in Metres

Rullard
Roost

Sacquoy Hd

Faraclett Hd

Scabra Hd

ROUSAY

Eynhallow Sound

WYRE

Point of
Graand

Gairsay Sound

GAIRSAY

MAINLAND

Linga
Skerry Q.3.10s

Wide Firth

p.53

Bay of
Kirkwall

Kirkwall

WESTRAY

Stanger Head

p.60

Faray

Fers Ness

Fersness
Bay

Westray
Firth

EDAY

Seal
Skerry

Tidal Energy
Test Site

EGILSAY

War
Ness

Muckle
Green
Holm

Fall of
Warness

Stronsay
Firth

Galt
Ness

Veantrow
Bay

Vasa Sound

p.53

SHAPINSAY

Helliar
Holm

See plan below

Shapinsay
Sound

The String

Bay of
Meil

Head of Work

Mull
Head

Rerwick Head

Bay of
Inganess

0 — 2
Nautical Miles

p.56

KIRKWALL TO WESTRAY

Admiralty Chart
2249, 2250, 2584,
1553

Imray Chart
C68

Ordnance Survey
6, 7

*Lighthouse on Saeva
Ness, Helliar Holm
looking towards
Rerwick Head*

John Albiston

Passages to and from Kirkwall

There are four entrances to Wide Firth and hence Kirkwall. Three of them - through Shapinsay Sound and The String; through Vasa Sound or via the main buoyed channel from the north which passes to the east of Gairsay - are described below. The fourth, the passage from Eynhallow Sound, is described on p.56.

Tide

In the String (the channel between southeast Stronsay and Orkney Mainland):
West-going stream starts –0135 Aberdeen (+0045 Dover)
East-going stream starts +0450 Aberdeen (–0600 Dover)

In channel to the northwest of Vasa Point:
South-southwest-going stream starts +0405 Aberdeen (+0045 Dover)
North-northeast-going stream starts –0230 Aberdeen (–0010 Dover)
Spring rates 3–4 kn except in Vasa Sound where they can reach 5 kn

Directions

Shapinsay Sound and The String The String is the body of water to the west of Shapinsay Sound between Car Ness and Head of Work to the south, and Helliar Holm and Strombery on Shapinsay to the north.

Making passage through through Shapinsay Sound and The String can be uncomfortable in certain adverse conditions of tide, wind and swell. There is turbulence off the headlands with wind against tide. Even in calm weather there can be a very lumpy sea off Head of Work, Helliar Holm, Holm and Rerwick Head.

When awaiting the tide, anchorage may be found east of Helliar Holm. South of Strombery the tide reaches 4kn in each direction at springs. If making west against east-going tide in Shapinsay Sound, hold well to the north, east of Helliar Holm. This may

ELWICK AND THE STRING

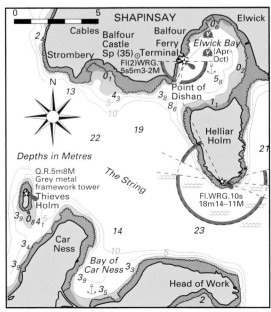

0 — 5
Cables

SHAPINSAY

Elwick

Balfour
Castle
Sp (35)

Balfour
Ferry
Terminal

Elwick Bay
(Apr–Oct)

Strombery

Fl(2)WRG.
5s5m3–2M

Point of
Dishan

N

13

4₃

3₈

8₆

1₁

22

19

Helliar
Holm

21

Depths in Metres

Q.R.5m8M
Grey metal
framework tower
Thieves
Holm

The String

3₉ 0₈4₁

Fl.WRG.10s
18m14–11M

3₄

Car
Ness

14

23

3₉

Bay of
Car Ness 3₃

3₅

Head of Work

3₉

allow further progress to reach Elwick Bay. The south point of Helliar Holm is clean close to. In bays on the south side of Shapinsay Sound there are eddies and slack water.

With caution the passage inside Thieves Holm (northwest of Car Ness) may be taken. Keep mid-channel to avoid 2m patch 1 cable south of Thieves Holm but after passing the patch keep well clear of the Car Ness shore avoiding Iceland Skerry.

Vasa Sound There is turbulence over the shoals. Going south, the leading line is picked up off Salt Ness (cathedral spire in line with west side of Strombery, the southwest headland of Shapinsay, bearing 194°). This course is held until Gairsay opens behind Skerry of Vasa Beacon (bearing 314°). Then steer to give Strombery a good offing.

Passage East of Gairsay Alternatively, use the main buoyed channel east of Hen of Gairsay. Pass west of the N cardinal buoy (Q) marking Skertours; pass 1 cable east of the S cardinal buoy marking Boray Skerries (Q(6)+Lfl.15s); pass east of E Cardinal buoy (Q(3)10s) marking Linga Skerry.

The Kirkwall sector light clears all obstructions from Linga Skerry onwards

Eynhallow Sound See p.56.

Kirkwall

Kirkwall, the main town of Orkney, lies at the head of Kirkwall Bay at the south of Wide Firth. It is a busy port for ferry communication, commercial shipping and cruise ships.

Tide

Kirkwall
Constant –0040 Wick (–0030 Dover)

Heights in metres

MHWS	MHWN	MTL	MLWN	MLWS
3·4	2·7	2·1	1·6	0·8

Directions

Before entering Kirkwall harbour area, vessels over 12m are required to report to Orkney Vessel Traffic Services (VTS) on Ch 11. Ch 14 is the working VHF channel for Kirkwall Harbour.

Before entering or leaving the marina, yachts should contact the harbourmaster on Ch 14 (or via ☎ 01856 873636) to check that there are no commercial shipping movements imminent.

Anchorage

Visitors' berths are available in the marina in depths of 2–4m. (Marina ☎ 01856 871313). Yachts may anchor to the northwest of the harbour area.

Good anchorages may be found to the north and east of Kirkwall at Bay of Carness (south of The String), Bay of Meil and Inganess Bay (south of Shapinsay Sound) and Elwick Bay (on Shapinsay, north of The String). All these anchorages have little tidal stream.

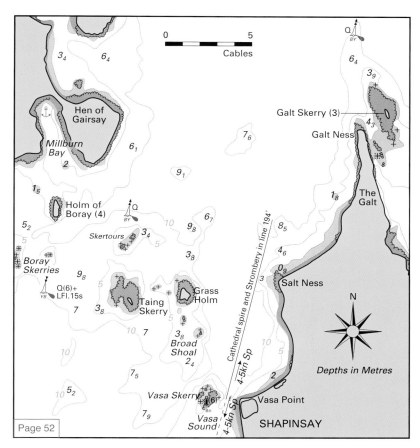

GAIRSAY AND VASA SOUND PASSAGES

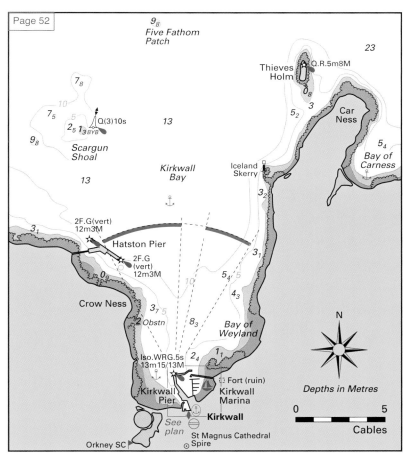

APPROACHES TO KIRKWALL

Alan Guthrie

Kirkwall Marina with Wideford Hill in the distance

Facilities

Water and all stores available in the town, 25-ton mobile crane, diesel, calor gas, fibreglass repairs, engine repairs, laundrette. Air and sea links with Scottish mainland.

Toilet and shower block at head of marina pontoon.

The Orkney Sailing Club is based in Kirkwall. Club facilities are available to visiting yachtsmen including advice on Orkney waters.

Local weather on Kirkwall Harbour Radio VHF Ch 16, 11(VTS) at 0915 hrs and 1715 hrs local time.

Interest

Many of the internationally important archaeological sites in Orkney can be accessed by bus from Kirkwall.

In Kirkwall there is St Magnus Cathedral, the Bishop's Palace and Tankerness House.

Kirkwall Harbour

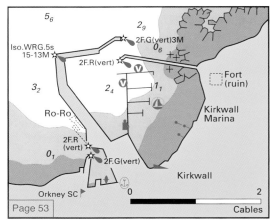

KIRKWALL

Orkney Tourist Board, 6 Broad Street, Kirkwall, Orkney KW15 1NX. ① 01856 872856 for guide books, maps and leaflets detailing places of interest in each of the main islands.

Orkney Islands Council

Shapinsay

An intensively cultivated island between Stronsay Firth and mainland Orkney.

Directions

For passage through Shapinsay Sound and The String see p.52.

To enter Elwick Bay pass west of Helliar Holm in mid-channel. Beware of tidal set in The String (rate 5kn at springs).

Anchorage

Elwick Bay Good shelter off Balfour in 2·5–3m. Note that the shores are fringed with a shallow bank. Bottom sand. Two visitors' moorings available in west of bay. Good place to anchor if crowded in Kirkwall.

Veantrow Bay on north of Shapinsay is reported as uncomfortable. Anchor on east side in 6–9m on sand.

Helliar Holm Temporary anchorage on east side in sand.

David Bowdler

Visitors' mooring, Shapinsay

Facilities

At Balfour there are toilets, water, a shop, Post Office and bar (open irregularly). Ferry service to Kirkwall.

Balfour Pier, Shapinsay

Orkney Islands Council

Eynhallow Sound

Barrie Waugh

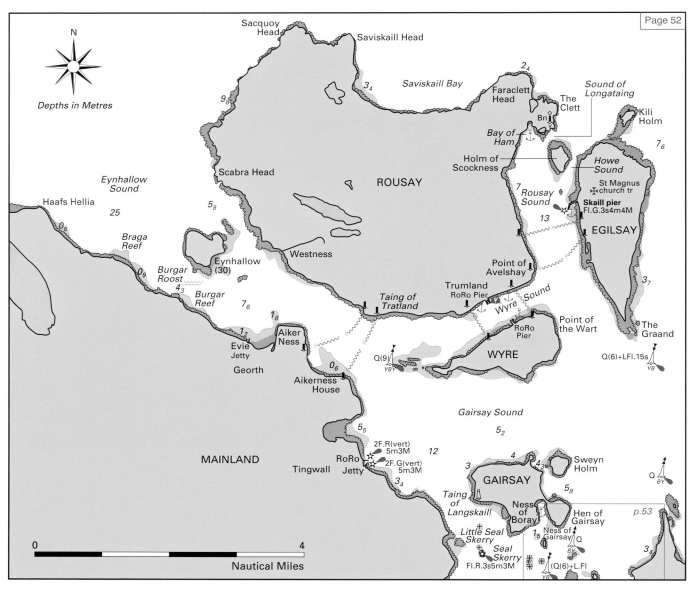

**ROUSAY, EGILSAY
AND WYRE AND
EYNHALLOW SOUND**

Admiralty Chart
2249
Imray Chart
C68
Ordnance Survey
6

Eynhallow Sound

The Sound is between Mainland Orkney and the island of Rousay. It is the main channel for access from the west of Orkney to Kirkwall.

Tide

In Eynhallow Sound:
Southeast-going stream starts +0420 Aberdeen (−0545 Dover)
Northwest-going stream starts −0205 Aberdeen (+0015 Dover)
Spring rates 2–3 kn in northwest entrance
Spring rates 7 kn in the channels northeast and southwest of Eynhallow

In the channel between Gairsay and Mainland:
Southeast-going stream starts +0435 Aberdeen (−0530 Dover)
Northwest-going stream starts −0150 Aberdeen (+0030 Dover)

Directions

Passage from Southeast to the Sound Steer for E Cardinal Linga Skerry Buoy and leave it to port. Then steer for Seal Skerry Beacon (334°) which should be left well to port.

When Ness of Boray and Ness of Gairsay are in line, alter course 20° to port to pass well clear of Little Seal Skerry. When Taing of Langskail (Tower (6m) on point) is abeam, steer for the cliffs at Taing of Tratland on the southwest of Rousay just open (325°).

Passage West through the Sound The principal problem to be faced on this passage is the Burgar Roost in in the narrows between the Burgar Reef and Eynhallow where heavy overfalls occur on the west-going tide, especially with wind against tide or when a westerly swell can increase the size of the roost.

Arrive at Aiker Ness at the east end of Eynhallow Sound during the last two hours of the west-going tide at neaps and not earlier than the last hour at springs.

From a position abreast of Aikerness, steer a course parallel to the Rousay shore until well clear of the rocks that extend to the northwest of Aikerness. Then head for the narrows between Eynhallow and the Mainland shore. (See photographs p.2 and p.55.)

Eynhallow Sound Narrows On arrival at Aiker Ness, if there appears to be too much sea at the roost, one can anchor either off Evie jetty or on the east side of Aiker Ness (in 5m off Aikerness House but in the approach keep within ¾ cable of the Aiker Ness shore to avoid shoal area to the east).

Much turbulence can be avoided by keeping nearer the Mainland shore and when approaching the roost hold close to the southern edge of the roost but watch the depth and avoid being drawn inshore where there is shoal water.

Having passed Eynhallow and the roost, give the Braga Reef a good berth

Passage west to east Entry from the northwest using the east-going tide does not present the same problems as with the west-going tide. There are no overfalls between Eynhallow and Orkney Mainland.

For the passage southeast after passing through the Sound, use the reciprocal courses to those given above for the northwest-going passage.

Rousay, Egilsay & Wyre

Rousay lies northeast of Mainland Orkney, separated from it by Eynhallow Sound. Rousay is a peat-covered hilly island (highest point 248m) with terraced slopes. Egilsay and Wyre are low-lying. St Magnus church tower at Skaill on Egilsay is a useful landmark.

Tide

The tidal streams in Rousay Sound are weak except at the narrows at the north entrance by the Sound of Longataing and Howe Sound where the spring rate is 6 kn. The tidal streams in Wyre Sound are weak.

Egilsay
Constant −0125 Wick (−0115 Dover)

Heights in metres

MHWS	MHWN	MTL	MLWN	MLWS
3·4	2·8	2·1	1·6	0·8

Directions

The approach to Rousay Sound through Eynhallow Sound should be made by keeping 4 cables off the Rousay shore to clear the shallows north of the west end of Wyre.

When approaching the Rousay Ferry Pier in Wyre Sound from Rousay Sound keep well over to the Rousay side which is steep-to and without dangers from the Point of Avelshay to the pier.

In Rousay Sound there are no dangers on the Rousay coast more than 1 cable offshore.

The Egilsay coast is clear up to 2½ cables south of Skaill Pier where there is a rock with 0·3m over it 1½ cables offshore. Another skerry which dries, lies 2 cables northwest of the pier.

The north entrance to Rousay Sound is obstructed by Holm of Stockness and should only be attempted under favourable conditions via the Sound of Longataing which has a fairway with a depth of 4m and is less than 1 cable wide.

Given fair conditions and a northeast-going tide it is easy enough to exit Rousay Sound via the Sound of Longtaing although there can be noticeable 'step' in a strong ebb. Entering from the north may be tricky as timing the tide to arrive at the narrow entrance at the start of the flood will be difficult and the southwest-going stream in the Sound of Longataing can be very strong.

Anchorage

Wyre Sound Anchor east or west of Rousay Ferry Pier; close inshore out of the tide gives reasonable shelter. Small vessels may lie alongside the east side of the pier if room permits. The west side is taken by the ferry. It is possible to lie on the west side of the old pier in an easterly. One visitors' mooring at Rousay Pier.

Anchorage may also be had off the Wyre shore east-southeast of the Wyre Ferry Pier. Berthing is possible on the 'T' of this pier.

Rousay Sound Shelter from the north and west can be found in the Bay of Ham at the north of the Sound in 3·5–5·5m.

Skaill (Egilsay) Anchor on a sandy bottom off the pier. Sheltered from the west but subject to swell from the northeast and the south.

Millburn Bay (Gairsay) (plan p.53) An inlet on the south side of Gairsay lying to the west of the Hen of Gairsay. Approach using Chart 2584 and anchor in mud at the head. Sheltered from all directions except south.

Facilities

Restaurant and craft shop near Rousay pier. On Wyre there are toilets at the pierhead.

Interest

Rousay Many objects of great archaeological interest. Outstanding tours.

Egilsay St Magnus Church

Wyre Cubbie Roo's castle. Remains of the oldest stone castle in Scotland.

Rousay pier

Orkney Islands Council

Admiralty Chart
2249, 2250, 2562-2

Imray Chart
C68

Ordnance Survey
5, 6,

Westray and Stronsay Firths

Westray Firth and Stronsay Firth form a channel which connects the Atlantic Ocean and the North Sea and divides the northern group of Orkney Islands from the rest of Orkney - see plan p.38.

Tide

The flood tide flows southeast and the ebb northwest.

A race, Rullard Roost, forms north of Sacquoy Head (northwest point of Rousay) during the northwest stream. This is violent in westerly gales. Another race, Rull Roost, forms north-northeast of Faraclett Head (northeast point of Rousay) in mid-channel. This is worst during the northwest-going stream and in northwest gales can spread across the Firth making it dangerous.

Safe Offings

War Ness Reef (The Kirk) 59°08'N 2°47'W. See clearance lines on Chart 2250.

Kili Holm and Muckle Green Holm off-lying reefs Keep Auskerry Lt just obscured by Rothiesholm Head (pronounced 'Rousam'). This line also serves to clear War Ness.

Light

Auskerry South End Fl.20s34m20M White tower

Bay of Carrick, Calf Sound, Eday has a solitary visitors' mooring, seen here in use

Passage between Fersness Bay (Eday) and Kirkwall

On the northwest-going tide Turn out of the bay close round Fers Ness and proceed south along the shore out of the tide to the south end of Seal Skerry. If the vessel has reasonable power, cut across the tide to the north end of Muckle Green Holm. If the vessel is of low power, turn into the bay south of Seal Skerry and follow the coast line round to War Ness, then cut across the tide to the north end of Muckle Green Holm. The fast running tidal stream to the west of Muckle Green Holm (plan p.52) extends only 2 cables and this should be quickly crossed making good a course for Galt Skerry Buoy (northwest of Shapinsay). From there proceed through Vasa Sound or anchor in the bight on the west of Shapinsay, just south of Galt Ness until the tide slackens off.

On the southeast-going tide Proceed from Fersness across the Firth towards the Egilsay shore making good a course for The Graand Buoy (south end of Egilsay). From there proceed through Vasa Sound with the tide, or use the west buoyed channel.

Rousay Sound Attempting to enter Rousay Sound through the Sound of Longataing from the north after crossing the Westray Firth can be difficult - see directions for Rousay, Egilsay and Wyre on p.57.

South coast of Eday There is a prolonged period of slack water off the south coast of Eday from +0500 Aberdeen to –0200 Aberdeen which can be useful when making passage to or from Stronsay.

Peter Bruce

Eday

The island of Eday lies in the middle of the north group of the Orkney Islands between Westray and Sanday.

Tide

Tidal streams in the south of The North Sound are weak. The spring rate in the narrows of the Sound of Faray is 4kn.

In Weatherness Sound and Sound of Faray
North-going stream starts +0155 Aberdeen (+0415 Dover)
South-going stream starts -0405 Aberdeen (–0145 Dover)
Spring rates in in both sounds 4 kn

In Calf Sound and Lashy Sound
South-going stream starts +0505 Aberdeen (+0500 Dover)
North-going stream starts -0250 Aberdeen (–0030 Dover)
Spring rates 6 kn in narrows east of Calf of Eday and in Calf Sound

A powerful roost forms at the north entrance to Calf Sound in strong north-northwesterly winds against a north-going tide and the area should then be avoided. There is calmer water at the sides of the entrance but beware of uncharted rocks on the west side of the north entrance close to the shore.

The narrows of Lashy Sound should also be avoided with north gales and north-going tide when a race forms in the narrows. Note that there is only 20 minutes' slack water in this sound.

War Ness Skerry (The Kirk) off the south point of Eday causes a race which, in southerly gales with wind against tide, can be dangerous.

Directions

Channel between Holms of Spurness and Sanday Chart 2562-2 notes that this channel, The Keld, is buoyed and gives a leading line through it - 240° on Ward Hill, Eday.

South Skerry is a significant unmarked hazard (1·5m) approximately 1 mile south-southeast of the N cardinal buoy marking Eday Gruna.

Calf Sound The entrance from the north is easily identified by Red Head and Grey Head which contrast with the low coastline. Red Head and Red Holm are quite red in colour.

A sectored light Fl(3)WRG.10s at the bend in Calf Sound shows white sectors over the north and southeast entrances to the sound. The white sector through the north entrance leads clear of the Holms of Ire at the northwest point of Sanday, but leads over shallow water on the west side of the sound where a rock with less than 2m has been reported to lie 1 cable offshore.

Anchorage

Fersness Bay at the south end of the Sound of Faray, gives shelter from all southerly winds. Anchor off the south shore out of the tide in 3·5m–7m. Vistors' mooring.

Bay of Backaland Anchor 2 cables northwest of the pier. Beware of cross tides. It may be possible to lie alongside the pier, clear of the ferry but not without keeping a constant watch. Visitors' mooring.

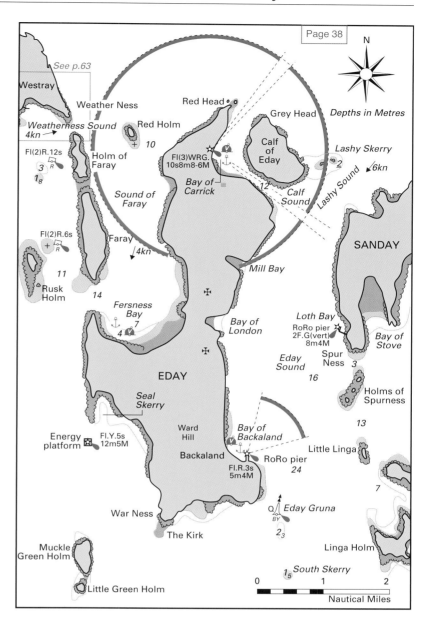

Bay of Carrick offers good shelter close inshore, out of the tide, in 3–4m below Carrick Visitors' mooring.

Facilities

Backaland. Water, petrol, auto-diesel, stores and Post Office. Ferry terminal pier.

Interest

Carrick House, where Gow, the Orkney Pirate, was finally captured in 1725. Ancient sites, RSPB reserve for Great Northern divers.

EDAY

Admiralty Chart
2250, 2562-2
Imray Chart
C68
Ordnance Survey
5, 6

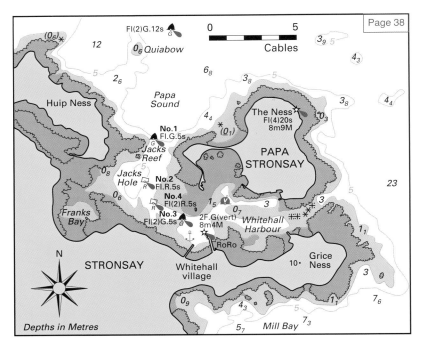

Page 38

PAPA SOUND,
STRONSAY

Admiralty Chart
2250, 2562-2

Imray Chart
C68

Ordnance Survey
5

Stronsay

Stronsay lies on the northeast side of Stronsay Firth. Papa Stronsay lies to its northeast, separated from it by Papa Sound.

Tide

Stronsay Whitehall
Constant   −0030 Wick (−0020 Dover)

Heights in metres

MHWS	MHWN	MTL	MLWN	MLWS
3·4	2·8	2·1	1·6	0·9

There is little tidal stream in Sanday Sound but it runs strongly through Spurness Sound where the southwest stream begins at −0310 Aberdeen (−0050 Dover) and attains 3·5kn at springs.

There is little tidal stream in Papa Sound.

Directions

Entry to Papa Sound The north entrance is between Huip Ness on Stronsay and a stony peninsula on Papa Stronsay. Six cables northeast of Huip Ness a G con buoy Fl(2)G.12s marks a submerged rock, Quiabow, with 0·6m over it.

Channel to Whitehall A spit east of Whitehall pier extends north 2 cables offshore. The east entrance is shallow and narrowed by reefs on either side and should not be attempted.

Anchorage

Whitehall Harbour Anchorage can be made anywhere space and soundings permit including to the north of the West Pier in depths of 2·4m–4m. There is one visitors' mooring.

The East Pier with the RoRo ferry has five yacht berths. Check with the harbourmaster, *mobile* 07901 984328 or ① 01857 616283, regarding availability.

Bay of Holland Anchor in depths of 3–8m. Well sheltered, except from the south.

St Catherine's Bay An occasional anchorage out of the tide on the east side of Linga Holm. The approach through Linga Sound is difficult especially as there is an uncharted rock, LD 0·4m, which can be avoided by holding towards Linga Holm.

Mill Bay Not recommended except for temporary shelter in northerly winds as the bottom is foul in places. When entering, avoid The Bow, a drying rock 4 cables northwest of Odness, and a drying rock 3 cables east-southeast of Grice Ness.

Facilities

Whitehall Village Post Office, shops, (early closing Thurs), building with museum and showers for visitors, hotel, fuel and water. Ferry to Kirkwall. Inter-island flights from Kirkwall, Sanday and Westray to airstrip northwest of Huip Ness. Museum. Departure point for access to monastic community on island of Papa Stronsay.

Whitehall Pier, Stronsay

Orkney Islands Council

Sanday

Sanday is an extensively cultivated island lying to the east of the northern group of Orkney Islands. It is low lying except for the southwest peninsula, which rises to 64m.

Tide

The tidal stream is weak in Sanday Sound but it runs strongly through Spurness Sound.

For Lashy Sound - see Eday p.59.

For North Ronaldsay Firth - see North Ronaldsay p.65)

Loth (southwest of Sanday on Eday Sound)
Constant –0030 Wick (–0040 Dover)
Heights in metres

MHWS	MHWN	MTL	MLWN	MLWS
3·1	2·5	2·0	1·5	0·9

Kettletoft Pier (south coast of Sanday)
Constant -0010 Wick (–0015 Dover)
Heights in metres

MHWS	MHWN	MTL	MLWN	MLWS
3·5	2·8	2·2	1·6	0·9

Directions

Start Point (see plan p.64) is the most easterly point on the island of Sanday. A race forms off it during the south-going stream and extends 1·5 miles offshore. It is violent in southeast gales. In the bay between Start Point and Tres Ness, there is an eddy on the south-going stream. In this bay the tidal stream is almost continuously northeast-going

Entry to Kettletoft Bay Kettletoft Bay is on the southeast of Sanday, opening south on to Sanday Sound. From the south, the bay should be entered to the west of Holm of Elsness, keeping at about 2 cables off the Holm, but note the 0·8m rock 4 cables west-southwest of Holm of Elsness. The leading line is the pierhead on a bearing of north.

If approaching the anchorage from the west, Bea Ness, the rocky point enclosing the bay on the west, should be given an offing of at least 3 cables but beware of shallow rocks (0·8m) to starboard.

Entry to Otterswick (See plan. p. 64.) The navigable entrance is considerably reduced by Long Taing, a reef which extends 5 cables offshore on the east side and Outer Skerry on the west side which is marked at its outer end by a G con. buoy (Fl.G.5s) 7 cables from the west shore.

North Bay (See plan. p.64.) On the west coast of Sanday, south of Holms of Ire. Enter from the northwest to clear Bow of Hermaness.

Anchorage

Kettletoft Bay Some protection from southerly winds is afforded by Holm of Elsness, a rocky islet surrounded by reefs extending about 1 cable offshore. There is a sectored light Fl.WRG.3s on the pierhead.

Use of the pier is not recommended. Anchorage may be found in the bay in 4m. Very exposed to southeast.

Otterswick (See plan p.64.) Situated on the north side of Sanday. Opens off North Ronaldsay Firth. It is a large, shallow bay with no tidal stream.

Anchor to suit the wind but give the shores a wide berth. Good shelter except in north and east winds.

North Bay Sheltered from north through east to south.

Facilities

Kettletoft Post Office and two hotels.

Admiralty Chart
2250, 2562-2
Imray Chart
C68
Ordnance Survey
5

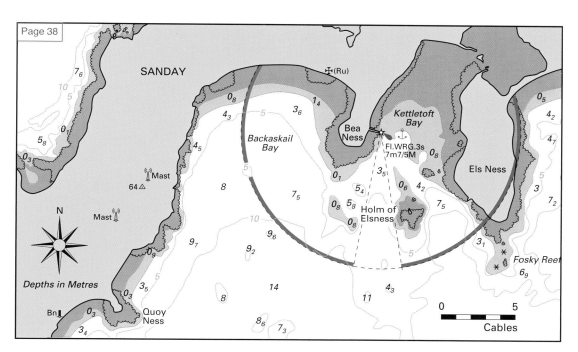

KETTLETOFT BAY, SANDAY

Admiralty Chart
2249, 2250, 2562-1

Imray Chart
C68

Ordnance Survey
5

WESTRAY AND
PAPA WESTRAY,
PIEROWALL

Westray and Papa Westray

Westray and Papa Westray, the northwest islands of the Orkney group, are separated by Papa Sound at the south end of which is Pierowall Road. There is a coastguard look-out (conspicuous) northwest of North Wick on Papa Westray.

A bay at the south end of Westray has the Rapness ferry terminal.

Tide

The tidal streams are weak in Papa Sound, except in the narrows at Holm of Aikerness where a roost forms with north wind and north-going tide.

A tide race forms off Mull Head, the north point of Papa Westray, known as the Bore Roost, on the west-going stream. Get clear of the area long before the west-going stream starts as the roost sets up very quickly.

In Papa Sound
South-going stream starts +0405 Aberdeen (−0600 Dover)
North-going stream starts −0220 Aberdeen (HW Dover)
Spring rates in narrows 2–3 kn

Rapnesss (south Westray)
Constant −0205 Wick (−0155 Dover)

Heights in metres

MHWS	MHWN	MTL	MLWN	MLWS
3·6	2·9	2·2	1·6	0·7

Pierowall (north Westray)
Constant −0150 Wick (−0140 Dover)

Heights in metres

MHWS	MHWN	MTL	MLWN	MLWS
3·7	2·8	–	1·4	0·6

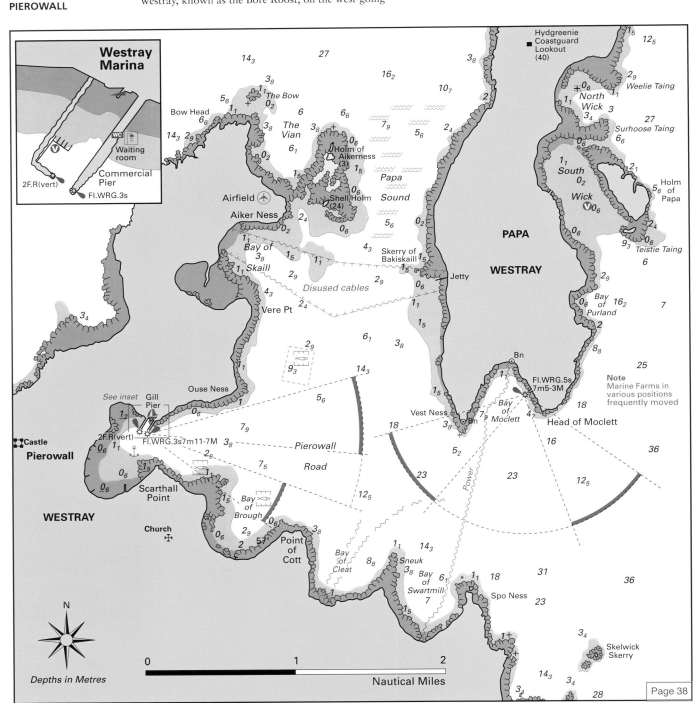

Directions

The approach to Pierowall from the east is straightforward but that from the north, through Papa Sound, requires care.

From the east keep well clear of Skelwick Skerry on the south side and the points between Spo Ness and Scarthall Point. In particular a drying reef extends for 3½ cables between the Bay of Cleat and the Bay of Swartmill. On the north side keep well clear of Vest Ness as there are rocks 1 cable offshore. Entering at night the white sector of Gill Pier lighthouse leads clear of all obstructions.

From the north keep well clear of the Holm of Aiker Ness and Shell Holm. The channel is shoal on the east side for 2 cables and is shallowest abreast of Shell Holm on the west side where the middle of the channel is 3 cables off Papa Westray. This offing should be maintained until on the leading line (216°) between the Coastguard Lookout on Papa Westray and the church on Westray can be followed in order to clear the shoal off Skerry of Backiskaill.

The church on the leading line is reported as difficult to identify.

Anchorage

Pierowall There is a marina on the West Pier with 80m of pontoons for visiting yachts. Depth MLWS 4m. There is 6m depth at the outer end of Gill Pier, which is used by trawlers. Contact the harbourmaster (VHF Ch 12, *mobile* 07787 364 934, ① 01857 677216,) to check berth availability.

There is good anchorage off Gill Pier in 6m. Good holding is reported. Pierowall Bay is a shallow bay where vessels can anchor in 2·5m. There is a visitors' mooring close to the pier.

Bay of Brough, Bay of Cleat and Bay of Swartmill It is possible to anchor in these bays but the holding is reported as not good.

Bay of Moclett This bay on Papa Westray is an excellent anchorage but open to the south. The island's main pier is also here, with the Kirkwall ferry calling on Tuesday and Friday. The passenger ferry based at Pierowall calls several times each day.

South Wick On the east side of Papa Westray, there is an attractive but shallow anchorage 1·5m off the pier. There is one visitors' mooring. Shop just over ½ mile.

Rapness Approaching from the south through Rapness Sound, note the 1·8m rock approximately 3 cables south-southwest of the red can buoy, Fl(2)R.12s, west of Holm of Faray. Approaching through Weatherness Sound keep more towards Holm of Faray to avoid drying rocks extending 1½ cables from Weather Ness. Anchor northwest of the ferry terminal keeping well clear of the ferry track.

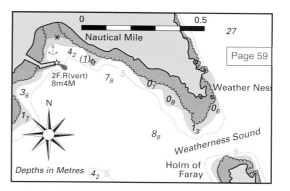

RAPNESS

Facilities

There is an air service between Westray and Papa Westray. The Westray to Kirkwall ferry terminus is at Rapness on the south tip of Westray.

Pierowall At Pierowall there is water and electricity at the marina and pier. Marine diesel and petrol in cans, gas. Post Office, good shops and hotel at Pierowall just over one mile from the marina. Laundry facilities at The Barn Hostel. Shower and toilet facilities on Gill Pier. Bicycle hire. Shellfish readily available from Westray Processors Ltd at the harbour.

The passenger ferry for Papa Westray is also based here.

Interest

Pierowall Notland Castle. Colonies of sea birds at Noup Head the west point of Westray; also the 'Gentleman's Cave' on south side of Noup Head. Active sailing club.

Orkney Islands Council

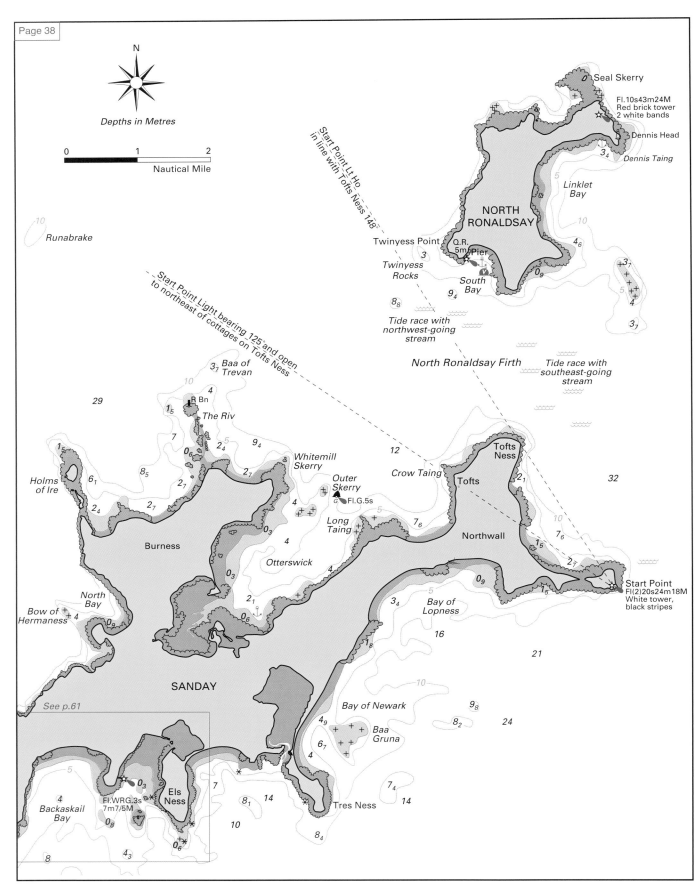

Page 38

N

Depths in Metres

0   1   2
Nautical Mile

Seal Skerry

Fl.10s43m24M
Red brick tower
2 white bands

Dennis Head

Dennis Taing

NORTH
RONALDSAY

Linklet
Bay

Runabrake

Start Point Lt Ho
in line with Tofts Ness 148°

Twinyess Point

Q.R.
5m Pier

Twinyess
Rocks

South
Bay

Tide race with
northwest-going
stream

Start Point Light bearing 125° and open
to northeast of cottages on Tofts Ness

North Ronaldsay Firth

Tide race with
southeast-going
stream

Baa of
Trevan

R Bn

The Riv

Whitemill
Skerry

Outer
Skerry

G Fl.G.5s

Crow Taing

Tofts
Ness

Tofts

Holms
of Ire

Long
Taing

Otterswick

Northwall

Burness

Start Point
Fl(2)20s24m18M
White tower,
black stripes

North
Bay

Bow of
Hermaness

Bay of
Lopness

SANDAY

See p.61

Bay of Newark

Baa
Gruna

Els
Ness

Backaskail
Bay

Fl.WRG.3s
7m7/5M

Tres Ness

Charles Tait

*North Ronaldsay
from the north*

North Ronaldsay

North Ronaldsay (see plan p.64) is the most northerly of the Orkney Islands. It is separated from Sanday by North Ronaldsay Firth, a particularly turbulent stretch of water.

Tide
Races form off Tofts Ness on Sanday and Twinyess Point on North Ronaldsay and extend across North Ronaldsay Firth on both the west-going and east-going streams.

In North Ronaldsay Firth
East-going stream starts +0535 Aberdeen (–0450 Dover)
West-going stream starts –0150 Aberdeen (+0030 Dover)
Spring rates 4 kn

Directions
Approaching from the south, keep well clear of Start Point and Tofts Ness on Sanday.

To clear Twinyess Rocks off the west point of North Ronaldsay, keep to the south of a line (bearing 148°) between Start Point light tower and the northeast point of Tofts Ness.

To clear Baa of Trevan north of The Riv keep north of a line (bearing 125°) between Start Point Lt Twr and the cottages on Tofts Ness.

Approaching from the north, avoid the shoal of Runabrake which lies 5¾ miles west of Twinyess Point, the southwest point of North Ronaldsay and on which the sea breaks heavily. Also stay at least 1 mile off the Holms of Ire and the beacon on The Riv on the north side of Sanday. Both Sanday and North Ronaldsay coastlines are low lying and distances off are deceptive. The tower on North Ronaldsay lighthouse can be seen, in good visibility, long before any land can be seen.

Anchorage
South Bay Anchor in the middle in 7–9m avoiding the submarine power cables. Sandy bottom. Open to the south and west. Subject to swell. There is one visitors' mooring.

On the west side there is a substantial modern concrete pier with diagonal rubber fendering. There is depth of water alongside at all states of the tide but liable to swell. There is always tidal motion in the bay.

Linklet Bay Anchorage may be found in 7 to 9m on a sandy bottom. Local lobster fishing boats moor on the north side of the bay, which is the best anchorage, just west of the jetty southwest of the beacon at Dennis Taing. Open to the east.

Neither South Bay nor Linklet Bay provide safe anchorages. A constant watch must be kept.

Admiralty Chart
2250
Imray Chart
C68
Ordnance Survey
5

5. Orkney to Shetland

Admiralty Chart
1234, 1119, 0219,
3299–5
Ordnance Survey
4

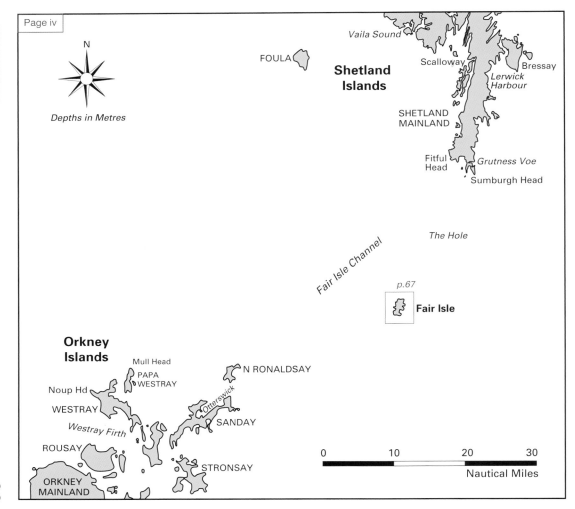

Passage from west of Orkney to west Shetland

Tides

Off Mull Head, Papa Westray
East-going stream starts +155 Aberdeen (+0415 Dover)
West-going stream starts -0405 Aberdeen (-0145 Dover)

Spring rate 2kn except close to the Head where the rate can attain 6kn

Roosts form in both directions and that on the west-going tide (the Bore Roost) can be particularly violent especially in west and northwest gales. Three miles off Mull Head the streams reach 2kn at springs.

In Fair Isle Channel
Southeast-going stream starts −0040 Aberdeen (−0050 Dover)
Northwest-going stream starts +0615 Aberdeen (+0605 Dover)
Maximum spring rate 2·5kn

The general trend of the direction of tidal streams in the channel is southeast and northwest but they both start with bearings to the east southeast and west northwest respectively and rotate clockwise during the periods of the streams.

Directions

In making the passage from the west of Orkney there is a tendency to keep too close to the northwest of Orkney. Mull Head (north point of Papa Westray) should be given a very wide berth.

The sea area between Noup Head and Shetland presents no special problems. Landfalls can be made at Scalloway or Vaila Sound (Walls) both of which have their entrances well marked by lighthouses. Foula to the north and Fitful Head to the south of these courses can be seen from a great distance in good weather. This route avoids the Sumburgh Roost.

Passage from east of Orkney to Shetland

The shortest passage between Orkney and Shetland (50 miles) is from Otterswick on Sanday to Grutness Voe, (close to Sumburgh Head). It is common to break this passage at Fair Isle.

Tides

Race off Sumburgh Head

East-going stream starts –00405 Aberdeen (–0410 Dover)
West-going stream starts +0055 Aberdeen (+0050 Dover)
East-going stream ends +0025 Aberdeen (+0020 Dover)
West-going stream ends -0405 Aberdeen (-0410 Dover)

For tides at Fair Isle see p.68.

Off Sumburgh Head the tide runs very strongly in both directions with eddies inshore. South of the head a violent roost forms under conditions of wind against tide and/or swell. This can be 3 miles wide and extends 6 or more miles south. The race forms in both directions with practically no slack period on the turn.

Directions

The sea area between Fair Isle and Shetland is known as the Hole, where in bad weather very difficult sea conditions have been reported.

Special care is needed at the Sumburgh Roost. If sailing to the east coast of Shetland steer to pass 2 miles east of Sumburgh Head. This offing can be modified when the situation of the roost is known. Similarly, if sailing to the west coast, steer to achieve an offing of 2 miles west of Fitful Head where a roost also forms with wind against tide. With a west-going stream it is possible to avoid the roost off Sumburgh Head by sailing close in round the Head and between Hog of the Ness and Horse Island.

For the passage inside Horse Island adopt a northwesterly course and pass close to the Hog of the Ness, not more than one third of the way across the width of the channel. It is not possible to avoid the roost off Fitful Head by an inside passage.

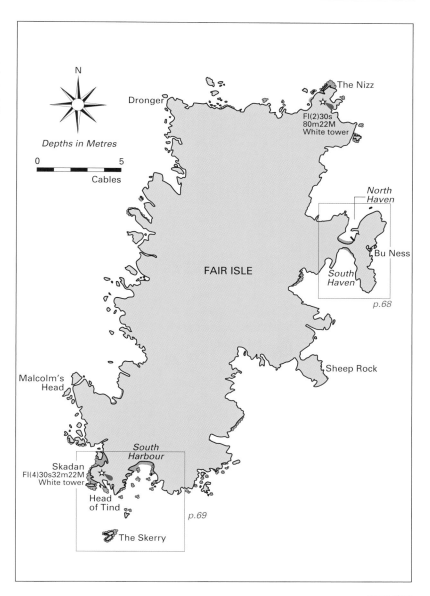

FAIR ISLE

Sumburgh Head

Admiralty Chart
3299-4, 3299-5
Ordnance Survey
4

Fair Isle

Fair Isle lies midway between Orkney and Shetland. The predominant feature of its coast is high inaccessible cliffs. All dangers are close inshore.

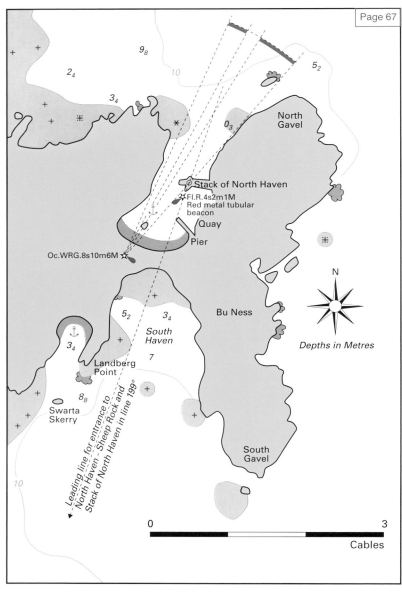

North Gavel

Stack of North Haven
Fl.R.4s2m1M
Red metal tubular beacon

Quay

Pier

Oc.WRG.8s10m6M

North Haven

South Haven

Landberg Point

Swarta Skerry

Bu Ness

South Gavel

Depths in Metres

N

Leading line for entrance to North Haven - Sheep Rock and Stack of North Haven in line 199°

0   3
Cables

NORTH AND SOUTH HAVENS, FAIR ISLE

Tide

At Fair Isle
Southeast-going stream starts +0535 Aberdeen (−0430 Dover)
Northwest-going stream starts −0200 Aberdeen (+0200 Dover)

Constant −0020 Lerwick (−0025 Dover)

Heights in metres

MHWS	MHWN	MTL	MLWN	MLWS
2·2	1·7	1·4	1	0·6

The streams which run northwest and southeast are very strong close to the island and at places reach 4–5kn at springs. Races form off the north and south ends. The race off the latter is known as the Roost of Keels and extends 2 miles off shore.

An eddy forms east of the island on the southeast-going stream and west of the island on the northwest-going stream.

Anchorage

North Haven on the northeast coast, is the only recommended anchorage.

The leading marks for entering North Haven are the Stack of North Haven inside the entrance in line with the summit of Sheep Rock bearing 199°. These are normally visible at night in summer. The photograph below is taken from a position to the west of the leading line. Sheep Rock shows prominently in the background with its steep face on the west side. The stack is the rock that is part of, but higher than, the breakwater. It is about a third of the way from the outer end of the breakwater just to right of the mist in the photo.

With binoculars one can pick out this rock above the breakwater, therefore hold the line up to the breakwater and then bear off round the end. The rocks at the entrance usually show breaks and swirls. In darkness the sectored North Haven Light leads in to the harbour.

The pier is of piled construction which is not suitable for yachts but there is also a quay where the *Good Shepherd*, the island's link with Shetland, lies alongside. Ahead of this boat there is room for two 40 ft yachts. Large fenders are available on the quay for use by visitors.

The entrance to North Haven, Fair Isle

Paul E.F. Wishart

North Haven, Fair Isle

North Haven is a safe anchorage even if uncomfortable in northeast winds. Bottom sand, with extensive kelp. Limited swinging room.

South Haven This anchorage can be used as shelter when the wind is from the north but the bottom is rock and boulders giving poor holding.

The way in is on the west side and is parallel to and ½ cable off Swarta Skerry and Landberg Point. Anchor inside the Point in 3m.

South Harbour is foul with rocks and must be approached with extreme caution. Enter from the southeast keeping Skarfi Stack (square rock less than 1 cable off the pier) in line with the door of Melville House, a white two-storey building just above the cemetery, bearing 331°. Continue on this course until Flure Stack, a rock on the east of the harbour entrance, is abeam to starboard. Then steer due north into the bay. Anchor in 4m east-southeast of the pier.

South Harbour, Fair Isle, in an autumn gale

Facilities

At North Haven there is water at the pier. Toilets and showers are situated at the Bird Observatory which is 300m from the harbour. Shop and Post Office approximately 2·5km from North Haven and 1km from South Harbour.

Accommodation and meals are available by arrangement at the Bird Observatory, ☎ 01595 760 258. For information about Fair Isle see www.fairisle.org.uk.

Interest

The Bird Observatory overlooks North and South Havens.

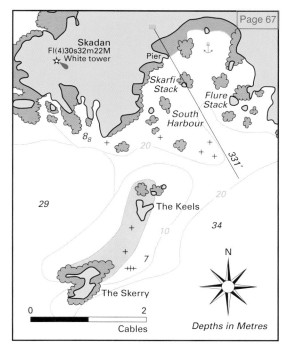

**SOUTH HARBOUR
FAIR ISLE**

6. Shetland Islands

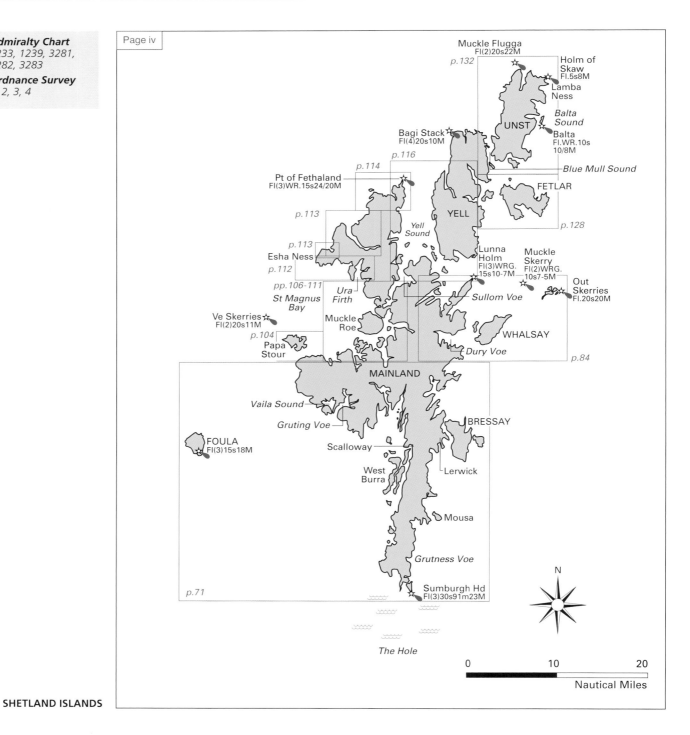

Admiralty Chart
1233, 1239, 3281,
3282, 3283
Ordnance Survey
1, 2, 3, 4

Page iv

Muckle Flugga
Fl(2)20s22M
p.132

Holm of
Skaw
Fl.5s8M
Lamba
Ness

Balta
Sound

Bagi Stack
Fl(4)20s10M

UNST

Balta
Fl.WR.10s
10/8M

p.116

Blue Mull Sound

p.114

FETLAR

Pt of Fethaland
Fl(3)WR.15s24/20M

YELL

p.128

p.113

Yell
Sound

p.113

Lunna
Holm
Fl(3)WRG.
15s10-7M

Muckle
Skerry
Fl(2)WRG.
10s7-5M

Esha Ness

p.112

Out
Skerries
Fl.20s20M

pp.106-111

Ura
Firth

Sullom Voe

St Magnus
Bay

Muckle
Roe

Ve Skerries
Fl(2)20s11M

WHALSAY

p.104

Dury Voe

Papa
Stour

p.84

MAINLAND

Vaila Sound

BRESSAY

Gruting Voe

FOULA
Fl(3)15s18M

Scalloway

West
Burra

Lerwick

Mousa

Grutness Voe

N

p.71

Sumburgh Hd
Fl(3)30s91m23M

The Hole

0   10   20
Nautical Miles

SHETLAND ISLANDS

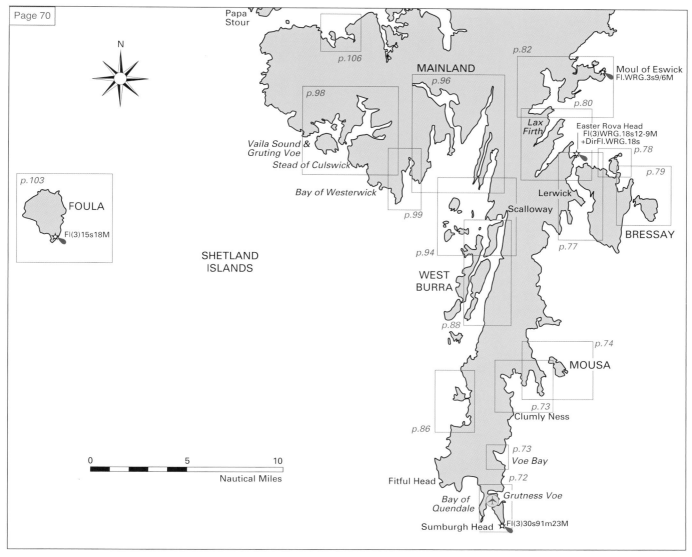

Page 70

SHETLAND ISLANDS

SOUTH MAINLAND

The Shetland Islands can provide an interesting and truly refreshing holiday. It is a most rewarding area to visit, with less rain than the west coast of Scotland, spectacular scenery and numerous sheltered anchorages. It is well suited to family cruising, exploring remote anchorages and visiting archeological sites. There is the satisfaction of making a comfortable anchorage and the welcome of the Shetlanders who will always advise and lend a sympathetic hand. For Scandinavian visitors particularly, cruising in the Shetland Islands is already well established and they are always most welcome.

Despite its small compass, the weather can vary across the islands. In summer when the east coast of Shetland has fog, the west coast can be in clear sunshine.

A common first port of call is Lerwick where there is very good visitor berthage and facilities. Other main centres with good, if limited, numbers of visitors' berths are at Scalloway, Skelda Voe, Symbister and Brae.

The people of Shetland are oriented towards the sea and small boat ownership is very common. Because of this there are many marinas around the islands the majority of which are for smaller boats and have limited facilities.

Some of the smaller Shetland Islands Council piers are not manned. General information about harbours can obtained be from the Shetland Islands Council, Ports and Harbours ✆ 01806 244200 and:
www.shetland.gov.uk/ports
See also Shetland Marinas:
www.shetlandmarinas.com

Shetland Islands Council provides inter-island air services, which are operated under contract by Directflight Limited Tingwall Airport, Tingwall. ✆ 01595 840246.

Anchored at Grutness

Ronnie Robertson

Admiralty Chart
3283, 3294
Ordnance Survey
4

Mainland East Coast

Grutness Voe

On the east coast 1½ miles north of Sumburgh Head this is a convenient first anchorage in Shetland if arriving from the south and proceeding up the east coast. It is also a convenient point of departure when waiting for suitable weather or tide if sailing round Sumburgh Head and Fitful Head (see passage directions on p.67) or when leaving Shetland for the south.

GRUTNESS VOE

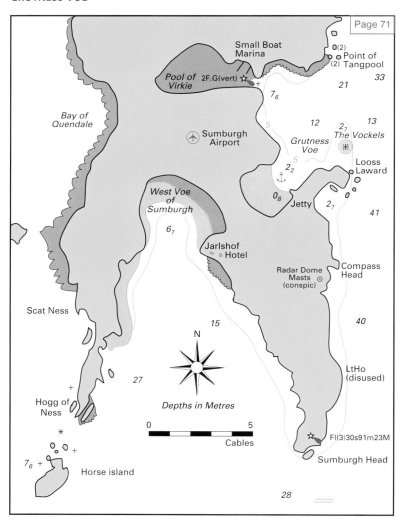

Tide

Constant +0005 Lerwick (HW Dover)

Heights in metres

MHWS	MHWN	MTL	MLWN	MLWS
1·8	1·4	1·1	0·7	0·4

Directions

Looss Laward, a stony peninsula forming the south side of the entrance, has a shallow tongue of rocks extending at least 3 cables north. These rocks, known as the Vockels, have at least 2 rocky areas projecting above LW springs. Coming from the south keep at least 4 cables north of Looss Laward before turning towards the west side of Grutness Voe. Once within the voe keep towards the southeast shore to avoid the 2·2m patch.

Anchorage

Grutness Anchor in 6m off the pier on the south side of the voe. If using this pier, depth alongside 3m, do not leave yacht unattended as it is used by the Fair Isle mail boat and by fishing boats. Well sheltered, but swell with northeast and east winds. Noisy due to closeness to the airport.

Ness Boating Club Marina The Ness Boating Club small boat marina is in the northwest of Grutness Voe at the entrance to the Pool of Virkie. There is one visitors' mooring but the minimum depth is only 1m. It is accessed by a very narrow channel with depth 1m at LW. The channel may be buoyed but the buoys can move in bad weather.

Facilities

Grutness Water from toilets at the pier; Post Office and stores at Toab 1½ miles; hotel ½ mile. Sumburgh, the main airport for Shetland, 1 mile; café, taxis, ferry to Fair Isle.

Ness Boating Club Marina Toilets, electricity, fresh water, slip.

Interest

Archaeology: Jarlshof and Scatness ancient habitations.
Ornithology: Sumburgh Head and Looss Laward. Sumburgh Head Lighthouse, visitor centre and nature reserve.

Sumburgh Head to Lerwick

Lights

Sumburgh Head Fl(3)30s91m23M White tower

Passage

From Sumburgh Head to Lerwick navigation presents no problems.

The area, however, is subject to fog and it must be remembered that there are magnetic anomalies for about 10 miles south of Bressay.

Tide

The tidal streams are weak. In Mousa Sound the spring rates in both directions are 1·25kn
North-going stream starts +0455 Lerwick (+0445 Dover)
South-going stream starts –0140 Lerwick (–0150 Dover)

Voe Bay

Voe Bay, two miles north of Grutness Voe, is considerably narrowed by shoal water on the north shore extending out more than 1 cable. Keep towards the southwest shore. The head of the voe is shoal. On the ebb keep clear of the point to the south of the entrance.

Anchorage

Voe Bay offers reasonable shelter in northeast winds. Anchor in 6m sand avoiding heavy patches of weed. Holding is variable.

Leven Wick and adjacent Wicks

Eight miles north of Sumburgh Head on the east coast of the Mainland this area has a choice of four well-charted anchorages, all of which are within a short distance of the Mousa broch and generally having sand on which to anchor.

Tide

Constant –0010 Lerwick (–0020 Dover)

Directions

From the south, after passing Clumly Ness 5 cables offshore to clear Clumly Baas, give the Mainland shore an offing of at least 1 cable as there are rocks up to ¾ cable off. There are magnetic anomalies in the area.

Anchorage

Leven Wick provides good shelter from south and west winds but swell sets in with east winds. Anchor 150m off the sandy beach in 6m towards the southeast corner in sand (see photograph).

Hos Wick, 1 mile further north, is sheltered from the north and east. Anchor at the northwest corner but take care as the head is shoal and there are rocky patches particularly on the west side. Temporary anchorage can be found in the bight south of Brownies Taing in 4m sand.

Channer Wick, although fully open to the southeast, this clean bay offers good anchorage in most other wind directions. Anchor at the head of the bay in 5m.

Sandwick Wick There are abandoned submarine cables in Sand Wick but these are shown on chart 3294 and can be avoided by anchoring in 4m in the northeast corner.

Facilities

Levenwick: Shop ¾ mile.
Hoswick: Stores and café, Visitor's Centre (May–Sept), knitwear factory and shop, swimming pool.

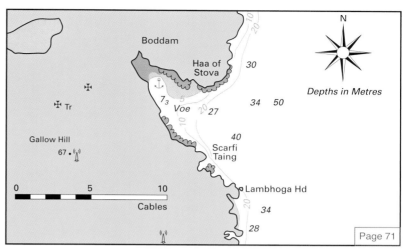

VOE BAY

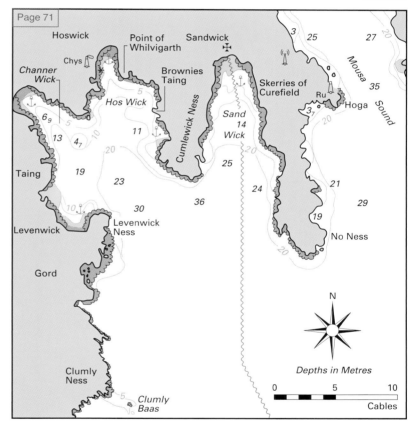

LEVEN WICK AND ADJACENT WICKS

Leven Wick, the anchorage is to the left of the photograph

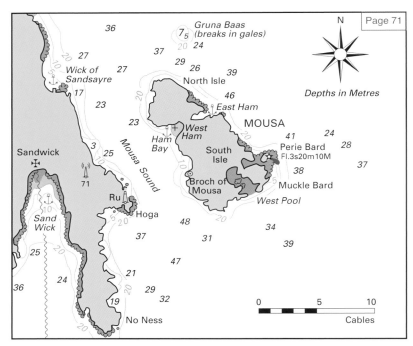

MOUSA

Admiralty Chart
3283
Ordnance Survey
4

Out from Lerwick for a day's sailing

Mousa

An island off the east coast 9 miles north of Sumburgh. In fine weather it is well worth while to anchor and visit the Broch of Mousa, the best preserved in Britain, which is clearly visible from Mousa Sound. Ornithology including storm petrels; seals.

Anchorage

West Ham Anchor in the bay ½ mile north of the broch where there is a cottage and boat slip. There is reasonable shelter from north to southeast but not in fresh southerly winds. 4m sand. Opposite the broch the bottom is rock.

Wick of Sandsyre There is a small bay on the mainland shore 1 mile west of the north end of Mousa. A rocky ridge extends 1 cable north from the south point of the entrance.

Anchor in the middle of the bay off the stone pier used by the ferry to Mousa.

Aith Voe (Helli Ness)

A narrow, rather shallow voe, west of Helli Ness and 2 miles north of Mousa. Hold close to the west side on entering to avoid rocks on the east side. There is a buoyed channel leading up to the marina.

Anchorage

Anchoring is not recommended but there is a small marina located from the entrance to the voe adjacent to a caravan park. It provides berths for about 43 boats. Depth in channel: 1·5 m. Depth at pontoon: 2m. A visitors' berth may be available but check availibility and depth. (☎ 07747 705278)

Facilities

Showers, toilets, waste disposal and laundry.

Helli Ness to Lerwick

Helli Ness to Lerwick (see plan p.71) is about 7 miles and a number of bays of varying size will be passed. Whilst not frequently used by yachts on passage they offer convenient occasional anchorages if day sailing from Lerwick or cruising slowly in fair, settled weather.

Anchorage

Bay of Fladdabister a rather featureless bay with a low-lying rock and shingle shoreline. A rock lies ½ cable of the north shore so tend towards the Ness of Fladdabister on entering. Anchor in the centre of the bay and avoid going too far south.

East Voe of Quarff The head of the bay and the south side are foul with drying reefs and submerged rocks. Enter on the north side, keeping about 75m off The Stack, which is steep-to, and anchor in 5m just over ½ cable further inshore. This is a temporary anchorage at best and not one to use with any swell running at all.

Gulberwick. Coming from the south, this is the first of three large bays all within 3 miles of Lerwick. The bay is reasonably clean, all of the rocks being within ½ cable of the shore. Anchor towards the head of the bay on one of the several areas of sand that can be seen.

Voe of Sound This bay has a submarine cable running out of it but anchoring is possible if the west side of the bay is used. Anchor a cable north of Point of Sandwell off the west shore in about 10m.

Brei Wick In the approach there are many rocks off the south shore of the bay; one off Skeo Taing lies over a cable from the shore. The bay is also used as an anchorage by quite large vessels but there is plenty of room for yachts to anchor inshore. Entering the bay from the north, be aware of Leake Rock (2·7m) which is over ½ cable south of The Knab. The north east corner has reasonable depths and is within easy walking distance of the centre of Lerwick.

Barbara MacLeod

The Broch of Mousa. Anchoring in the bay beneath the broch is not recommended but there is temporary anchorage in Ham Bay, ½ mile to the north

The marina at Aith Voe (Helli Ness)

Admiralty Chart
3271, 3272, 3282, 3283

Ordnance Survey
4

Lerwick

Lerwick harbour is much frequented by oil rig supply vessels, ferries and other commercial traffic. Yachts must keep clear of the commercial traffic, especially in the approaches and in the narrow channels where larger vessels cannot deviate from the channel due to draught restrictions. Accordingly, attention is drawn to the International Regulations which require that a vessel of less than 20m in length or a sailing vessel shall not impede the passage of a vessel which can safely navigate only within a narrow channel or fairway. Lerwick Port Control (Ch 12) should be advised of yacht movements.

Tide

The tidal streams are generally weak in Bressay Sound except in the narrows at the north entrance.

At the north entrance to Bressay Sound at Point of Scattland:
South-going stream starts (–0400 Lerwick (–0410 Dover)
North-going stream starts +0130 Lerwick (+0140 Dover)

There is no slack water at springs between these streams. Spring rates 2kn

Constant Standard Port –0010 Dover

Heights in metres

MHWS	MHWN	MTL	MLWN	MLWS
2·1	1·7	1·4	0·9	0·5

Directions

In Bressay Sound the flood tide sets north; the channel is marked by green buoys to the east side and red to the west side. The main route for shipping into the harbour is from the south through the wide entrance between Kirkabister Ness and Ness of Sound and is straightforward.

If coming from the north hold a course from the Moul of Eswick to leave the E cardinal (VQ(3)5s) Unicorn Rock buoy to starboard and the W cardinal (Q(9)15s) Brethren buoy to port (plans pp.80,81). In heavy weather keep well to the east of the shoal patch South Baa, 5 cables southwest of Hoo Stack, (plan p.81). When the Brethren buoy is abeam, take a southerly course until the white beam of the Point of Scattland directional light (Oc 214-216°, visible in daylight) is picked up. Follow this into the channel. With a north going tide against a strong northeasterly, an uncomfortable sea can build up in the channel north of Turra Taing.

At night the green sector of the Easter Rova Head light shows over the Brethren. The red sector of the Moul of Eswick light shows over the Unicorn.

If coming from the east hold a course of 252° for Rova Head Light. This leads clear of all dangers until the white sector of the Point of Scattland light is picked up.

Follow the directional light into the entrance of Bressay Sound until well past Green Head. The channel then passes between two well marked dangers:

Skibby Baas, off Mainland 3½ cables SSW from Easter Rova Head, is left to starboard. Another reef, extending ¾ cable west from Turra Taing, the point of Bressay opposite Greenhead, is left to port. Here the fairway is just over ½ cable wide.

Further south two shallow patches, Middle Ground and Loofa Baa, considerably narrow the fairway, are left to port. The light on North Ness shows G over Middle Ground and Loofa Baa. At Loofa Baa, the channel turns southeast and is deep on the Mainland side to South Harbour in the R sector of Maryfield Ferry Terminal light (on Bressay). Proceed to the pontoons as below. Note the ferry to Bressay.

Anchorage

Visiting yachts should contact Port Control for Lerwick Harbour Ch 12 (or ☎ 01595 692991) to report intentions and to seek berthing availability.

A Visiting Yachts Welcome Pack detailing the facilities and services at the Port is available on request and can be downloaded via: www.lerwick-harbour.co.uk

Crew from visiting yachts can use the Lerwick Boating Club (☎ 01595 692407), a very short walk from Victoria Pier), for toilet, shower and laundry facilities. The key can be collected from the Lerwick Port Authority Office at Albert Building on the Esplanade.

Small Boat Harbour is the principal berth for visiting yachts. It has a 70m floating pontoon which offers good shelter and can accommodate up to seven yachts alongside, and many more when rafted up, at all states of tide. There is 8m at the mouth of the dock and 1·2m at the inner corner.

Albert Dock A pontoon alongside the Albert Wharf is available for visiting yachts and a pontoon alongside the Victoria Pier may also be used when not needed for cruise ship tenders. Dates of use by tenders are displayed on the pontoon and at the Port Authority office in the Albert Building.

Lerwick Marina, Gremista is situated at the north end of Lerwick Harbour, 2 miles from the main harbour. It is run by the Marina Users Association, with whom arrangement can be made to use a vacant berth for longer, temporary stays. Port Control will advise on contact to be made. There is 2·5m depth at the outer pontoons and 1·8m at the inner ones. It has a slipway and a hoist.

Facilities

Toilet, showers, electricity, fuel, water, chandlery, laundry, waste oil disposal points.

Numerous shops, including supermarkets, hotels and full engineering and electrical repairs for yachts. Duty free stores also available.

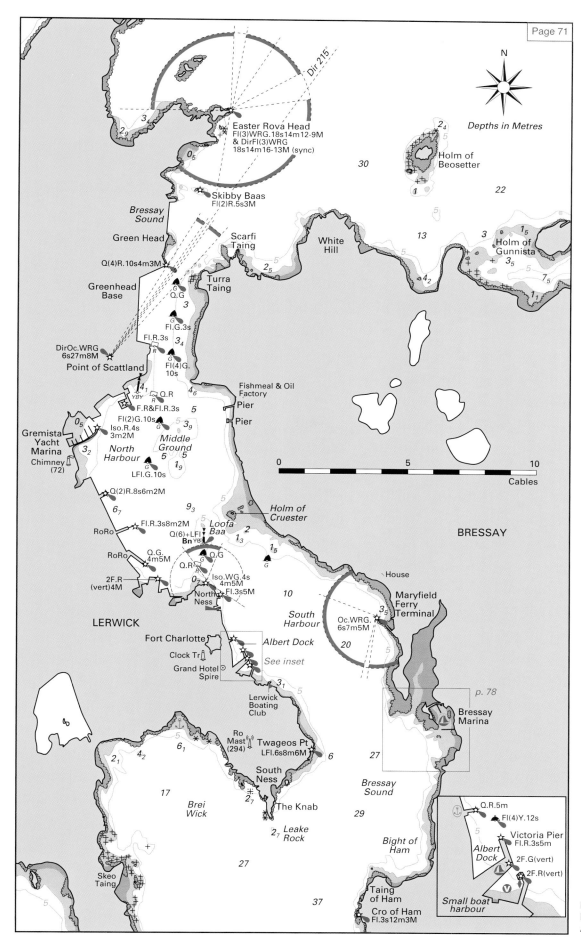

N

Depths in Metres

Easter Rova Head
Fl(3)WRG.18s14m12-9M
& DirFl(3)WRG
18s14m16-13M (sync)

Holm of
Beosetter

Skibby Baas
Fl(2)R.5s3M

Bressay
Sound

Green Head

Scarfi
Taing

White
Hill

Holm of
Gunnista

Q(4)R.10s4m3M

Greenhead
Base

Turra
Taing

Q.G

Fl.G.3s

Fl.R.3s

DirOc.WRG
6s27m8M

Fl(4)G.
10s

Point of Scattland

Fishmeal & Oil
Factory

Q.R

Pier

F.R&Fl.R.3s

Pier

Gremista
Yacht
Marina

Fl(2)G.10s
3m2M

Middle
Ground

Chimney
(72)

North
Harbour

LFl.G.10s

Q(2)R.8s6m2M

Holm of
Cruester

Fl.R.3s8m2M

RoRo

Loofa
Baa

Q(6)+LFl
Bn

BRESSAY

Q.G

RoRo

Q.G.
4m5M

Q.R.

Iso.WG.4s
4m5M

2F.R
(vert)4M

North
Ness

Fl.3s5M

House

0   5   10

Cables

LERWICK

South
Harbour

Maryfield
Ferry
Terminal

Oc.WRG.
6s7m5M

Fort Charlotte

Albert Dock

Clock Tr

See inset

Grand Hotel
Spire

p. 78

Bressay
Marina

Lerwick
Boating
Club

Ro
Mast
(294)

Twageos Pt
LFl.6s8m6M

South
Ness

Bressay
Sound

Brei
Wick

The Knab

Skeo
Taing

Leake
Rock

Bight of
Ham

Q.R.5m

Fl(4)Y.12s

Victoria Pier
Fl.R.3s5m

Albert
Dock

Taing
of Ham

2F.G(vert)

2F.R(vert)

Cro of Ham
Fl.3s12m3M

Small boat
harbour

LERWICK AND
BRESSAY
APPROACHES

Bressay Marina

Barbara MacLeod

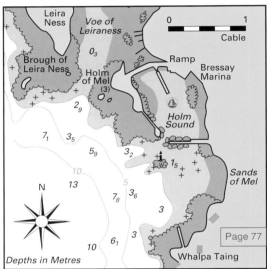

BRESSAY MARINA

Depths in Metres

Bressay Marina

Opposite Lerwick on Bressay is Bressay Marina, 1km south of the Lerwick-Bressay Ferry (Maryfield) Terminal in Holm Sound. It provides a quiet alternative to Lerwick.

Directions

In the approach about 1 cable southwest of the entrance pick up a transit of the church door centred on the gap between the two breakwaters. A shoal area has been reported south of the pontoons approximately midway between the entrance and the pontoon end.

Care should be exercised on entering/leaving the marina at low water.

Anchorage

The number of visitors' berths is limited, ☎ 01595 820377. Minimum 1·5m depth at pontoon.

Facilities

Electricity, water, waste disposal, Post Office. Toilets at Ferry Terminal. There is also a slipway for small craft.

Interest

East of Bressay is the National Nature Reserve island of Noss, which has a daytime anchorage at Nesti Voe. See Voe of the Mels; Nesti Voe (Noss) p.79.

AITH VOE (BRESSAY)

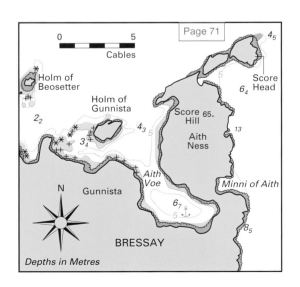

Admiralty Chart
3272, 3283

Ordnance Survey
4

Depths in Metres

Aith Voe (Bressay)

A sheltered voe on the north coast of Bressay 1 mile southwest of Score Head.

Directions

Holm of Gunnista lies in the middle of the approach ½ mile from the entrance. Keep to the east of this where there is a minimum depth of 4·6m in the channel and deeper water nearer the Bressay shore. There is a 3·5m bar at the narrows into Aith Voe.

Anchorage

There is a minimum of 5·5m in the middle of the voe to within 1 cable of the head. Perfect shelter in all weathers. Good holding.

Interest

There is a first world war gun on Score Hill. Good walking.

Voe of the Mels; Nesti Voe (Noss)

Voe of the Mels lies on the south side of the Isle of Noss and Nesti Voe is the bight 3 cables to the west.

Directions

The passage through Noss Sound should not be attempted except for shallow draught craft with local knowledge. Enter both the Voe of the Mels and Nesti Voe in mid-channel. In Voe of the Mels there is an awash rock 1 cable east of the point on the west side. In Nesti Voe there are rocks close to the shore on the west side

Anchorage

There is 4m in Voe of the Mels almost to the head. Anchor in the middle of Nesti Voe. Sand. Both anchorages are convenient for visiting the island but should not be used in south winds.

Interest

Ornithology: Noss is a nature reserve. The ledges on the faces of the cliffs on the east side are the breeding places for many thousands of sea birds.

Looking over Noss Sound from Bressay. Nesti Voe is the bay beyond the building with Voe of the Mels beyond it

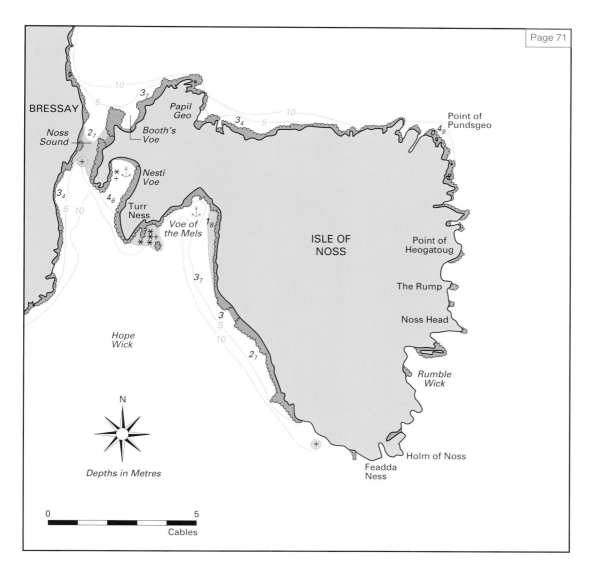

ISLE OF NOSS

Admiralty Chart
3282, 3272, 3271

Ordnance Survey
3, 4

Passage Lerwick to Moul of Eswick

Tide

For the tidal streams in Bressay Sound and Lerwick Harbour see Lerwick.

Passage

Care must be taken when leaving Lerwick by the north entrance. With a north-going tide against a strong northeasterly an uncomfortable sea can build up in the channel north of Turra Taing. Pick up the powerful directional light on Point of Scattland (2° beam visible in daylight) before passing Green Head and stay in the beam, course 035°, until the Brethren are open east of Rova Head light. Keep to the east of this line (017°) to clear Skibby Baas which contains a dangerous awash rock marked by a beacon.

When Rova Head light is abeam, alter course to pass west of the Brethren marked by W cardinal buoy Q(9)15s. When these rocks are abeam 2 cables off, steer to make good a course 020° for Moul of Eswick passing ½ mile west of Hoo Stack. In heavy weather keep east of South Baa.

At night when setting a course from Rova Head keep in the north white sector of that light towards the east boundary with the G sector but not in the G sector as this leads to the Brethren. The white sector of Moul of Eswick Light should be picked up at once. Keep in this sector also and do not cross the boundary of the R sector of the Moul Light to the west as this leads on to the Unicorn, another dangerous rock marked by E cardinal buoy VQ(3)5s.

DALES VOE & LAX FIRTH

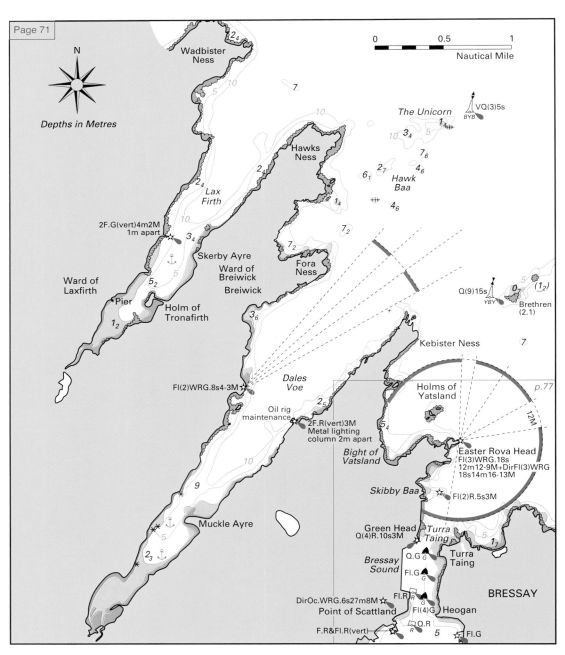

Pass west of Hoo Stack. There is an isolated rock (1·8m) 5 cables northeast of Hoo Stack. By taking the inner passage past the Moul of Eswick the problem of identifying the rocks and islets which form a chain known as the Stepping Stones between the Moul of Eswick and Whalsay is avoided.

Fru Stack lies ½ cable off below the Moul Light and 4 cables north of this is Hevda Skerry 1 cable offshore. Give these at least an offing of ½ cable. Nearly 1 mile northeast of the light is the Inner Voder Rock marked by a W Cardinal buoy Q(9)15s. It should be passed on the west side. The narrow white sector of the Moul Light leads clear between the Inner Voder to the east and the dangerous Climnie Reef to the west.

Dales Voe (Kebister Ness)

One mile northwest of Rova Head; open to the northeast but there is shelter at the head.

Directions

There are numerous dangers off the entrance (see passage from Lerwick to Moul of Eswick p.80). Enter between Kebister Ness on the east and Fora Ness. Keep at least one cable off as the shores are foul. There is an oil rig maintenance base on the east shore. Keep 1 cable off when passing Muckle Ayre.

Anchorage

Anchor in 6m, mud, either on west side short of two rocks shown on plan or in 4m further in. Be aware of a mussel farm behind the ayre.

Facilities

Golf course at head of the voe. Clubs and trolleys available for hire.

David White - Geograph

North & South Voes of Gletness

These voes are useful passage anchorages just off the direct route from Lerwick to Moul of Eswick.

Directions - North Voe of Gletness

A rock spit extends south from the north shore of the bay, with Eswick Holm at the inshore end and Aswick Skerries at the outer extremity, 4 cables offshore. There is a passage through the Skerries but it is not recommended. Exposed to the north and east.

The approach is clear between Aswick Skerries, 3 cables to the northeast, and Colsie (3·0m rock) the same distance to the southeast of the point of Gletness. Do not pass inshore of the North Isle of Gletness.

Anchorage

North Voe of Gletness Anchor in 4m near the head of the voe. Sand. Attractive views towards Noss and the Moul of Eswick.

South Voe of Gletness Temporary anchorage can be found on the west side of the South Isle of Gletness on sand in 4m but beware extensive hazards. Chart 3272 essential and see plan on p.82.

The North Isle of Gletness from the mainland with Hoo Stack on the far left

Admiralty Chart
3272, 3282
Ordnance Survey
3, 4

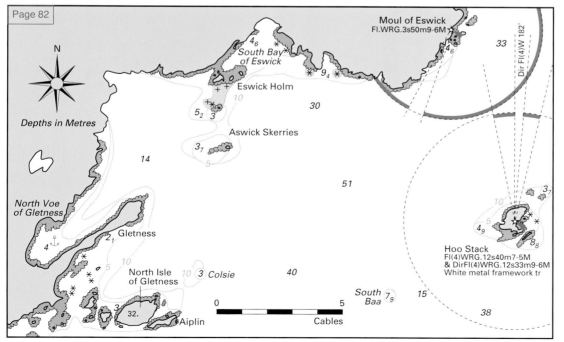

NORTH VOE OF GLETNESS

Page 82

N

Depths in Metres

Moul of Eswick
Fl.WRG.3s50m9-6M

South Bay of Eswick

Eswick Holm

Aswick Skerries

33

Dir Fl(4)W 182°

30

51

North Voe of Gletness

Gletness

North Isle of Gletness

Colsie

40

South Baa

15

Hoo Stack
Fl(4)WRG.12s40m7-5M
& DirFl(4)WRG.12s33m9-6M
White metal framework tr

38

Aiplin

0   5

Cables

Admiralty Chart
3272, 3282

Ordnance Survey
3

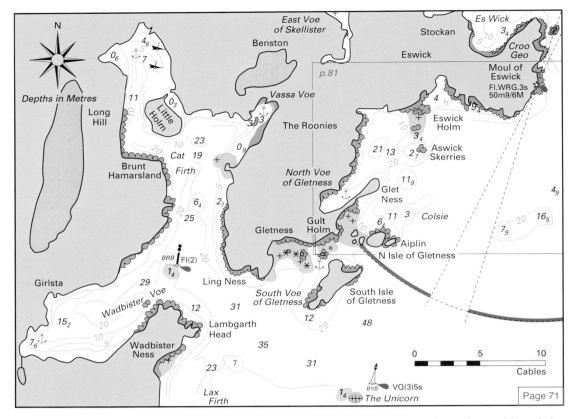

CAT FIRTH,
WADBISTER VOE

Lax Firth; Wadbister Voe; Cat Firth; Vassa Voe

This area lies 3 miles northwest of Rova Head providing sheltered anchorages but there are normally many large fish farms.

Directions

The entrance to this system of voes is between Hawks Ness in the south, and South Isle of Gletness to the north. The Unicorn rock lies mid-channel off the entrance, and Hawk Baa, with 2·7m over it, lies 3 cables southeast of the point of Hawks Ness.

Within the entrance, Lax Firth (plan p.80) and Wadbister Voe lie to the southwest and west, and Vassa Voe lies to the north. There is a dangerous rock in the middle of the entrance to Wadbister Voe marked by an isolated danger buoy Fl(2) northeast of it. If making for Cat Firth keep to the north and east until well within the Firth; then keep mid-channel to avoid a rock off a small promontory on the east side at the entrance to Vassa Voe. At this point a channel opens to the west between Little Holm and Brunt Hamarsland leading to the inner part of Cat Firth.

Anchorage

Lax Firth (plan p.80) Enter on the west side to avoid foul ground 1 mile within the entrance on the east side stretching almost to mid-channel. Anchor in 6m north of the ayre to Holm of Tronafirth; shoal draft vessels can proceed into the pool at the head beyond the ayre (shingle beach) opposite the stone pier on the west side.

Wadbister Voe The rock in the middle of the entrance can be avoided by keeping close to either the northwest or the southeast shores. Excellent shelter in southwest winds.

Cat Firth There is excellent shelter in 6m north of Little Holm between the 2 burns and clear of the 2 wrecks which show at LW. Anchor carefully as the holding is reported as not good.

Vassa Voe At the northeast corner of Cat Firth. After passing the reef and offlying rock at the entrance on the east side of the voe proceed towards the head of the voe where an islet (1m) with extensive reefs limits a clear passage into the landlocked pool at the head of the voe. The channel, depth 3m, on the west side of the islet is the more straightforward. Hold towards the west shore in the approach to avoid the reef extending southwest from the islet. When abeam of the north end of the islet alter course immediately towards the centre of the pool to avoid a reef running out from the west shore. Good holding in mud but space is usually limited due to small boat moorings.

Facilities

Post Office and shop at Skellister ¾ mile from Vassa Voe.

Dock of Lingness

This is a very sheltered anchorage in the south of South Nesting Bay to the west of Lingness.

Directions

There are numerous below water rocks but these are all within 100–170m of the visible rocks. Approach on a course of 245° to pass midway between Gaat of Brough and Ling Ness until Cunning Holm is abeam to starboard. Alter course to approximately 170° keeping Limey Holm, the islet at the entrance to the Dock, close to port. Alternatively, if approaching from the northeast and unsure of the position of the below water rocks, steer to leave Fiska Skerry about a cable to port on a course of 225°. Pass midway between Cunning Holm and Corn Holm before heading for Limey Holm and leaving it to port.

Anchorage

Turn northeast into the Dock and anchor where depth allows. There is adequate depth for yachts of up to 2m draft to anchor anywhere in the Dock between the entrance channel close southwest of Limey Holm and a line between a wall on the southeast shore and the southwest point of Ling Ness. Avoid anchoring in the southwest part of the Dock where there is a shallow patch. Good holding in sand.

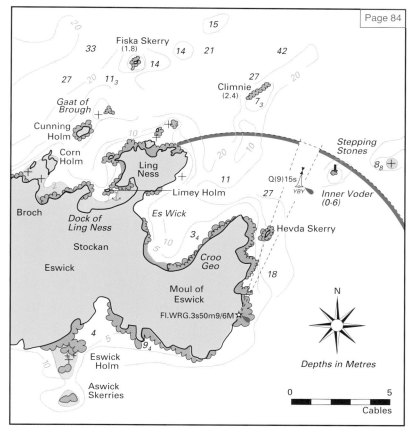

DOCK OF LINGNESS

Admiralty Chart
3284

Ordnance Survey
3

Dock of Lingness: do not anchor any further in than the dinghy on the left

Vassa Voe
(see opposite page)

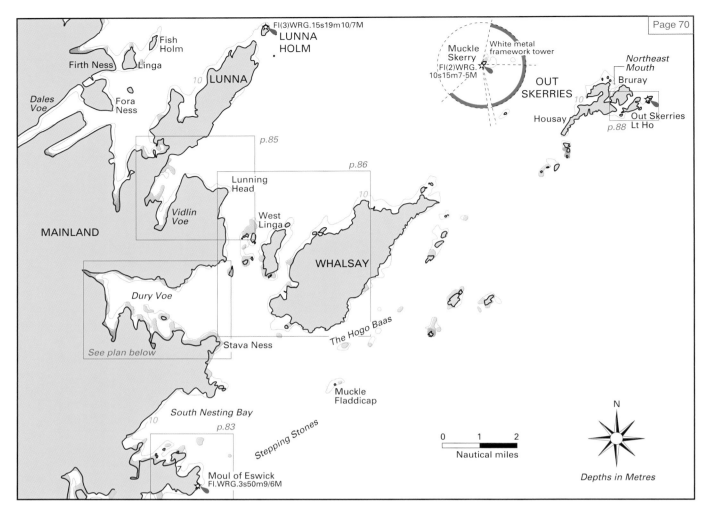

Page 70

MOUL OF ESWICK TO LUNNA HOLM

Admiralty Chart
3284

Ordnance Survey
3

Dury Voe and Grunna Voe

Dury Voe is a wide voe running 3 miles into Mainland where the Whalsay ferry terminal is situated. Grunna Voe lies on its south side.

Most of the south shore is foul up to 5 cables offshore and only Grunna Voe offers secure anchorage for yachts.

Tide

Constant –0020 Lerwick (–0030 Dover)

Heights in metres

MHWS	MHWN	MTL	MLWN	MLWS
2·1	1·6	1·2	0·9	0·3

Directions

In Dury Voe keep at least 1 cable north of Green Isle and Swarta Skerry. Grunna Voe is entered ½ mile beyond Swarta Skerry round Muckle Ness. The east and north shores of Muckle Ness should be given an offing of more than 1 cable.

Anchorage

Grunna Voe provides much the better anchorage. Anchor in 5–10m, black mud, good holding, sheltered. Use a tripping line as there may be old fish farm moorings.

Dury Voe There is a temporary anchorage giving shelter from the west at the head of Dury Voe, just to the west of the ferry pier.

DURY VOE

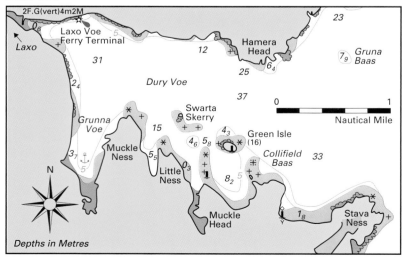

Vidlin Voe

Vidlin Voe lies on the east side of Lunna Ness. The outer part, 6 cables wide, is foul to halfway across on the west side and shoal up to 1 cable off the east shore at Catta Ness. From there the voe narrows at Vidlin Ness to 2 cables wide up to the head. The shores become progressively shoal, especially on the east side. The ferry terminal for Out Skerries and bad weather terminal for the Whalsay Ferry is on the west side before it opens out. The pool at the head is well sheltered and provides good anchorage.

Directions

The approach is clear up to the entrance to the voe. Keep well to the east of the middle in the outer wide part and slightly to the west of the middle in the narrow southern part of the voe.

Anchorage

Anchor in 4m at head of Vidlin Voe. Some patches of heavy weed. The RoRo Terminal is unsuitable for lying alongside.

Vidlin Marina provides good shelter and is accessible at all states of the tide. There are berths at the end of the pontoons for visitors. Depth 1·7m. Marina contact ☎ 01806 577326.

Facilities

Marina: Toilets, water and electricity on pontoons, waste disposal, launching slip.
Vidlin: Stores and Post Office. Out Skerries ferry terminal is 200 yards along the shore.

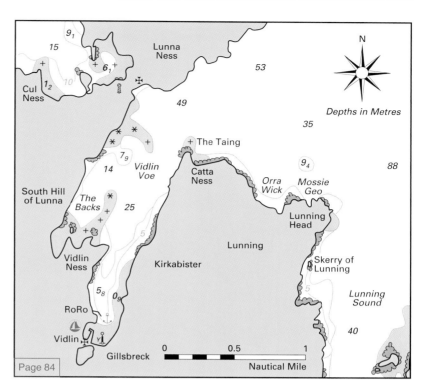

VIDLIN VOE

Vidlin Voe with Lunna beyond

The Whalsay ferry entering Dury Voe

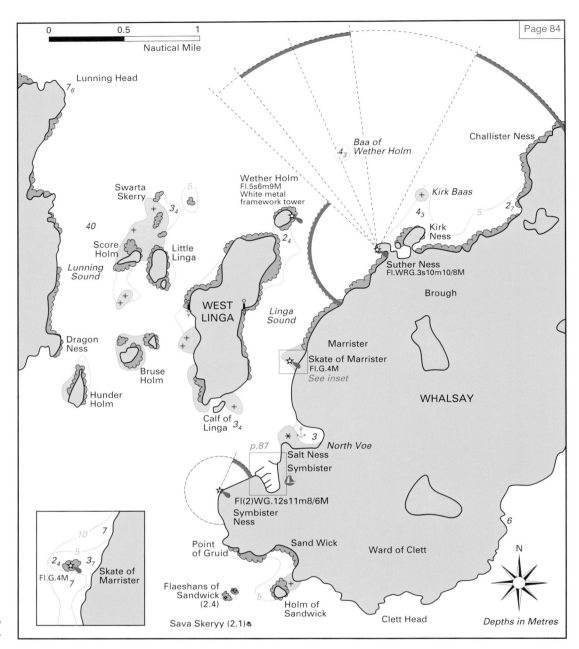

Page 84

LINGA AND
LUNNING SOUNDS

Admiralty Chart
3284
Ordnance Survey
3

Linga Sound

Linga Sound, between West Linga and Whalsay, is the main shipping channel.

Tide

In Linga and Lunning Sounds:
The south-going stream starts –0430 Lerwick (–0435 Dover)
The north-going stream starts +0215 Lerwick (+0210 Dover)

The northeast-going stream is strongest (4kn springs)
At the narrower parts of Linga Sound the spring rate is 5–6kn.

Directions

Coming from the southeast it is advisable to keep outside Sava Skerry and the Flaeshans of Sandwick.

From the south these skerries are cleared by keeping the east side of West Linga open off Symbister Ness (i.e. bearing more than 012°).

From Symbister Ness keep to the east of a line between Symbister Ness and Skate of Marrister bearing 023° until the north end of Calf of Linga is abeam. From there the leading line (Neap Manse in line with the southeast corner of West Linga) bearing 212° over the stern leads clear out of the Sound between Kirk Baas and the shoal patch Baa of Wether Holm.

From the north, enter Linga Sound on a course of 215° leaving Suther Ness 2 cables to port. This avoids Kirk Baas, a dangerous rock lying 5 cables northeast of Suther Ness and Baa of Wether Holm, 6 cables west-northwest of Suther Ness, where seas break in heavy weather. Maintain the course of not less than 215° until abeam Skate of Marrister light which should be left 1½ cables to port. This will clear the sunken rock 1 cable west of Skate of Marrister light.

There is a clear passage (½ cable wide, depth 4m) inside the Skate of Marrister. This can be used to lessen the effect of an adverse tide in Linga Sound.

At night, from the south, approach in the white sector of Symbister Ness light. When this light is abeam, alter course towards Skate of Marrister light and acquire the G sector of Symbister Ness light astern. Steer to keep on the W/G boundary of that light until the R sector of Suther Ness light shows when course should be altered to 005° until abeam of Skate of Marrister light. Thereafter a course of 035° will lead out of the sound.

Lunning Sound

Lunning Sound is between West Linga Island and the Mainland shore. There are a number of islands west of West Linga and considerable foul ground. From the south enter Lunning Sound west of Hunder Holm or between Hunder Holm and Bruse Holm.

Tide

For tidal streams see Linga Sound.

There are several eddies and strong turbulence in the Sound when the tide is running at full strength and, when the stream is south-going, there is an easterly set across the shoals of Swarta Skerry and a westerly set across the shelf at the north end of Hunder Holm.

Whalsay and Out Skerries

Symbister

Symbister harbour lies in a small bay with its entrance opening northwest and is well sheltered with two substantial breakwaters. The harbour is used by large pelagic trawlers, which principally use the outer basin.

Directions

See Directions for Linga Sound.

When entering Symbister Harbour keep well clear of the north breakwater by passing outside the red buoy and the red post both of which are unlit.

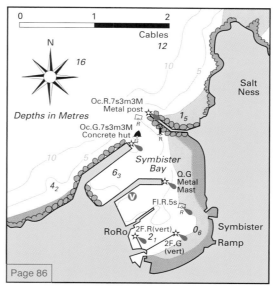

Anchorage

Symbister Visiting boats are are advised to tie alongside the south of the inner breakwater (depth 5m). Berthing may be available, by prior arrangement, at the marina where there are depths of 2m. ☎ 01806 566476.

North Voe This anchorage, sheltered from the southwest, is foul in parts with old moorings. Use of tripping line essential. Beware the dangerous rock off Salt Ness in the approach.

Facilities

Town Stores, Post Office, leisure centre, swimming pool, taxi service. Ferry to Laxo (Mainland).

Marina Toilet, showers, fuel, waste and waste oil disposal, yacht engineering repairs, Boating Club.

Admiralty Chart
3284, 3284-1, 3282
Ordnance Survey
2

Symbister, Whalsay

Barbara MacLeod

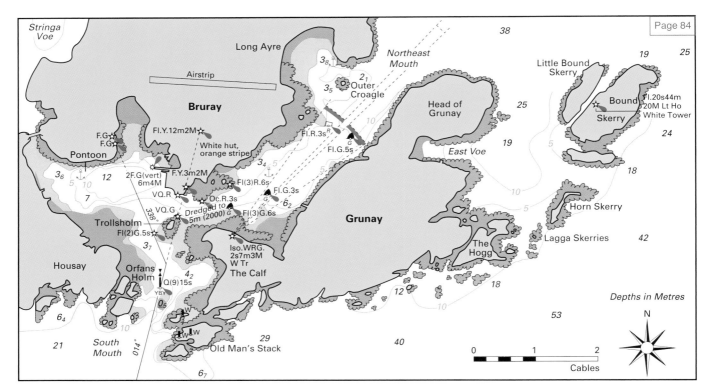

OUT SKERRIES

Admiralty Chart
3282, 3284-2
Ordnance Survey
2

Out Skerries

A group of islands lying 4 miles northeast of Whalsay. The main harbour lies between the three largest islands of Housay, Bruray and Grunay. The easiest entrance is the Northeast Mouth.

In the South Mouth there are covered rocks and there may be swell.

A bridge separates the main harbour, where local boats are moored all the year round, from the North Mouth which is badly exposed to the north and northeast and should not be considered as an anchorage.

It is a good starting point for the 164 miles to Norway.

Tide

Constant –0020 Lerwick (–0040 Dover)

Heights in metres

MHWS	MHWN	MTL	MLWN	MLWS
2·2	1·7	1·3	0·9	0·4

Directions

Except in strong winds from northwest to northeast, the Northeast Mouth presents no difficulties. Reefs and navigational aids are shown on the plan. Approaching from the southeast, Bound Skerry can be kept close aboard.

The approach through the South Mouth should only be attempted when there is minimal swell and in light to moderate or northerly winds. The orange transit leading marks (arrowheads) on Bruray bearing 014° should be acquired as early as possible and this leading line followed in until the W cardinal buoy is abeam. Care must be taken when approaching the buoy from the south to clear the patch of rock (dr 0·5m) lying south of the buoy. After the W cardinal buoy alter to follow the transit marks on the northwest shore which lead west of the green beacon (Fl(2)G.5s) marking the skerry (Trollsholm) in the harbour.

Out Skerries

Charles Tait

Anchorage

This is a convenient anchorage in the Northeast Mouth well in on the northwest side in 4m. Should this part be affected by a northeast swell proceed to the west side of the harbour, through the narrows south of Bruray. Alongside berths at the pier (depth 3m) are usually available. Contact ☎ 01806 515236. The pier has large tyres hung along its full length.

The west part of the harbour is deep in the middle and the best positions for anchoring are occupied by moorings. The most likely anchorage is towards the bridge on the north side. Off the school (white building) on Bruray there is a 6m depth where there is shelter from any sea which might enter by the South Mouth. Use a tripping line because the bottom is foul with old moorings.

Facilities

Bruray Water, electricity, stores; Post Office, showers and toilet block. Waste disposal, fuel by arrangement, slip.
Ferry service to Lerwick and Vidlin.
Air service to Tingwall for Lerwick.

The Out Skerries ferry pier with a yacht lying alongside

The Out Skerries from the northeast

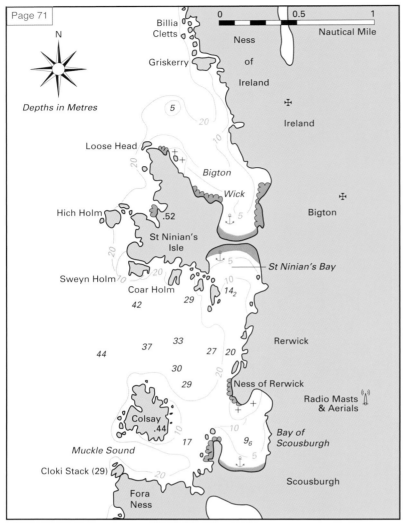

Page 71

N

Depths in Metres

0   0.5   1
Nautical Mile

Billia
Cletts
Griskerry

Ness
of
Ireland

Ireland

5
20

Loose Head
Bigton
Wick

Hich Holm
.52

St Ninian's
Isle

Bigton

Sweyn Holm
Coar Holm
42
St Ninian's Bay
29
14₂

44
37
33
27   20
30
29

Rerwick

Ness of Rerwick

Radio Masts
& Aerials

Colsay
.44
17
9₆
Bay of
Scousburgh

Muckle Sound

Cloki Stack (29)
20

Fora
Ness

Scousburgh

ANCHORAGES NORTH OF FITFUL HEAD

Admiralty Chart
3283, 3295-5

Ordnance Survey
4

Mainland West Coast

For the passage from Sumburgh Head to Fitful Head see *Orkney to Shetland*, p.67.

Bay of Quendale

In the south of mainland Shetland (plan p.71) this is a large sandy bay, fully open to the south, and it can only be considered as a temporary passage anchorage in settled weather.

Tide

Constant −0030 Lerwick (−0040 Dover)

Heights in metres

MHWS	MHWN	MTL	MLWN	MLWS
1·7	1·4	1·1	0·9	0·6

Fitful Head to Fugla Ness

Except in settled weather this stretch of the Mainland coast should be given a wide berth.

Bay of Scousburgh

Three miles north of Fitful Head. Open to the west. Sandy beach at the south end. Free of dangers.

Directions

Enter north of Colsay or through Muckle Sound. There are many isolated rocks off Colsay and Ness of Rerwick both of which should be given a berth of at least 1 cable.

Anchorage

Anchor in 6–8m off the beach; sand. Sheltered from southerly winds but subject to swell and to be used in settled conditions only.

Facilities

Hotel. Fine sandy beach.

St Ninian's Bay; Bigton Wick

These two bays are south and north respectively of the tombolo (sand bar) connecting St Ninian's Isle to the Mainland.

Directions

All dangers entering St Ninian's Bay are visible. In Bigton Wick give the northeast shore of St Ninian's Isle a berth of at least 1 cable. A 5m patch in the entrance to Bigton Wick causes the seas to break in severe weather.

Anchorage

These bays provide shelter depending on the direction of the wind, though the west side of St Ninian's Bay is reported to give reasonable protection from the southwest due to the islets extending south from the west side of the entrance.

Anchor as far into the bays as possible on the west sides for shelter. Both these bays provide good holding in sand although there is likely to be some swell.

Facilities

Post Office; stores.

Interest

Archaeological; ornithological.

May Wick

Two miles north of St Ninian's Isle.

Anchorage

In 3m sand. The bay shoals extensively. Use in settled conditions only.

South Havra

Three miles north of St Ninian's Isle.

Anchorage

There is a very confined, temporary anchorage in the most southerly inlet on the east side, with a depth of 2m. Lie in the middle of the gut with warps ashore or with bow and stern anchors. The north inlet is foul with rocks. Avoid the bays on the south side of the island.

Interest

Remains of the only windmill in Shetland and deserted croft houses at the edge of the cliff.

St Ninian's Bay with Bigton Wick on the far right

Charles Tait

Looking south from St Ninian's Isle towards the Bay of Scousburgh

Edwatrd Mason

*Approaching the narrow inlet,
North Ham, on South Havra*

Peter Bruce

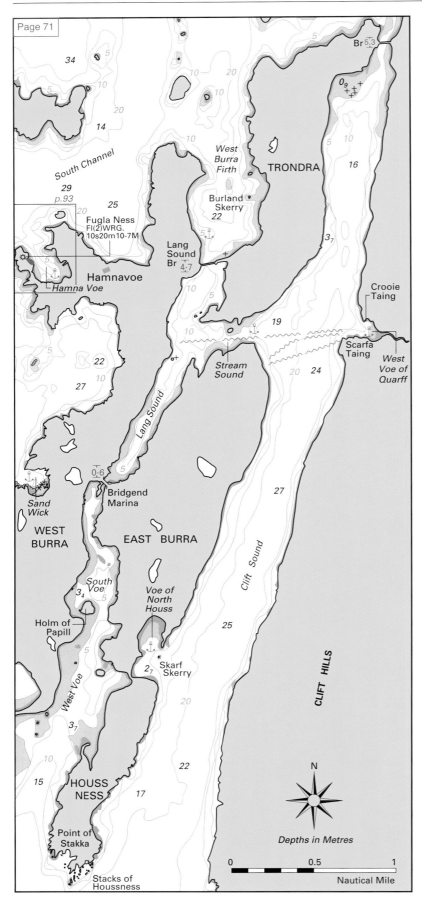

Page 71

34

5

5

5

10

10

20

20

10

10

14

20

South Channel

29
p.93

25

Br 5·3

0 9

West
Burra
Firth

TRONDRA

16

10

5

7

5

20

25

Fugla Ness
Fl(2)WRG.
10s20m10-7M

Burland
Skerry
22

Lang
Sound
Br 4·7

10

5

3 7

Hamnavoe

Hamna Voe

5

10

Crooie
Taing

5

22

27

10

10

19

10

0

Scarfa
Taing

West
Voe of
Quarff

Stream
Sound

20 24

Lang Sound

5

5

27

5

Clift Sound

0·6

Sand
Wick

Bridgend
Marina

WEST
BURRA

EAST BURRA

South
Voe

Voe of
North
Houss

25

3 4

5

Holm of
Papill

5

20

Skarf
Skerry

2 7

West Voe

3 7

22

10

CLIFT HILLS

15

HOUSS
NESS

17

N

Point of
Stakka

Depths in Metres

Stacks of
Houssness

0   0.5   1

Nautical Mile

CLIFT SOUND

Ruth Sharville - Geograph

Looking south down Clift Sound

Clift Sound

The south entrance is 8 miles north of Fitful Head and the Sound, about 5 cables wide, runs north-northeast for 6 miles between Mainland Shetland and Houss Ness, East Burra and Trondra.

Directions

Clift Sound shallows at the extreme north end and narrows to 1 cable wide where a bridge crosses to Trondra. At this point the depth in the channel is 1·8m and the headroom 5·3m. Within these limitations, the Sound provides a sheltered approach to Scalloway for small power vessels.

From the west, pass between South Havra and Houss Ness. Keep at least 2 cables off the Point of Stakka at Houss Ness.

From the south, pass between South Havra and Holm of Maywick but do not go east of a north-south line through Holm of Maywick until the whole of South Havra bears south of west.

Anchorage

Clift Sound is open to the south but some shelter can be found. Care must be taken in the north of Clift Sound as the northwest corner is foul with rocks.

Voe of North Houss or *Stream Sound* Good shelter can be found in north or west winds in these.

West Voe of Quarff A cable runs from the head round Scarfa Taing and down Clift Sound. Another cable runs from Scarfa Taing through Stream Sound. Anchor to avoid these.

Bridgend

Located at the bridge between West Burra and East Burra, Bridgend has a marina for shallow draft boats. There is a partially buoyed channel but access is not recommended without local knowledge. It is a main kayaking centre.

Dennis Geldard

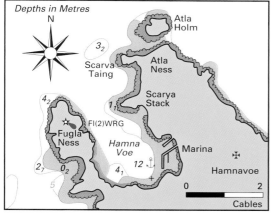
HAMNA VOE, WEST BURRA

West Burra Firth (Scalloway)

Approached from the South Channel leading to Scalloway, West Burra Firth (plan p.92) offers shelter from all directions except north.

The firth is clean apart from a small islet and Burland Skerry which lie close to the east shore. South of these the east shore should be given a berth of at least a cable but otherwise there are no dangers, apart from fish farm equipment. Anchor anywhere in the southwest corner of the firth where suitable depth can be found.

It is about a mile from Lang Sound bridge, at the southern end of the firth, to Hamanavoe village.

Hamna Voe marina (West Burra), with the new breakwater and pontoons

Admiralty Chart
3281, 3299-3
Ordnance Survey
4

Hamna Voe - West Burra

This is an almost landlocked harbour just inside Fugla Ness and at the northwest of West Burra offering good shelter. Once a busy fishing port, it has restricted room and most boats go to Scalloway. The bottom is foul with old moorings but it remains a safe haven in bad summer weather, except when a swell is running, and in strong northwesterly winds.

A small boat marina has been built behind a new breakwater south of the pier. A visitors' berth may be available but check availibility and depth, ☎ 01595 859444. Otherwise anchor southwest of the pier or lie alongside the pier (3·4m) for a short stay.

Facilities

Water, electricity, & toilets at marina. Shop and Post Office in village.

Occasional anchorage - West Burra

Sand Wick, (plan p.92) lying about 1½ miles south of Fugla Ness on the west coast of West Burra, offers a temporary passage anchorage in settled weather or offshore winds. Anchor in the centre of the bay, but no further in than half way, as the head is foul. Subject to swell. Whale Wick, just over ½ mile south of Sand Wick is not recommended.

Scalloway Harbour looking over the East Voe Marina

Dennis Geldard

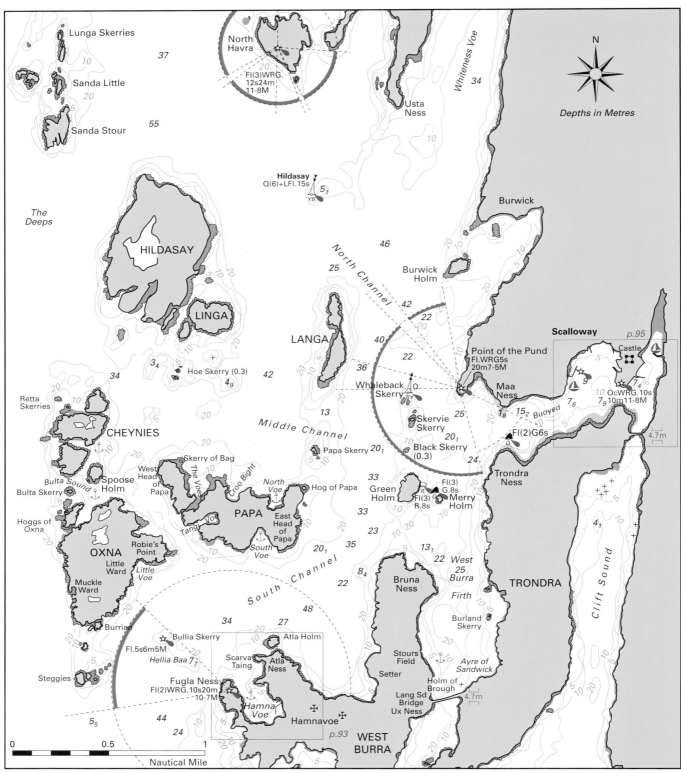

SCALLOWAY

Depths in Metres

0   0.5   1
Nautical Mile

p.95
p.93

Admiralty Chart
3294-1, 3294-2, 3281,
3283
Ordnance Survey
4

Scalloway

Scalloway offers sheltered anchorage on the west coast of Mainland Shetland about 20 miles north of Sumburgh Head. It is a convenient port for arrival from the south and west. (photograph p.93) and has all the stores and services that could be needed prior to starting a cruise on Shetland's west coast.

Tide

Constant −0155 Lerwick (−0205 Dover)

Heights in metres

MHWS	MHWN	MTL	MLWN	MLWS
1·6	1·3	1	0·6	0·5

Directions

Scalloway Harbour (Ch.12) or ☎ 01595 880566 should be contacted on arrival. The harbour is protected by a number of islands through which there are various channels of approach. Although great care is needed in strong onshore (southwest) winds it is possible to enter in all weathers.

There are three channels into the harbour:

South Channel Head for Green Holm leaving it to port via the buoyed channel between it and Merry Holm. Take a course that leaves Scalloway Castle open off Trondra Ness.

Enter the harbour between Trondra Ness and Maa Ness and follow the buoyed channel.

Note that there are two dangers equally spaced between Fugla Ness and Oxna, the island 7 cables northwest of Fugla Ness (plan p.94). These are Bullia Skerry (1·2m) and Hellia Baa (7·8m). In southwest gales the seas break over the latter and sometimes right across the entrance. In these conditions use of the North Channel is advisable.

Middle Channel Keep well south of Hoe Skerry (0·3m). Leave Papa Skerry to starboard and Green Holm close in to starboard to avoid Black Skerry. Not recommended at night or in poor visibility.

North Channel Pass between the island of Hildasay and the S Cardinal Hildasay Buoy (Q(6)+LFl.15s) northeast of it. The channel between Point of the Pund and Whaleback Skerry (dr. 1.5m, marked by a N Cardinal Buoy (Q)) is 3 cables wide.

Anchorage

Scalloway Bay Anchor off the west side of the bay in 8m soft mud. Use of a tripping line is advisable. In southwest winds better shelter may be found in East Voe in 4m north of the East Jetty but well clear of it. Use a tripping line.

Harbour Contact the Harbourmaster (Ch 12/16 ☎ 1595 744 221) for berth alongside the quay.

Port Arthur Marina is on the west side of the harbour.

Scalloway Boating Club Pontoon This is to the south of the main part of the marina and has berths for visitors. Depth alongside 4m. ☎ 01595 880388.

East Voe Marina This marina is on the east side of the East Voe of Scalloway. It is run by a Users Association and has limited space for visitors, ☎ 01595 880476. Depth 2m. It may be possible to arrange berthing for a short period during crew changing.

Facilities

Scalloway Shops, Post Office, hotels, restaurants, swimming pool, garage.

Scalloway Boating Club welcomes visitors and has toilets, showers and laundry facilities. Excellent fish restaurant at the North Atlantic Fisheries College (not open Saturday and Sunday) close by the Boating Club. Water and electricity on pontoon.

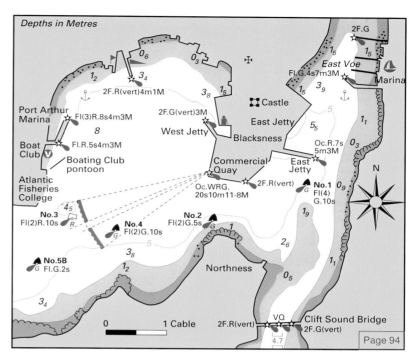

SCALLOWAY
HARBOUR

East Voe Marina Water and power on pontoons.

Blacksness Water, electricity and waste oil disposal. Crane hire, engineering services, boat repairs, electrical services, taxi service can be arranged. Marine diesel is available from a pontoon berth behind the West Jetty at Blacksness.

Interest

Scalloway Vistor Centre/Museum has the history of the 'Shetland Bus' in the second world war which took agents to and from Norway. Scalloway Castle.

Occasional anchorages

The islands to the west of Scalloway, whilst giving shelter to the harbour entrance, also offer occasional anchorages in fine weather.

Papa, the island north of Fugla Ness (plan p.94), has two voes on opposing sides, North Voe and South Voe, giving a choice of shelter. Both are straightforward to approach but both can be subject to swell.

Oxna anchorage is best approached from the east, though the passage through Bulta Sound can be used with care if there is no swell. If approaching from the south give Robie's Point a berth of at least a cable to avoid an awash rock. Anchor bewteen Spoose Holm and Oxna.

Cheynies This anchorage gives the best protection from the west. Anchor between Cheynies and Spoose Holm.

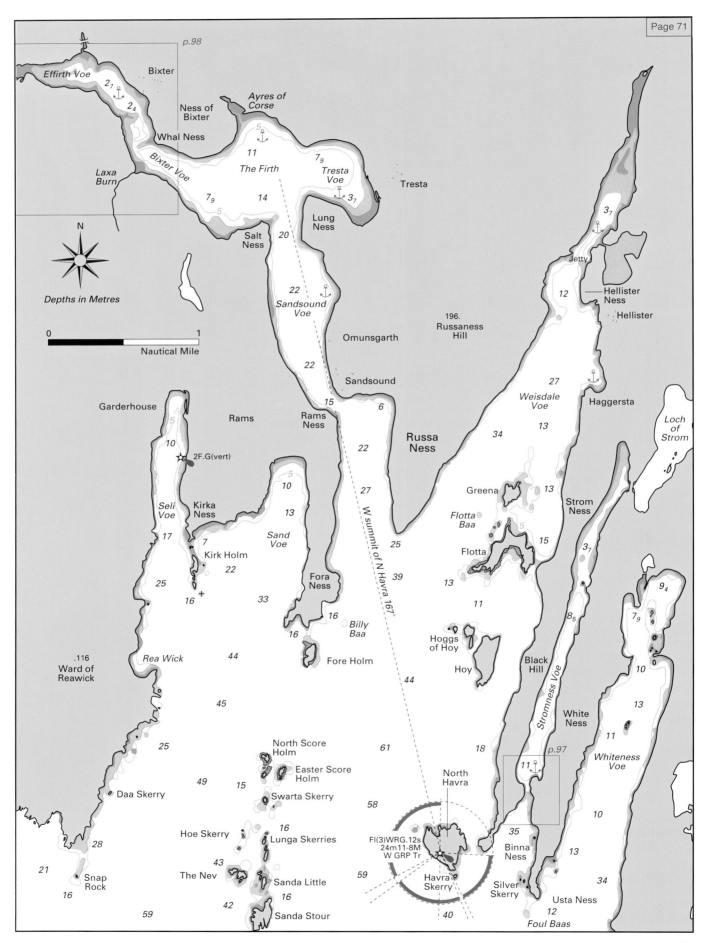

p.98

Effirth Voe

Bixter

2₇

2₄

Ness of
Bixter

Ayres of
Corse

Whal Ness

Bixter Voe

5

Laxa
Burn

The Firth

11

7₉

Tresta
Voe

Tresta

N

7₉

14

3₇

Depths in Metres

Salt
Ness

Lung
Ness

20

3₇

Jetty

0   1

22

Nautical Mile

Sandsound
Voe

22

Omunsgarth

196.
Russaness
Hill

Hellister
Ness

12

Hellister

Sandsound

Garderhouse

Rams

Rams
Ness

15

6

Weisdale
Voe

27

Haggersta

5

10

22

Russa
Ness

34

13

Loch
of
Strom

2F.G(vert)

10

27

Seli
Voe

Kirka
Ness

13

Greena

13

Strom
Ness

17

7

Sand
Voe

Flotta
Baa

5

15

3₇

9₄

Kirk Holm

22

25

16

+

33

Fora
Ness

Flotta

13

8₅

7₉

16

Billy
Baa

11

10

.116
Ward of
Reawick

Rea Wick

44

16

Fore Holm

Hoggs
of Hoy

Hoy

Black
Hill

13

45

Stromness Voe

White
Ness

11

25

18

p.97

Whiteness
Voe

North Score
Holm

61

11

49

15

Easter Score
Holm

North
Havra

35

10

Daa Skerry

Swarta Skerry

58

Binna
Ness

13

Hoe Skerry

16

Lunga Skerries

Fl(3)WRG.12s
24m11-8M
W GRP Tr

28

59

Silver
Skerry

13

34

21

43

The Nev

Sanda Little

Havra
Skerry

Usta Ness

16

Snap
Rock

16

42

Sanda Stour

40

12

59

Foul Baas

W summit of N Havra 167°

25

39

44

Colin Smith - Geograph

The Deeps

The Deeps is a large bay lying to the north and west of Scalloway. A number of islands lie in the bay and many voes are connected to it. The whole area is an attractive small scale cruising ground and a good place to spend some time. For this, the Admiralty Chart 3294 is recommended. Tidal constants are approximately the same as Scalloway throughout.

Suitable voes with shelter from the worst of normal summer weather are Stromness Voe, Weisdale Voe, Sandsound Voe with the connected voes to the north of it and Skelda Voe. Voes not suitable for an overnight stay, except in settled weather, are Whiteness Voe, Sand Voe, Seli Voe and Rea Wick.

Weisdale Voe

This lies 5 miles to the north of Scalloway, between Stromness Voe and Sandsound Voe.

Directions

The west shore is free of dangers more than 100m offshore as far as the channel north of Hellister Ness, near the head of the voe, which is 3 cables wide and clear.

On the east side of the entrance to the voe are the low-lying islands of Flotta and Greena which should not be approached closely. Note especially the isolated 2m rock, Flotta Baa, which lies 2 cables west of them, almost in the centre of the mouth of the voe. There is a narrow clear channel between Flotta and Strom Ness with a minimum depth of 1·8m.

Anchorage

The voe is sheltered from all winds except the south but can be gusty due to surrounding hills.

Bay of Haggersta or the pool at the head of the voe can provide some shelter from the south.

Facilities

Shop, auto diesel and Post Office at Hellister on the east side of the voe. Weisdale mill, gallery and café at head of voe.

Stromness Voe

Due to the restricted entrance and strong tide, care is required at the narrows where the rock in the approach must be passed on the west side. Then pass east of the inner rock and anchor in 8m in the sheltered bay on the east side of the voe just past the narrows. An attractive spot recommended by local yachtsmen.

Looking south towards the mouth of Weisdale Voe. The dark island, slightly left of centre, is Hoy with the Hoggs of Hoy lying off it

Admiralty Chart
3294-2, 3294-3, 3281, 3283
Ordnance Survey
3, 4

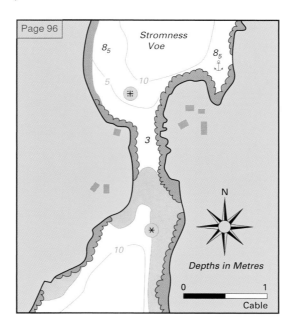
STROMNESS VOE NARROWS

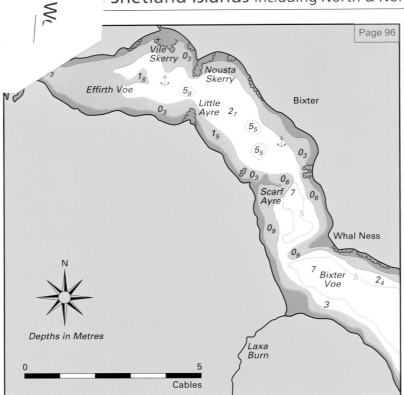

Page 96

Vile Skerry
Nousta Skerry
Effirth Voe
Little Ayre
Bixter
Scarf Ayre
Whal Ness
Bixter Voe
Laxa Burn

N

Depths in Metres

0   5
Cables

BIXTER VOE AND EFFIRTH VOE

Admiralty Chart
3294-3, 3281
Ordnance Survey
3

Sandsound Voe from the west shore looking due east towards the first narrows

Sandsound Voe, Tresta Voe & The Firth

Sandsound Voe lies immediately west of Weisdale Voe and, together with the voes leading off it, offers the most sheltered natural anchorages in the whole area. Sandsound Voe leads to The Firth and Tresta Voe is a bight off the east side of The Firth.

Directions

The entrance to the voe is clear. Between Sandsound and Rams Ness keep mid-channel in the first narrows and to the east of mid-channel off Salt Ness to avoid the spit that extends 1 cable northeast off Salt Ness. If heading towards Bixter Voe give the south shore of The Firth a berth of at least a cable as it is shoal for the next ½ mile.

Anchorage

Sandsound Voe, anchor in the bight north of Omunsgarth

Tresta Voe Excellent anchorage can be found in the south-southeast corner of Tresta Voe with good holding and shelter but subject to strong gusts in east winds.

The Firth Anchor at the head in Ayres of Corse or off the southwest shore once clear of the shallows mentioned above.

Bixter Voe and Effirth Voe

Bixter Voe is little more than a channel leading to Effirth Voe, an almost landlocked pool providing shelter from all winds.

Directions

The entrance to Bixter Voe from The Firth is clean as far as the mouth of the Laxa Burn on the southwest side, where a sandy shoal extends out from the shore. A little over a cable beyond this a spit runs out from Whal Ness on the east shore for about ¾ of the width of the voe.

Hold close to the west shore at this point then steer north-northeast across the channel to avoid a second spit, Scarf Ayre, extending ⅔ of the way across the voe from the west shore. Do not keep too close to the east shore to pass this spit as drying rocks extend a little distance from the shore. From here onwards keep to the centre of the voe.

Anchorage

Bixter Anchor off the houses in sand and shingle.

Effirth Voe anchor 1½ cables off the mouth of the burn on the north shore. Do not go any further west than Vile Skerry.

Facilities

Bixter: Water, stores, Post Office, auto diesel.

D Mayes - Geograph

Skelda Voe (Skeld)

This is the most westerly of the voes of The Deeps. The main part of it is short with a wide entrance open to the south and so can be subject to heavy seas and swell from that direction.

In settled weather, Westerwick Bay and Stead of Culswick are worth visiting (plan p.71). They lie on the heavily indented coast between Skelda Ness and Vaila. However, they are not included on the larger scale chart 3295-2 and great care should be taken when entering.

Directions

Approaching Skelda Voe there are several dangers:

Braga Rock (shows 2m) and a drying rock 1 cable south of it lies 1 mile south of the entrance in the middle of the fairway.

Snap Rock (shows 3·5m) lies 2½ cables south of Roe Ness with foul ground inshore of it.

A rocky spit six cables northwest of Snap Rock runs 2½ cables south.

When entering at the narrows avoid the shallow water on the west side.

Anchorage

The pool to the south of the marina provides a secure anchorage for yachts in 5m.

Skeld Marina has visitors' berths at a pontoon just north of the breakwater. Depth 2·5m. ☎ 01595 860287. There are two other pontoons. An adjacent caravan site overlooks the marina.

Facilities

Village: shop, Post Office. Bus and taxi service.
Pier: Diesel by arrangement.

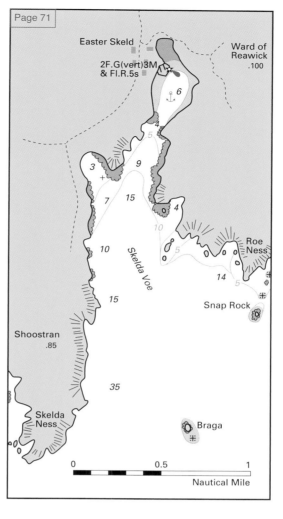

Page 71

Easter Skeld
2F.G(vert)3M
& Fl.R.5s

Ward of Reawick .100

6

3

9

4

5

7 15

10 5

10

Roe Ness

14 5

15

Snap Rock

Shoostran .85

15

35

Skelda Voe

Skelda Ness

Braga

0   0.5   1
Nautical Mile

SKELDA VOE

Admiralty Chart
3281, 3283
Ordnance Survey
4

Skeld marina at the head of Skelda Voe

Patrick Roach

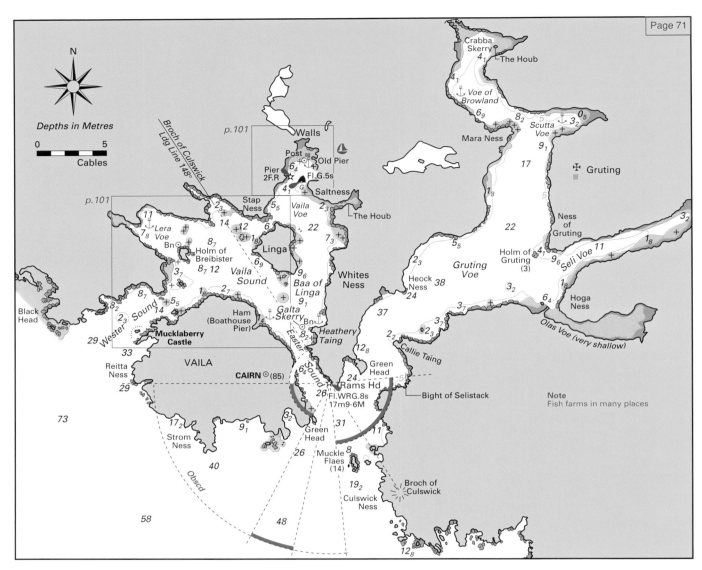

GRUTING VOE & VAILA SOUND

Admiralty Chart
3295-2, 3281, 3283
Ordnance Survey
3, 4

Gruting Voe

Gruting Voe lies on the south side of Shetland's West Mainland. Its entrance is east of the island of Vaila and leads to Voe of Browland, Scutta Voe and Seli Voe. Good shelter can be found within the main voe and in Browland, Seli and Scutta Voes.

Directions

There is usually swell in the entrance to Gruting Voe. North of Green Head the west shore is steep-to and clear to Mara Ness.

On the southeast side, the bight northeast of Callie Taing is foul with above and below water rocks. Keep on a course of less than 055°.

Thereafter, for 1 mile up to the entrance to Seli Voe, the shore should be given a berth of 1 cable. Holm of Gruting lies off the north side of the entrance to Seli Voe, and the shore due north from there is clear to Scutta Voe. A spit with under 3m runs 1½ cables northwest and narrows the entrance to Scutta Voe.

The entrance to Browland Voe is narrow and foul with rocks for 1 cable off Mara Ness.

The channel lies towards the north side of the entrance. A course 298° with the chapel in Gruting over the stern leads in clear. The voe shoals towards the head and is foul on the east side from the head for ½ mile.

Anchorage

This can be made in any of the voes clear of the numerous fish farms. Mud generally.

Vaila Sound (Walls)

An area of sheltered water on the southwest of Shetland Mainland enclosed by Vaila Island.

On the northwest of Vaila Sound lies Lera Voe and on the northeast Vaila Voe with Walls at the head (see aerial photograph p.102).

Directions

Approaching from the west and south, the shores of Vaila Island are clean and steep-to with any dangers visible.

Easter Sound The approach through this sound is straightforward provided the east shore of Vaila Island is given a berth of ½ cable. The

Whites Ness shore is clean and steep-to up to the narrows where a shoal extends north-northwest to Galta Skerry marked by a concrete beacon. Just over 2 cables northwest of Galta Skerry is a dangerous sunken rock, Baa of Linga, in mid-channel. If proceeding to Walls, the Baa must be passed well clear on the east side, so keep about 1½ cables off the east shore of Linga.

Vaila Voe to Lera Voe If leaving Vaila Voe by the channel between Stap Ness and Linga, the rock northwest of Holm of Stapness is not shown on older versions of Chart 3295. Note the rocks off the north shore of Lera Voe and those to the north of Holm of Breibister.

Wester Sound The dangerous underwater rock 'The Streng' lies mid-channel northwest of the islet of Gluibuil. The Streng is steep-to on the south side so will not show on the echo sounder before you hit it. On no account attempt to pass to the north of it.

If heading west, hold close to Gluibuil and when the reef at its west end is abeam take a west-northwesterly course to clear the reef to port that extends from the Vaila shore. Further west the mid-sound shoal (2·3m) lying northwest of the prominent Mucklaberry Castle is the final hazard before reaching open water.

Anchorage

Walls This is the best anchorage in Vaila Sound. A green buoy, Fl.G.5s, marks the west extremity of the shoal off Saltness. Anchor northeast of the public pier, clear of moorings.

Public Pier There is gale proof berthing at the pier depending on space left available by commercial users. 150m berthing, 3 to 7m depth. ☎ 01595 809293.

Temporary use of the pontoon for the Foula Ferry is possible but check the ferry times.

Walls Marina A red perch marks a rock towards the head of the sound. Leave this to port and follow the port and starboard channel buoys round into the marina leaving the small islet well to starboard. There are two visitors' berths. Depth 1·5m. ☎ 01595 809 311.

Boating Club Pier Depth 1·5m max. ☎ 01595 809277.

Facilities

Walls Shop, Post Office, shop, swimming pool with toilet and shower facilities within 1¼ mile, fuel at shop, diesel and chandlery within 1 mile; café, bus service, ferry to Foula.

Public Pier Toilets, water, electricity.

Marina Water, fuel, electricity (by arrangement), waste disposal, launching slip, Boating Club (open weekends).

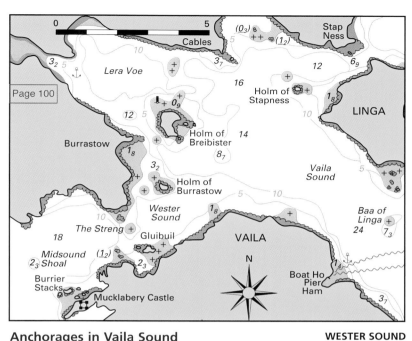

Anchorages in Vaila Sound

Lera Voe Anchor towards the west end.

Heathery Taing The bay to the north of Heathery Taing and to the east of Galta Skerry affords good anchorage.

Vaila Anchor off the boathouse and pier at Ham. Note the charted submarine cables.

WESTER SOUND

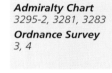

Admiralty Chart
3295-2, 3281, 3283
Ordnance Survey
3, 4

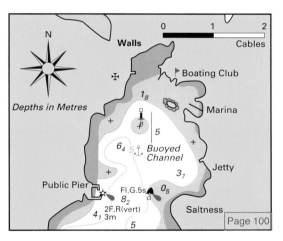

**WALLS,
VAILA VOE**

The new public pier at Walls offers good alongside berthing for yachts

Dr Julian Paren - Geograph

Patrick Roach

Walls and Vaila Sound (p.100) from the northeast. This was taken before the new pier on the west shore was built

Foula

Lying 27 miles west of Scalloway, Foula is one of the most isolated inhabited islands in the UK. There is an airstrip and regular communication by motor boat from Foula to Walls. If a visit is contemplated a telephone call to the sub-postmaster, ☎ 01595 753236 is suggested to find out if the conditions for landing are suitable.

Tide

Constant −0140 Lerwick (−0150 Dover)

Heights in metres

MHWS	MHWN	MTL	MLWN	MLWS
1·6	1·3	1	0·6	0·5

Ham Voe, Foula

Barrie Waugh

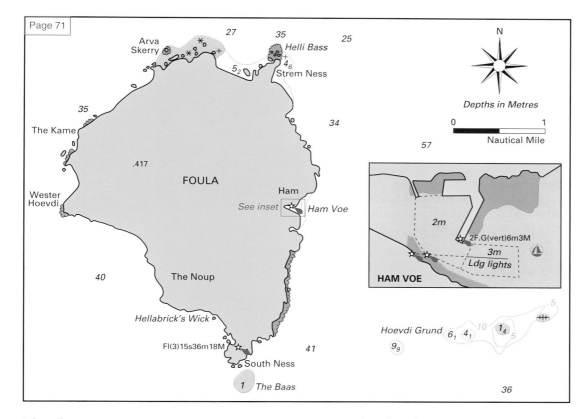

Arva Skerry

27 35 25

Helli Bass

Strem Ness

The Kame

35

FOULA

.417

Ham

See inset Ham Voe

Wester Hoevdi

The Noup

40

Hellabrick's Wick

Fl(3)15s36m18M

South Ness

The Baas

N

Depths in Metres

0   1
Nautical Mile

34

57

2m

2F.G(vert)6m3M

3m

Ldg lights

HAM VOE

Hoevdi Grund 6₁ 4₁ 10 1₄ 5

9₉

41

36

FOULA

Admiralty Chart
3281, 3283
Ordnance Survey
4

Directions

In the approach to Foula from the south or east note well the Hoevdi Rocks. These dangerous rocks lying up to 2½ miles east of Foula must be avoided and given a wide berth beyond the location indicated on Chart 3283. Take into account the tidal flow across this area. There appears to be less water than is stated on the chart. There is no possible anchorage anywhere round the coast except in the very narrow Ham Voe inlet mid-way up the east coast.

There are rocks on the south side of Ham Voe. Coming from the south do not turn into the voe till the whole of the footbridge over the burn at the head is well open of the high ground on the south side of the voe. There are rocks on the north side also and shoal water the full length of the pier on its east side. Keep well clear. Approach on the 270° leading line shown on the inset plan, to a point just off the southwest corner of the pier which runs north and south. There are 2G (vert) lights exhibited 7m from the south end of the pier. Do not be misled into thinking that these lights mark the south end of the pier.

Anchorage

Ham Voe There is a pier on the north side with davits to lift out the mail boat. Boats drawing 1·8m can lie alongside the west side of the pier. Good fendering is essential. The depth at the outer end of the pier is 2·3m. Since it is difficult to turn a longer boat inside the harbour, it is advantageous to lie bow out.

It is only safe to lie in the harbour when the wind is between south and northwest. There can be a nasty swell with strong northwest winds and the harbour is subject to down draughts. If the wind shifts to the southeast and freshens, it is necessary to clear out.

Facilities

Water at pier. No shop. Public telephone at the air strip, mobile (Vodafone) signal at air strip.

Interest

Ornithology, spectacular cliffs.

The stacks off the north coast of Foula

Dr Julian Paren - Geograph

Admiralty Chart
3281
Ordnance Survey
3

Sound of Papa

Sound of Papa separates Papa Stour from Mainland Shetland and provides a convenient route to avoid the very severe overfalls which occur off the northwest of the island.

Tide

The tide runs strongly through the Sound of Papa
SW-going stream starts –0355 Lerwick (–0400 Dover)
NE-going stream starts +0355 Lerwick (+0330 Dover)

Passage

Passage through the Sound requires great care as there are dangers extending well offshore on both sides. Strong tides can raise considerable seas with wind against tide and make course keeping difficult.

In the west approach, the shores of both Mainland and Papa Stour should be given a berth of at least 2 cables. The west entrance is narrowed to 5 cables wide by Huxter Baas which extends 4 cables northwest from Mainland. 1 mile within the entrance lies Midsound Baas which, together with Forewick Holm and a dangerous drying rock 1 cable further south, effectively reduces the channel width to 2½ cables.

South-southeast of Forewick Holm lies Holm of Melby off the Mainland shore, surrounded by foul ground and with a dangerous sunken rock 4 cables east-northeast.

Entering from the west in mid-channel make good a course of 060° for Forewick Holm.

Hold this course until 3 cables off this island then turn to starboard making good a course 115° for the north point of Holm of Melby. When 2 cables off the nearest part of Holm of Melby turn to port making good a course 070° for Muckle Roe Light Tower. This leads clear of the sunken rock off Holm of Melby.

Entering the Sound from the east make good a course 230° to keep the Mainland shore west of Ness of Melby well open north of Holm of Melby which should be passed 1 cable off. When Holm of Melby is abeam to port turn to starboard to make good a course of 295° to pass 2 cables southwest of Forewick Holm. When Forewick Holm bears 060° turn to a course of 240° keeping it on the reciprocal bearing 060° over the stern. This leads clear of all dangers.

Papa Stour

Papa Stour lies 1 mile off the west coast of Mainland Shetland at the south of St Magnus Bay. It has has a spectacular coastline and some of the finest sea caves in the UK

Directions

The approach from the south and west is clear to the south of the island but note that for 4 miles southwest of Papa Sound the north and south-going streams reach 3–4 kn at springs. To reach the north and east it is necessary either to traverse the Sound of Papa or to sail west-about.

PAPA SOUND

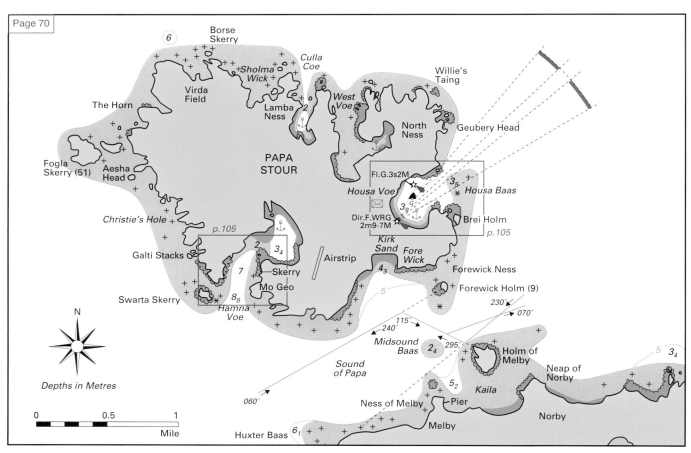

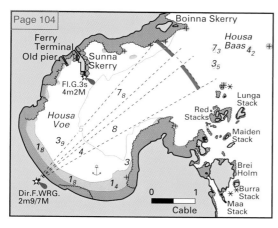

HOUSA VOE, PAPA STOUR

The passage west-about between Ve Skerries, (3 miles northwest of Papa Stour, plan p.70), and Papa Stour is only advisable in quiet weather with no wind against tide or swell. Otherwise pass over ½ mile west of Ve Skerries as the seas break over the whole area between Ve Skerries and Papa Stour.

The approach from St Magnus Bay is clear to the north of the island but the above remarks about Ve Skerries apply.

Anchorage

Housa Voe On the east coast of Papa Stour with entrance facing northeast. It has a pier and is the main harbour for the island. It offers reasonable shelter from normal summer weather.

There is a sunken rock, Housa Baas, mid-channel 2 cables east of the point on the north side of the entrance and just over 1 cable north of the stacks on the south side of the entrance. Enter the voe parallel to and 1 cable off the northwest shore. The white sector of the Dir F light bears 226°– 230°.

Anchor anywhere in the voe in 4–6m. Sand, good holding but subject to swell. An alongside berth in depth 2·5m is available at the end of the old pier, west of the ferry pier. Water and toilets at ferry waiting room.

Hamna Voe (Papa Stour) The only voe on the south of the island is an almost completely landlocked lagoon giving shelter from all weather. Access is not possible in strong south winds nor to deep draught vessels at LW.

From the south, the entrance can be recognised by Mo Geo in the red cliffs on the east and by Swarta Skerry on which the seas break almost continuously on the west. Enter mid-channel to avoid sunken rocks on either hand then steer 015° towards where the channel narrows and turns northeast. Keep on this course until a small skerry, (reported to cover at HWS) off the south point of the narrows can be identified. When this is abeam bear slowly round to the east and aim to pass well north of the skerry.

Here the channel is narrowed to about 30m by a drying reef running south from the north shore and another drying reef extending northeast of the skerry. Keep slightly north of mid-channel and enter the lagoon. The depth in the narrows is 2m at LWS.

Anchor in 4–6m anywhere to suit. Keep clear of the rocky spit and the remains of a ruined slipway on the east shore.

Culla Voe On the north coast of Papa Stour to the west of West Voe it is entered to the east of Lamba Ness. It offers shelter from most weather but would be difficult to leave if the wind increased from any northerly direction.

Keep to mid-channel to avoid sunken rocks on either hand. Once inside the voe all dangers are visible. Anchor near the head of the voe. Good holding apart from patches of heavy weed. Shallow with limited swinging room.

West Voe Keep to the west side of the voe when entering until an inlet opens up on the east side. Head towards the inlet and anchor in 4-6m, just inside its mouth. Not much protection from the north and heavy weed reported.

Facilities

There is a piped water supply, an airstrip and a ferry to West Burra Firth on Mainland Shetland. Water, toilets, Post Office at Housa Voe.

Papa Sound from the east with Holm of Melby on the extreme right

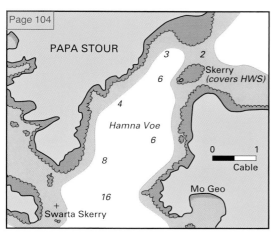

HAMNA VOE NARROWS, PAPA STOUR

Charles Tait

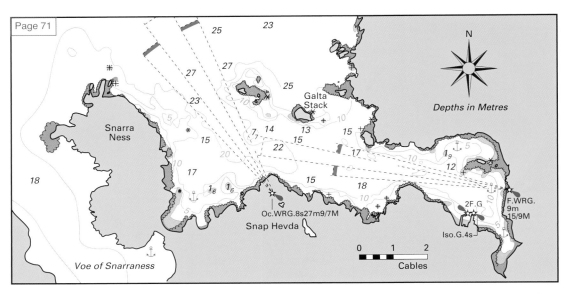

Page 71

Snarra Ness

Galta Stack

Depths in Metres

N

Oc.WRG.8s27m9/7M

Snap Hevda

F.WRG. 9m 15/9M

2F.G

Iso.G.4s

Voe of Snarraness

0   1   2

Cables

VOE OF SNARRANESS & WEST BURRA FIRTH

Admiralty Chart
3281, 3299-3
Ordnance Survey
3

Sound of Papa to Swarbacks Minn

The anchorages in this section are on the south shore of St Magnus Bay that lies between Papa Stour and Esha Ness.

Voe of Snarraness

Directions

There are no unseen dangers up to the head of this voe if the shores are given an offing of ½ cable. At the head of the voe there is a drying shoal patch in the centre

Anchorage

Anchor anywhere in the voe in 9-14m mud, good holding. The bay in the northeast corner is shallower but may be obstructed by fish pens. The shelter for anchoring is generally better than West Burra Firth. Use a tripping line as there may be discarded fish farm moorings and anchors.

West Burra Firth

West Burra Firth (West Mainland)

This firth is located on the north coast of west Mainland, on the south of St Magnus Bay and southeast of Papa Stour.

Tide

Constant –0205 Lerwick (–0215 Dover)

Heights in metres

MHWS	MHWN	MTL	MLWN	MLWS
2·2	1·7	1·4	1·0	0·6

Directions

Keep at least 1 cable off Snarra Ness to avoid a dangerous rock (drying 1·3m) lying to the east of it. The approach course of 146° on the white tower of West Burra Firth Outer Light on Snap Hevda is the middle of the white sector of that light and leads clear of the sunken rocks off the skerries northwest of Galta Stack. Then keep mid-channel through the narrows into the head of the Firth.

Anchorage

Snarraness Anchor in the bay southeast of Snarra Ness. Note the drying rock ¾ cable off the east side of Snarraness and two 1·6m patches off Snap Hevda.

North of harbour Anchor in 7m in the centre of the bay on the north shore. Note the rock on the west side of the bay and rocks extending ½ cable southeast of the islet.

East of the harbour Anchor as far east of the ferry pier as depth and swinging room allow, but note that the head of the firth is shallow.

The well fendered pier is 'L' shaped and provides good shelter in 4m. Keep clear of the ferry berth. (① 01806 244200).

Facilities

Water, fuel, waste and waste oil disposal, launching slip. Ferry to Papa Stour.

Interest

Pictish broch.

Arthur Houston

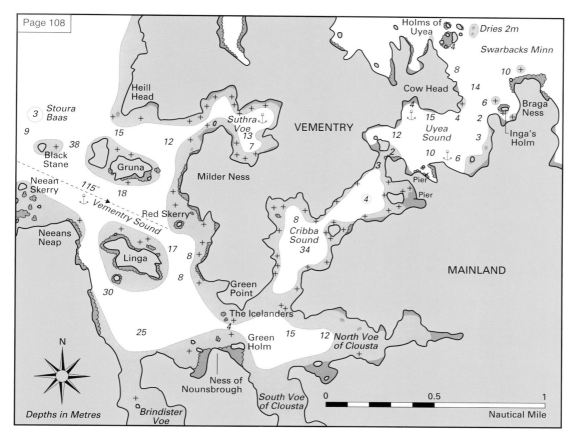

Page 108

Holms of Uyea

Dries 2m

Swarbacks Minn

8

10

Cow Head

14

Heill Head

Stoura Baas 3

9

15

Suthra Voe 13 7

VEMENTRY

4

15

Uyea Sound

4

6

Braga Ness

2

Inga's Holm

38

Black Stane

Gruna

12

Milder Ness

0

12

3

10

6

0

Neean Skerry

115°

18

Vementry Sound

Red Skerry

2

3

Pier

Pier

Neeans Neap

Linga

17

8

8

4

8

Cribba Sound 34

30

Green Point

MAINLAND

25

The Icelanders

4

Green Holm

15

12

North Voe of Clousta

N

Ness of Nounsbrough

South Voe of Clousta

0

0.5

1

Nautical Mile

Depths in Metres

Brindister Voe

VEMENTRY

Vementry Sound including Suthra Voe, Voes of Clousta & Brindister Voe

Two miles northeast of West Burra Firth, Vementry Sound and the connected voes comprise an area of sheltered water suitable for sailing and making overnight anchorage.

Directions

Vementry Sound contains many rocks and shallows which necessitate careful pilotage. In particular there are a number of dangers off the entrance which lies between Heill Head on Vementry Island and Neeans Neap.

A course of 115° leads in clear past Stoura Baas, Black Stane and Gruna to port, and Neean Skerry and Linga to starboard. The most difficult passage is rounding Green Point, the south tip of Vementry. A reef known as 'The Icelanders' extends south from this point, partly visible at LW, for 1 cable. Another reef extends north for 1¼ cables from Ness of Nounsbrough. These dangerous reefs effectively reduce the channel to ½ cable and depth 4m.

Entry is possible also for small craft at suitable states of the tide from Swarbacks Minn through Cribba Sound, a narrow channel with a minimum depth of 1m between Vementry Island and Mainland. The tide runs strongly through it. It is best tackled near HW.

Anchorages

Anchor in any of the voes as weather and soundings permit.

Interest

Take a walk to the three world war one naval guns on Swarbacks Head, the north point of Vementry.

Uyea Sound (Swarbacks Minn)

This Sound is 1½ miles inside the entrance to Swarbacks Minn, on the south side, and for most yachts it is best entered from Swarbacks Minn, though small shoal draught vessels might choose to use Cribba Sound.

Directions

Entering from Swarbacks Minn keep well clear of the drying rocks east of Holms of Uyea. Otherwise the west side is reasonably clear of unseen dangers. The east side of the entrance is foul and should be given ¾ cable berth off the shore including Inga's Holm.

There is a channel for small craft from the southwest corner of the pool of Uyea Sound leading round the south of Vementry Island to Cribba Sound.

For entry to Cribba Sound from Uyea Sound see directions for Vementry Sound.

Anchorage

The Sound is generally deep and, depending on the position of the fish cages or mussel lines, anchorage may be had in the bay on the north side in 4-8m, weed, but good holding may be found. Anchorage is also possible off the south shore but thick weed can cause difficulties.

Admiralty Chart
3281, 3295-1
Ordnance Survey
3

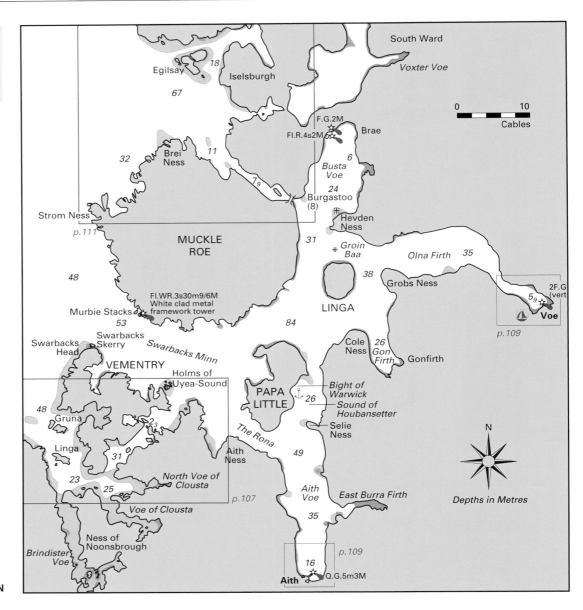

Admiralty Chart
3281, 3295-1
Ordnance Survey
3

SWARBACKS MINN

Swarbacks Minn

Swarbacks Minn is an extensive complex of voes, islands and sounds forming a large area of sheltered navigable water with numerous anchorages suitable for both large and small craft. It lies in the southeast corner of St Magnus Bay and, like The Deeps (p.97), it is a good place to explore.

Swarbacks Head from Muckle Ward, Vementry Island

Ruth Sharville - Geograph

Directions

Swarbacks Minn is entered between Vementry Island on the south and Muckle Roe Island on the north. Swarbacks Skerry lies ½ cable north of Swarbacks Head, the northwest point of Vementry Island. This headland is conspicuous for the three 1914–18 war guns mounted on the cliff top. The southwest corner of Muckle Roe has a light tower and the Murbie Stacks lie just west of it.

The white sector of Muckle Roe Light to the west shows over clear water in the approach, and the white sector to the south can be picked up in the entrances to Uyea Sound and The Rona (the sound to the southwest of Papa Little). Within the entrance to Swarbacks Minn, the south shore of Vementry Island is steep-to and clean for 1 mile up to Holms of Uyea Sound ½ cable east of which are 2 drying (1·5m) rocks. The shore of Muckle Roe Island should be given a berth of 1 cable.

Aith Voe

A large voe on the south of Swarbacks Minn. Access is either east or west of Papa Little Island which lies in the entrance. The village of Aith lies at the head.

This voe gives shelter from all weather except north. If caught at the head in a northerly gale, shelter can be found in the entrance to the shallow East Burra Firth or in the Bight of Warwick in the Sound of Houbansetter (see below) east of Papa Little.

Directions

The Rona, the passage to the southwest of Papa Little, is 3 cables wide at its narrowest and clear of hidden dangers more than ½ cable offshore.

The east entrance through the Sound of Houbansetter quickly narrows to 1½ cables with shoal water on either shore. There is a skerry on the outer end of a drying spit running south-southeast from the Papa Little shore 2 cables within the narrows. There is an awash rock 6 cables further in, ½ cable off Selie Ness on the Mainland shore. Apart from these there are no off-lying dangers.

Inside Aith Voe there are no hidden dangers apart from one sunken rock just northwest of the skerry that is 1½ miles from the head on the east side.

Anchorage

Anchorage can be made anywhere round the shores but only Aith offers any facilities

Aith Anchor northwest of the pier in 5-7m. Alternatively a visitor's berth may be available at the pier. ☎ 01595 810378.

Aith Marina for small boats with 2 visitors' berths. Depth 1·2m.

Facilities

Village: Shop and Post Office, leisure centre with swimming pool and showers; bar in Aith Public Hall Friday and Saturday.

Pier: Water and diesel; lifeboat station.

Marina: Water, electricity, toilets, waste and waste oil disposal; slip, repairs; engineering services; Boating Club.

Sound of Houbansetter; Gon Firth

Sound of Houbansetter This is the channel between Papa Little and the Mainland.

Anchor in the Bight of Warwick in the Sound of Houbansetter, east of Papa Little. Anchor at the north end of bay in 4m. Good shelter in northerly weather.

Gon Firth South of the entrance to Olna Firth. There are no unseen dangers in Gon Firth.

Anchor towards the bight at the southeast corner. Good shelter. Weed can cause difficulties.

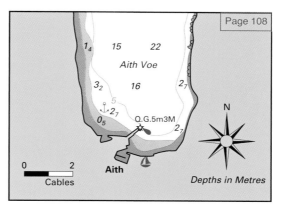

HEAD OF AITH VOE

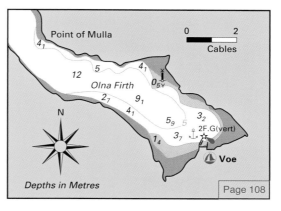

HEAD OF OLNA FIRTH

Olna Firth

The most easterly of the firths leading off Swarbacks Minn.

Directions

The main channel south of Linga Island is wide and clear. Groin Baa, a sunken rock 1½–2 cables north of Linga Island, lies in the middle of the north channel. Otherwise this channel is clear. Nearly 1 mile within the entrance of Olna Firth a drying rock lies 1 cable off the south shore. This is the only unseen danger but there may be mussel farms. After 1½ miles Olna Firth narrows to 1 cable and widens again at the head where there is the village of Voe.

Anchorage

Voe at the head of Olna Firth. Anchor in 4–8m north or northwest of the pier.

Voe Marina is a small boat marina with two pontoons either side of the pier. Depth 3·75m. ☎ 01806 588708.

Facilities

Village Shop up the hill; pub/restaurant; joinery and welding services; bakery. Bus service.

Marina Toilets, showers, water and electricity, fuel, launching slip.

Voe marina at the head of the Olna Firth (p.107)

Busta Voe (Brae)

This is the most northerly of the voes in Swarbacks Minn. The town of Brae is at the head of the voe.

Directions

The island of Linga lies south of the entrance to Busta Voe. The passage to the west of Linga Island presents no difficulties but a sunken rock, Groin Baa, lies 1½–2 cables to the north of Linga Island.

On the west side of Busta Voe, just north of the entrance, is the east entrance to Roe Sound but this passage is closed by a drying bank and a road bridge. Burgastoo, an 8·5m rock, lies to the east of the entrance to Roe Sound in Busta Voe.

On the east side of Busta Voe, opposite Roe Sound is a dangerous awash rock 1 cable northwest of Hevden Ness.

Five cables north of the entrance to Roe Sound is a small private harbour below Busta House. The bottom is clean gravel.

Anchorage

Brae at the head of Busta Voe, is a main town in Shetland and is a major sailing centre. Anchoring is possible off Brae in 6m but in thick weed. Ensure anchor is well dug in.

Delting Boating Club Marina on the northwest shore of Busta Voe has 54 fully serviced berths. Minimum depth 2m. Visitors' berths are available and yachts should berth initially on the hammerhead pontoon from where a berth will be allocated. ☎ 01806 522524.

Facilities

Brae Hotels, restaurants and shops, Post Office and leisure centre; marine and auto diesel; petrol; garages, chandlery.

Marina Showers, toilets and laundry available at the Delting Boating Club. The club is open every night and visitors are welcome to use the bar facilities.

The Delting Boating Club marina at Brae, Busta Voe

Roe Sound

This sound runs northwest/southeast and separates Muckle Roe on the north side from Shetland Mainland. The southeast end is spanned by a low bridge and drying bank which prevents the passage of vessels.

Directions

There is an isolated above water rock, the Lothan, in the middle of the entrance with a sunken rock 1 cable southeast of it. Approach may be made either northeast or southwest of these dangers but the northeast is recommended as being the wider channel. If coming from the south give the west coast of Muckle Roe a berth of at least 1 cable beyond visible dangers and the north coast a berth of over 2 cables as there is a sunken rock off Brei Ness.

Coming from the west or north, approach The Lothan on a course 130° with Isle of Stenness, at the southwest point of Esha Ness, on the reciprocal bearing over the stern. Leave the Lothan skerry to starboard and once in the Sound hold over to the Mainland shore to avoid the dangerous reef which extends 1 cable northwest from Staba Ness.

Anchorage

Anchor just west of Crog Holm clear of any cages. There is no passage for yachts north of Crog Holm. Limited swinging room and poor holding.

Hams of Roe

These are two spectacular inlets on the northwest of Muckle Roe. It is reported that the North Ham anchorage is foul and the South is preferable. In South Ham care must be taken to avoid the rocky patch off the south beach. There is an occasional anchorage off the easterly beach but proceed with care as soundings of less than 1m have been reported up to a considerable distance from the shoreline.

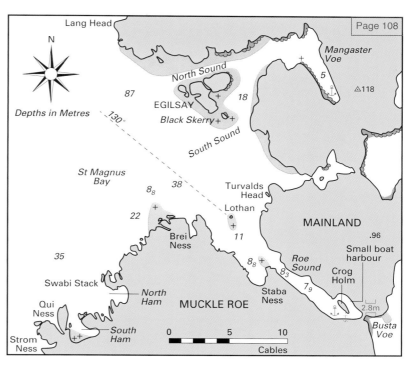

ROE SOUND

Admiralty Chart
3281, 3295-1

Ordnance Survey
3

Mangaster Voe

This voe lies in the middle of St Magnus Bay 1½ miles north of Roe Sound.

Directions

The Egilsay Isles and Black Skerry lie in the entrance and have many outlying sunken rocks.

There are channels north and south of these islands which must be given a berth of at least 1 cable. Keep ¾ cables off the Mainland shore and at least 1 cable off Black Skerry if using the South Sound.

Anchorage

The voe offers shelter from all winds except west. Anchor at the head in 4–6m avoiding the small boats moored there.

An occasional anchorage on the south coast of Muckle Roe

David Gillibrand

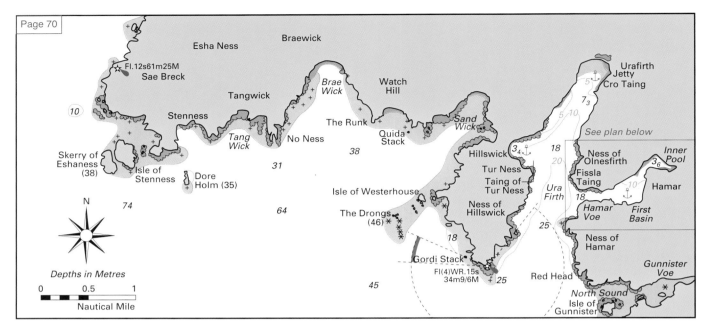

Admiralty Chart
3281, 3295-3
Ordnance Survey
3

Ura Firth; Hamar Voe; Hills Wick

The entrance to Ura Firth, which leads to Hamar Voe and Hills Wick, is at the northeast of St Magnus Bay.

Tide

Constant −0215 Lerwick (−0235 Dover)

Heights in metres

MHWS	MHWN	MTL	MLWN	MLWS
2·0	1·6	1·25	1·0	0·4

Directions

The entrance to Ura Firth is about 1 mile wide and can be approached in any weather, night or day. It is marked on the west by the sectored Hillswick Light showing red over The Drongs, Dore Holm and Skerry of Eshaness, and white over the clear water in St Magnus Bay. There is a sunken rock 1½ cables south of the light but otherwise the dangers are visible if the shores are given a ½ cable offing as far as Hills Wick.

Do not turn into Hills Wick until a cleft in the hills beyond is seen over the low neck of land connecting Hillswick Ness to the Mainland.

The west side of the Ura Firth, north of Hills Wick, is foul.

The entrance to Hamar Voe is 1 cable wide or less for 4 cables and leads into the first basin. At the northeast end of this there is a rocky spit extending south from the north shore where the channel to the pool narrows to ½ cable.

Anchorage

The firth offers good shelter.

Urafirth Anchor northwest of Cro Taing in 4–10m.

Hillswick The holding in Hills Wick is not good.

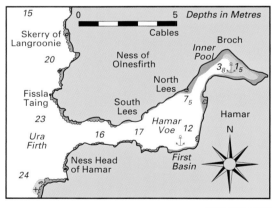

HAMAR VOE

Hamar Voe Anchor anywhere in the first basin in depths between 10–16m. The pool at the head, which is shoal at its east end, is almost completely landlocked offering security in all weather.

Facilities

Hillswick Hotel, shop, toilets, auto diesel, healthcare centre.

The Drongs, an unmistakable group of stacks southwest of the Ness of Hillswick

Mike Pennington - Geograph

Hamna Voe (Esha Ness)

On the northwest coast of Mainland Shetland 2 miles northeast of Esha Ness Light.

Tide

Constant –0150 Lerwick (–0200 Dover)

Heights in metres

MHWS	MHWN	MTL	MLWN	MLWS
2·3	1·9	1·5	1·1	0·6

Directions

The entrance is reduced to 0·3 cable by rocks on either hand. There are rocks 3 cables offshore west from the entrance to Head of Stanshi. Approach from the north or northwest and enter on the leading line: old single-storey house on the south shore in line with the prominent rock off the point on the west shore 3 cables within the entrance bearing 153°. If the entrance is difficult to see in bad light the hole through Muckle Ossa, the small island (55) to the west of Ockram Head, open astern may help to indicate the general direction.

Anchorage

Anchor in the bay either in the east of the voe (but note that it shoals rapidly towards the beach) or in the south part of the bay. Avoid pier as it is used by work boats.

Temporary anchorage may be found off the landing beaches on the southeast side. It is reported that the bottom is foul with old moorings. Good holding.

Facilities

Small museum close by.

Ronas Voe

A spectacular voe five miles long on the northwest coast of Mainland Shetland.

Directions

Running southeast from the entrance for 2½ miles there are red cliffs to port and black cliffs with green vegetation to starboard. It then narrows to a little over 1 cable and the cliffs give way to more gentle slopes.

Keep mid-channel from the entrance to 5 cables before The Blade, a promontory on the southwest shore, where it shoals for 2 cables. Tend towards the northeast shore which is clean until the narrows are reached. Beyond this there are no dangers more than ½ cable offshore.

There is a fish factory at Skeo Head where the voe turns east. East winds are funnelled through the narrows between the cliffs and accelerate, producing violent squalls which blow the tops off the waves in spindrift. Violent down-draughts from Ronas Hill to the northeast can be experienced.

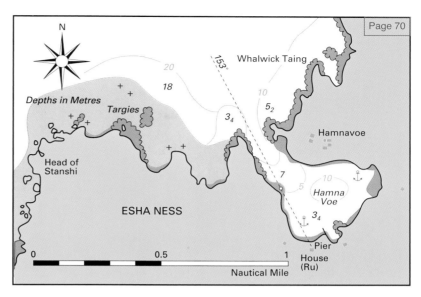

HAMNA VOE

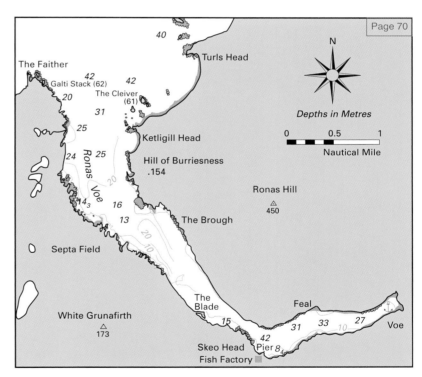

RONAS VOE

Anchorage

There is sheltered anchorage in 4–10m near the head of the voe but even here the wind may come from all directions causing vessels to range about their anchors.

To climb Ronas Hill (450m), the highest point of Shetland, temporary anchorage can be found off Feal, the bay on the north shore 1 mile from the head of the voe. There are rocks off each end of the beach.

Admiralty Chart
3281, 3295-4

Ordnance Survey
3

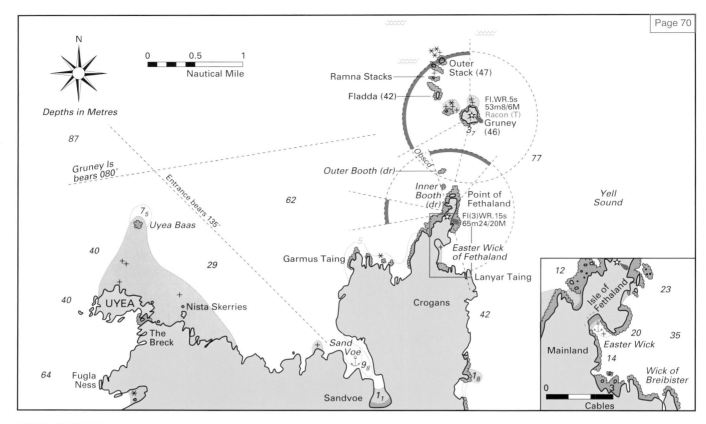

UYEA ISLAND TO RAMNA STACKS

Admiralty Chart
3281, 3282, 3298

Ordnance Survey
1,2

Uyea to Point of Fethaland and Ramna Stacks

Uyea is a tidal island at the northwest tip of Mainland Shetland (not to be confused with the island of the same name at the south of Unst). The Point of Fethaland is at the northeast tip. To the north from the Point of Fethaland lie the Island of Gruney and the Ramna Stacks.

Directions

Uyea Baas, a group of dangerous rocks, some of which dry, lies 7 cables north-northeast of Uyea. The shore east of Uyea is foul for a considerable distance. Do not attempt to pass inshore of the Uyea Baas.

When proceeding either east or west past the Point of Fethaland hold to Gruney Island to avoid the Outer and Inner Booth rocks, both of which dry.

The Gruney light is obscured in the southwest sector where Outer Booth would make it dangerous to attempt the passage between Gruney Island and Point of Fethaland in darkness.

Sand Voe

This spectacular voe is situated on the northwest coast of Mainland Shetland 2 miles southwest of Point of Fethaland with a narrow entrance between steep-to rocks. There is a fine sandy beach at the head of the inner part beyond the narrows.

Directions

Coming from the south or west hold a course where Gruney Island bears not less than 080° until the entrance to the voe bears not less than 135°.

Anchorage

Good anchorage can be found in the outer part of the voe except in northwest winds when it is subject to swell. Better shelter can be found in the inner part close to the rocks on the west side in 3m. It can be difficult to get out if swell sets in.

Easter Wick of Fethaland

This small wick on the east side of Fethaland just north of the Wick of Breibister (see inset above) is suitable as a temporary anchorage in settled weather. A rock lies in mid-channel in the approach. Pass south of this rock. Depth in the anchorage is 2·7m; sand. Ropes ashore can help stay in position as swinging room is limited.

The Point of Fethaland and Ramna Stacks

Yell

Whale Firth

The entrance to Whale Firth is 5 miles due east of Ramna Stacks, lying on the west coast of Yell immediately north of the entrance to Yell Sound. Whale Firth is 4 miles south of Bagi Stack at the extreme northwest point of Yell and it is the only secure anchorage on the west coast of Yell, north of Yell Sound.

Directions

At the entrance a sunken rock lies 2 cables northeast of Nev of Stuis. Numerous mussel farms are on east side of the voe. Be aware of two rocks just north of the shore at Grimister.

Anchorage

Anchor at the head of the voe giving quiet and secluded anchorage even with bad weather outside. Excellent holding in mud. Keep in mind the tide and weather conditions in Yell Sound in north and west winds before leaving.

Interest

Splendid base for coastal walks. Mid Yell is a pleasant two-mile walk away. Otters. The 'haunted' ruins of Windhouse.

Gloup Voe and Wick of Breckon

These are two inlets on the north coast of Yell.

Gloup Voe This is to be avoided as it dries out halfway and considerable seas penetrate the voe with strong north and northwest winds.

Wick of Breckon Can be used as a temporary daytime anchorage only.

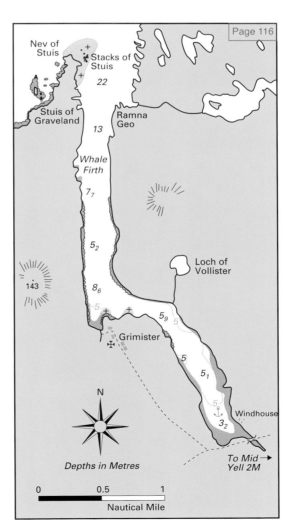

WHALE FIRTH

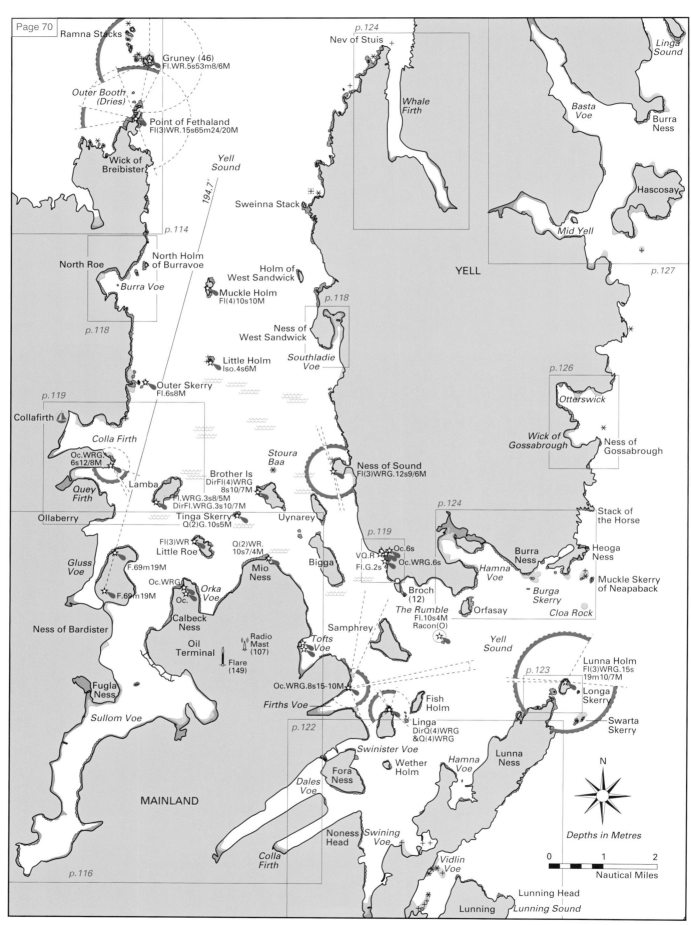

Page 70

Ramna Stacks

Gruney (46)
Fl.WR.5s53m8/6M

Outer Booth
(Dries)

Point of Fethaland
Fl(3)WR.15s65m24/20M

Wick of
Breibister

Yell
Sound

194.7°

Nev of Stuis

p.124

Whale
Firth

Linga
Sound

Basta
Voe

Burra
Ness

Hascosay

Sweinna Stack

p.114

North Roe

North Holm
of Burravoe

Burra Voe

p.118

Holm of
West Sandwick

Muckle Holm
Fl(4)10s10M

Ness of
West Sandwick

p.118

Southladie
Voe

Mid Yell

YELL

p.127

Little Holm
Iso.4s6M

Outer Skerry
Fl.6s8M

p.119

Collafirth

Colla Firth

Oc.WRG
6s12/8M

Quey
Firth

Lamba

Ollaberry

Brother Is
DirFl(4)WRG
8s10/7M
Fl.WRG.3s8/5M
DirFl.WRG.3s10/7M

Tinga Skerry
Q(2)G.10s5M

Stoura
Baa

Uynarey

Ness of Sound
Fl(3)WRG.12s9/6M

p.126

Otterswick

Wick of
Gossabrough

Ness of
Gossabrough

p.124

Burra
Ness

Stack of
the Horse

Heoga
Ness

Hamna
Voe

Muckle Skerry
of Neapaback

Burga
Skerry

Cloa Rock

Fl(3)WR
Little Roe

Q(2)WR.
10s7/4M

Bigga

VQ.R
Fl.G.2s

Oc.6s

Oc.WRG.6s

Gluss
Voe

F.69m19M

Oc.WRG
Orka
Voe

F.69m19M

Oc.

Calbeck
Ness

Ness of Bardister

Oil
Terminal

Mio
Ness

Radio
Mast
(107)

Flare
(149)

Broch
(12)

The Rumble
Fl.10s4M
Racon(O)

Orfasay

Samphrey

Yell
Sound

Lunna Holm
Fl(3)WRG.15s
19m10/7M

Longa
Skerry

Tofts
Voe

Oc.WRG.8s15-10M

Fugla
Ness

Sullom Voe

Firths Voe

p.122

Fish
Holm

Linga
DirQ(4)WRG
&Q(4)WRG

Swinister Voe

Dales
Voe

Fora
Ness

Wether
Holm

Hamna
Voe

Swarta
Skerry

Lunna
Ness

MAINLAND

Noness
Head

Swining
Voe

Colla
Firth

Vidlin
Voe

N

Depths in Metres

p.116

Lunning Head

Lunning

Lunning Sound

0   1   2
Nautical Miles

Yell Sound

Yell Sound lies between Mainland Shetland and Yell and is approximately 16 miles long. From the Point of Fethaland in the north, the sound runs due south for 9 miles. Here it narrows to 1½ miles and heads southeastwards for 3 miles. Then it finally runs due east for a further 3 miles before reaching the southern entrance between Yell and Lunna Ness.

The entire area of Yell Sound and Sullom Voe, from the Point of Fethaland to Samphrey Island in the southeast, is defined as the Sullom Voe Harbour area. All vessel movements are controlled by Port Operations based at Sella Ness in Sullom Voe.

Yachts are advised to contact the Port Controller on VHF Ch 14, call sign 'Sullom Voe Harbour Radio' to check on shipping movements and for notification of intentions. Vessels should keep clear of the main ship channel on the west of Yell Sound when traffic is expected.

Vessels under 300 ton GRT are exempt from pilotage requirements. Very large oil tankers and LPG carriers making to and from Sullom Voe Oil Terminal can frequently be encountered in Yell Sound. Accordingly, attention is drawn to the International Regulations which require that a vessel of less than 20m in length or a sailing vessel shall not impede the passage of a vessel which can safely navigate only within a narrow channel or fairway.

Tide

In Yell Sound:

South-going stream starts −0525 Lerwick (−0530 Dover)
North-going stream starts +0105 Lerwick (+0100 Dover)

At the wide part of the Sound the spring rates are:

South-going 1½kn, North-going 2½kn

At the narrow part in the south of the channel the spring rate is 6–7 kn.

In the channel between Shetland Mainland and the south end of Yell and to the east of Samphrey Island the tidal streams run east and west starting about 1 hour later than those in the narrows at the south end of the sound.

When the tide is running full in either direction there is violent turbulence close to The Rumble.

A tidal eddy runs counter to both streams along the south coast of Yell Sound north of a line between Cloa Rock and Orfasay and extending to Holm of Copinsay.

East-going eddy stream starts −0455 Lerwick (−0500 Dover) and runs for 3 hours.

West-going eddy stream starts −0155 Lerwick (−0200 Dover) at a spring rate of 7kn.

There is considerable turbulence between the west-going eddy stream and the east-going main stream.

At Toft Pier:

Constant −0105 Lerwick (−0115 Dover)

Heights in metres

MHWS	MHWN	MTL	MLWN	MLWS
2·3	1·8	1·2	0·8	0·4

Passage

There are numerous islands, skerries, banks and dangerous rocks in the sound and care is required. These hazards can be avoided by following recognised channels.

The sound is extemely well marked and lit with many sectored and directional lights provided for commercial shipping. These can be seen in full detail on chart 3298 and are summarised on the adjacent plan.

The tidal streams are significant, especially towards the southern end, where they can reach 7 knots. A passage under sail can normally only be made with a fair tide.

Where the stream passes over shoal areas it is accelerated and causes turbulence which, in wind over tide conditions can cause severe overfalls. These are marked on the chart and in unsettled weather they should be given a wide berth.

The north entrance to the sound is over 3 miles wide and unobstructed apart from the islands of Muckle Holm and Little Holm, both of which can be passed on either side. In this wide part of the sound the streams are no more than 2 knots in both directions. However, in strong northwest winds against a north-going stream, particularly bad seas can be experienced at the northern entrance.

The south entrance is a little over 2 miles wide between Lunna Holm and Burra Ness, at the south end of Yell. Lying 2 miles within this entrance are the significant dangers of The Rumble, a low-lying rock with a beacon, and an adjacent drying rock 1 cable southeast of it. Due to the strong tides and consequent turbulence in the vicinity of The Rumble it should be given a wide berth in bad weather or bad visibility by using the channel west of Samphrey Island.

Note also Cloa Rock (LD 1·8m) lying ½ mile south-southwest of Muckle Skerry of Neapaback and the drying Burga Skerry 3 cables south of Burra Ness.

Approaching from the south, a short cut can be taken by passing inside Lunna Holm (p.123).

The central part of the sound between Little Holm and Samphrey Island contains many islands and there is a choice of channels: east or west. In moderate conditions either can be taken but in heavy weather holding towards the Mainland side of the sound and passing west of Samphrey Island, Bigga and Tinga Skerry and east of Lamba, will avoid the worst of the overfalls. Give all these islands, and Mio Ness on Mainland, a berth of at least 2½ cables.

Occasional anchorages in Yell Sound

There are a large number of voes opening off Yell Sound and many of these provide excellent anchorages which are described later. Smaller voes suitable for short daytime stops are:

Tofts Voe Much ferry traffic makes this an unpleasant anchorage.

Quey Firth Anchor in the centre of the bay on sand (see plan of Colla Firth p.119).

Firths Voe and *Orka Voe* have both been used as anchorages but major pipelines come ashore in them and they cannot be recommended.

Admiralty Chart
3282, 3298
Ordnance Survey
1,2,3

Looking from the village of North Roe towards the anchorage in the north bay of Burra Voe (northwest Yell Voe)

Colin Smith - Geograph

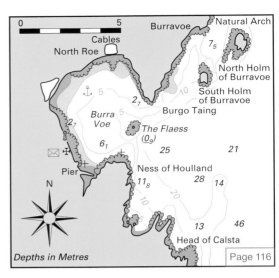

BURRA VOE, NORTHWEST YELL SOUND

Burra Voe (northwest Yell Sound)

On the west of Yell Sound, 3½ miles south of Point of Fethaland. Locally known as North Roe.

Directions

Outside and just north of the entrance, North Holm and South Holm have foul ground between and inshore of them. Keep at least 3 cables offshore to clear them. The approach requires attention to the tidal streams in Yell Sound.

In the middle of the entrance lie drying rocks (The Flaess), with navigable water on either side. On the south side of the entrance there is foul ground inshore and the north passage is recommended.

Entering Burra Voe keep less than ½ cable off Burgo Taing, the north point of the entrance. This shore is clear of dangers.

There is a rocky patch close northwest of the pier in the southwest corner. The southwest shore is shoal.

Anchorage

The north bay of the voe is the best anchorage.

Admiralty Chart
3281, 3282, 3298
Ordnance Survey
1, 2

Southladie Voe

A narrow and shallow inlet in Yell Sound on the east shore of Yell Sound and 2¼ miles north of Ness of Sound Light.

Directions

The depth is 3–4m or less but the shores are clean. This is a good anchorage except in south winds. Towards the head of the voe, Urabug, a shingly ayre, runs out from the east shore leaving a narrow passage through to a landlocked pool. As there is only 0·6m in the channel and less than 1·5m in the pool, anchoring here is only for shoal draught craft.

SOUTHLADIE VOE

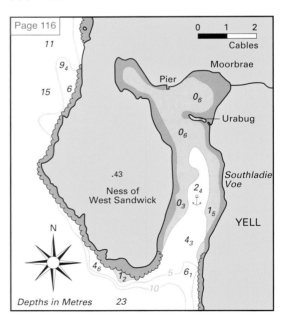

Southladie Voe from the north with the shingle ayre of Urabug on the right

Robbie Work - Geograph

Colla Firth (Yell Sound)

On the Mainland shore 6 miles south of Point of Fethaland.

Directions

Give the shores on each side of the entrance a berth of at least 1 cable to clear sunken rocks. At night keep in the white sector of Lamba (S) Light to clear the rock on the south side at the Ness of Queyfirth.

Anchorage

The best yacht anchorage is off the pier at Collafirth Brig but leave space for large trawlers to berth. Otherwise anchor anywhere on the west shore giving shelter from west winds. The southwest arm is a pleasant anchorage although weed may be a problem. Convenient for climbing Ronas Hill.

Alternatively it may be possible to berth inside the pier ☎ 01806 544296, the outside of which is used by the trawlers.

Collafirth Marina This is a small boat marina and has a berth for visitors but check first for availability ☎ 01806 533288. Depth 2m max.

Facilities

Water from hose at pier. Waste disposal. Slip. Electricity can be arranged at marina. Bus and taxi service.

Bay of Ulsta

This is in the southwest of Yell. The terminal for the RoRo ferry from Tofts on Mainland Shetland is here.

Ulsta Marina adjacent to the ferry terminal. Depth 2·3m max. Toilets at ferry terminal. Shop, Post Office and fuel.

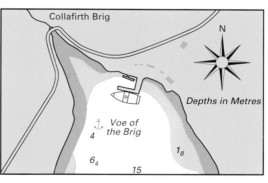

COLLA FIRTH, YELL SOUND

Admiralty Chart
1233, 3281, 3282, 3298
Ordnance Survey
2, 3

COLLA FIRTH MARINA

Collafirth Marina on Yell Sound

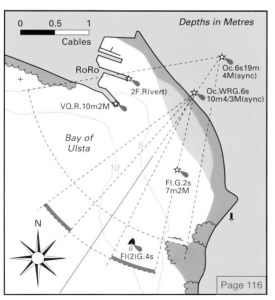

BAY OF ULSTA

Barbara MacLeod

Page 116

Ollaberry

Otter Hadd

South Head

LAMBA
Fl.WRG.3s8/5M
Dir.Fl.WRG.3s10/7M

Brother Isle

43

47

14

4₆

42

14

15

22

34

39

Tinga Skerry
Q(2)G.10s9m5M

Pier

Bay of Ollaberry
East Ness

45

35

32

21

Sligga Skerry

Gluss Voe

43

Trumba

43

Fl(3)WR.10s
16m5/4M

Little Roe

37

32

40

20

F.39m19M
Grunn Taing

No.5
Fl.G.2s

40

21

16

Mio Ness
Q(2)WR.10s7/4M

R Fl.R.6s

Yarfils Wick

Gluss Isle

43

Fl(4)Y.12s

Skaw Taing
Fl(2)WRG.5s
21m8-5M

Swarta Taing

North Gluss

Tivaka Taing

No.4
Fl(3)G.4s

Fl(4)Y.12s

Roe Clett

Brough

Boom
Fl(4)Y

35

Calbeck Ness

Fl(2)5s
35m8M

Orka Voe

Ness of Bardister

43

26

Brei Wick

Sullom Voe

The Kames

25

Dale Voe

No.2
Fl(2)G.5s

26

Sullom Voe
Oil Terminal

Iso.4s27m14M

The Houb

6₅

VQ(2)s

5₆

No.1
Fl.G.2s

26

Fugla Ness

4₄

Ungam

22

Fl.Y.2s

Fl(4)Y.12s

23

Q.G.

Sullom

16

26

20

Voe of Scatsta

Garths Voe

Gaza Jetty

23

Booms

Sella Ness
DirOc.WRG.10s16-3M

Markiness

Houb of Lunnister

Ness of Haggrister

Spit

21

The Narrows

Fl(4)Y.12s
Booms

Bight of Haggrister

Voxter Voe

Mavis Grind

20

41

Ell Wick

41

Brae

N

Depths in Metres

0   1   2

Nautical Miles

The tanker 'Hanne Knutsen' at Sullom Voe terminal. This is not a viewpoint that the sailor following these Directions is likely to experience

John Bateson - Geograph

Sullom Voe

A 6½ miles deep-water voe running south-southwest from Yell Sound to the narrow isthmus of Mavis Grind which separates it from Culsetter Minn, a voe off St Magnus Bay.

The entrance to Sullom Voe, as far as the village of Sullom, is part of an industrial complex but south of Sullom the attractive scenery of Shetland reasserts itself.

Yachts entering Sullom Voe must report to the Port Controller on VHF Ch 14 to check on shipping movements and for notification of intentions.

Tide

Constant –0130 Lerwick (–0140 Dover)

Heights in metres

MHWS	MHWN	MTL	MLWN	MLWS
2·1	1·7	1·2	0·7	0·3

Directions

For approaches see Yell Sound (p.117).

The entrance is between Calback Ness and Gluss Isle.

The Fl(4)Y buoys shown on the plan of Sullom Voe are positioned to assist in the laying of booms when there is a threat of oil pollution.

The shores of Sullom Voe are clean beyond ½ cable offshore apart from Ungam, a group of above-water rocks, northeast of Fugla Ness. There is 4m depth 1 cable off the visible rocks between Ungam and the shore to the west.

Keep well to the west side of the entrance and pass west of Ungam. Between Ungam and Sella Ness is the tanker swinging area and this should not be entered.

Three miles further south the channel is narrowed to under 2 cables by The Spit extending 1 cable off the west shore. Thereafter the voe widens with Voxter Voe to the east, Bight of Haggrister to the west and Ell Wick to the south.

Anchorage

There are two temporary anchorages in the outer voe, south of Gluss Isle and Dale Voe, but the better anchorages are to be found further in, south of The Narrows.

Voxter Voe is shoal at the head. Anchor one third of the way in, in 4–5m mud and gravel. Good holding but wind funnels down the voe in east and northeast winds.

Ell Wick Anchor in 6m in the centre of the bay, mud and gravel.

Bight of Haggrister Anchor as shown on the plan.

Facilities

At Brae, which is less than a mile from the anchorages in Voxter Voe and Ell Wick (p.110).

Gluss Voe and Bay of Ollaberry

Gluss Voe lies on the west side of Yell Sound just north of the entrance to Sullom Voe. It is very deep, the shores are steep-to except where there are rocks on either hand inshore of ½ cable. The Bay of Ollaberry lies just north of the entrance to Gluss Voe.

Directions

There are no dangers in the approach to Gluss Voe and the tidal streams in this part of Yell Sound do not exceed 2kn. At night keep within the red sector of Lamba Light until well into the voe.

Anchorage

Gluss Voe Good anchorage can be found in the pool at the head which gives shelter from all weather. It is a good place to wait for the tide when heading east through the narrows of Yell Sound. Anchor in the pool in 4–12m; sand. At the west end, the pool dries and there is a large shoal area. Generally good holding.

Bay of Ollaberry offers good shelter from westerly weather. Anchor at the head of the bay in 5m. Stores, Post Office.

Admiralty Chart
3297, 3281, 3282, 3298
Ordnance Survey
2, 3

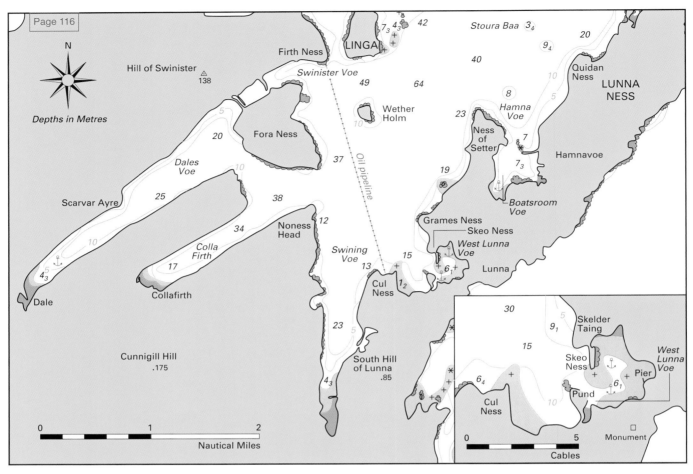

N

Depths in Metres

Firth Ness

Hill of Swinister △ 138

Swinister Voe

Fora Ness

Dales Voe

Scarvar Ayre 25

Colla Firth

Dale

Collafirth

Cunnigill Hill .175

Noness Head

Swining Voe

Cul Ness

South Hill of Lunna .85

Wether Holm

Oil pipeline

LINGA

Stoura Baa

Quidan Ness

LUNNA NESS

Hamna Voe

Ness of Setter

Hamnavoe

Boatsroom Voe

Grames Ness

Skeo Ness

West Lunna Voe

Lunna

Skelder Taing

Skeo Ness

Cul Ness

Pund

West Lunna Voe

Pier

Monument

0   1   2
Nautical Miles

0   5
Cables

DALES VOE, WEST LUNNA VOE (INSET) & HAMNA VOE

Admiralty Chart
3282, 3295-6

Ordnance Survey
2, 3

Looking over the West Lunna Voe pier towards the anchorage and The Pund

Robbie Work - Geograph

Dales Voe (Yell Sound)

Dales Voe and Colla Firth share a common entrance on the south side of Yell Sound 5 miles inside the east entrance. Colla Firth is narrow and deep and exposed to the east and so is not recommended.

Directions

Halfway up Dales Voe on the northwest shore a spit extends ½ cable off the point of Scarvar Ayre. Otherwise the shores are clean. Many mussel farms.

Anchorage

Dales Voe offers good holding and shelter from swell but is liable to severe gusts in strong westerlies. Anchor southwest of Scarvar Ayre in 5–15m. Excellent holding in mud.

West Lunna Voe

On the west side of the narrowest part of Lunna Ness.

Directions

From the northwest head for West Lunna Voe keeping clear of the rock ¾ cable northwest of Cul Ness. When abreast of Skelder Taing alter course towards the point of Skeo Ness.

When ½ cable off the shore steer south towards the east side of Pund to avoid a drying rock ½ cable off the northwest of Pund. When due east of the point of Pund turn southeast and follow the coast about ½ cable off avoiding the rock south of Skeo Ness.

The passage through to the inner pool is restricted to less than 1 cable. Great care is required in negotiating this passage and manoeuvring within the pool as the north part is shoal for up to 2 cables offshore and there are rocks off the east shore.

Anchorage

About ½ cable offshore below the monument (tower) in 10–12m or to the east of Skeo Ness.

Interest

This was the original base for the 'Shetland Bus' operations to occupied Norway during the second world war.

Hamna Voe (Lunna Ness); Boatsroom Voe

Hamna Voe is on the west side of Lunna Ness, 2 miles southwest of the north point of Lunna Ness. The village of Hamnavoe is in Boatsroom Voe which is separated from the outer Hamna Voe by a shingle ayre forming a natural breakwater.

Directions

The approach is clear from the north with the exception of Stoura Baa, a shallow patch 5 cables northwest of Quidan Ness. The west shore of Lunna Ness should be given a berth of over 1 cable as it is shoal and foul.

The ayre extends west from the east shore with an extensive drying reef extending north northwest from the end of the breakwater. This restricts the passage into Boatsroom Voe to ½ cable. Hold towards Ness of Setter to clear the reef.

Anchorage

Anchor in the southwest bay of Boatsrooom Voe. Good holding. There are rocks off the southeast shore and the east is shoal.

Robbie Work - Geograph

Directions

Heading north pass between Lunna Holm and Sand Skerry (1m) holding a northerly course in mid channel (depth 3·7m) but do not turn west until three quarters way up the Lunna Holm shore in order to avoid the dangerous rock lying 1 cable northwest of Sand Skerry. (This rock lies northeast of a skerry which has a height of 0·3m.) If proceeding south approach the passage between Lunna Holm and Sand Skerry from the northwest holding well towards the north of Lunna Holm.

The shingle ayre dividing Hamna Voe from Boatsroom Voe, on the left, and protecting the anchorage in the latter

Admiralty Chart
3282, 3284

Ordnance Survey
2, 3

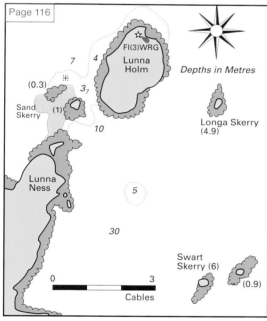

Page 116

Fl(3)WRG
Lunna Holm

Depths in Metres

7 4
(0.3) ※
3 7
Sand Skerry
(1)
10
Longa Skerry (4.9)

Lunna Ness

5

30

Swart Skerry (6)
(0.9)

0 3
Cables

LUNNA HOLM

The pier, storehouse, and, on the horizon, Lunna House, which in the early years of WW2 was the headquarters of the 'Shetland Bus' operation

Lunna Holm

When entering or leaving Yell Sound from the south some distance can be saved, and the tidal conditions north of Lunna Holm (off the northeast point of Lunna Ness) avoided, by taking the inside passage to the southwest of Lunna Holm.

Tides

In the southeast entrance to Yell Sound off Lunna Ness:
The west-going stream starts at HW Lerwick (–0050 Dover)
The east-going stream starts at +0500 Lerwick (+0450 Dover)
North of Lunna Holm the tide sets strongly and a steep sea is likely.

Robbie Work - Geograph

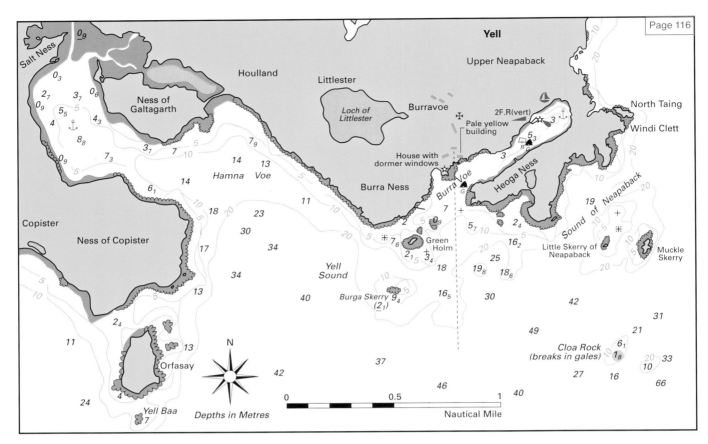

Depths in Metres

Nautical Mile

Admiralty Chart
3282, 3292, 3298
Ordnance Survey
1, 2, 3

Burravoe (Southeast Yell Sound)

Burravoe lies just inside the east entrance to
Yell Sound on the Yell shore.

Tide

Constant –0030 Lerwick (–0040 Dover)

Heights in metres

MHWS	MHWN	MTL	MLWN	MLWS
2·3	1·8	1·4	0·9	0·4

Directions

There are many dangers in the approach to the
entrance and these are clearly shown on Chart
3292 and the plan above.

The voe is approached between a drying reef
northeast of Green Holm and rocks southwest
of Heoga Ness. The leading line through this
channel bears due north. It is defined by a
point midway between two doors of a grey two
storey house and the midway position between
the east end of a white house with four dormer
windows and the west end of a pale yellow
building (see photo below).

When the voe is fully open to the northeast
alter course to pass over the bar (depth 2·5m)
leaving a green buoy to starboard.

To reach the pier and marina in the inner
part of the voe, pass between the red and green
buoys where the channel is narrow (depth 3m).

Anchorage

Anchor at the head of the voe where indicated
on plan. Good holding in mud. Alternatively
berth alongside the substantial pier at the head
of the voe or on the end berth of the marina
where there is 1·75m at LWS.

Facilities

Burravoe Pier Trust has a building close to the
marina with very good facilities: toilet,
showers, laundry.
Marina electricity, fresh water, waste disposal
at caravan park, slip, fuel by arrangement.
℡ 01957 722315.
Old Haa, Burravoe musuem, heritage centre
and café.

Burra Voe leading line

Hamna Voe (South Yell)

An inlet on the southwest of Yell on East Yell Sound (see plan p.124). The entrance is 1 mile west of Burra Voe.

Directions

Rocks extend 3 cables south of Burra Ness on the east of the entrance. Orfasay Island on the west side, is foul to the east and south for 2 cables. Once inside the entrance there are no dangers.

Anchorage

In the inner part above the narrows in 8–10m; good holding. It is open to the southeast.

The pontoons at Burravoe Marina with the anchorage beyond

Edward Mason

Barbara Macleod

Burravoe, Yell, shore facilities

Patrick Roach

Burra Voe, southeast Yell with Hamna Voe in the distance

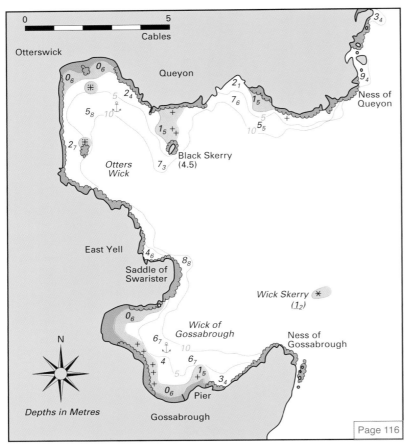

WICK OF
GOSSABROUGH &
OTTERS WICK

Wick of Gossabrough; Otters Wick

On the east side of Yell, approximately half way between Heogha Ness and Mid Yell Voe, a large bay, wide open to the east, opens up between Ness of Gossabrough and Ness of Queyon. This offers two occasional anchorages.

Directions

Entering the bay, especially from the south, care must be taken to avoid the unmarked Wick Skerry (drying 1·2m) which lies ¼ mile north-northeast of the Ness of Gossabrough.

Further in to the bay, Black Skerry (4·5m) lies 2 cables off the north shore and should be left to starboard.

Anchorage

Wick of Gossabrough Approaching from the south, hold to the Ness of Gossabrough, which is steep-to, to pass inside Wick Skerry. Anchor in the centre of the bay in 6m.

Otters Wick is the bay in the northwest corner. Entering the bay, do not pass inside Black Skerry which is foul, and anchor well offshore to avoid drying rocks extending a cable off the west and north shores.

Mid Yell Voe with Fetlar on the horizon

Patrick Roach

Mid Yell Voe

Lying half way up the east coast of Yell behind the island of Hascosay this voe offers good anchorages and facilities.

Tide

Constant –0030 Lerwick (–0040 Dover)

Heights in metres

MHWS	MHWN	MTL	MLWN	MLWS
2·4	1·9	1·5	1·1	0·6

Directions

The approach from the south is clear through South Sound and from the north through Hascosay Sound. Coming from the east, Baa of Hascosay, 3½ cables south of Ba Taing and connected to Hascosay by a rocky ledge, should be given a good offing to the south.

Mid Yell Voe extends 2 miles west but the head dries for nearly 5 cables. The south shore is foul from Ness of Lussetter at the entrance almost to the pier at Mid Yell. Keep at least 1 cable off. Further west the shore shoals. Kay Holm lies on the north side of the entrance. Keep south of this where there are no outlying dangers. The north shore is clear to where the voe widens.

Anchorage

There is good anchorage anywhere in the inner part of the voe in 2·5–10m. Good holding to north of marina in 6m between south shore and mussel farm. If anchoring off the pier at Mid Yell beware of shallows northeast of the pier. It should be possible to lie alongside the pier which is 90m in length and depth 2–3·5m.

Alternatively, for vessels with draught not exceeding 1·5m there is a small marina for one larger or two smaller visiting boats in the inner part of the voe. (☎ 01957 702317).

There is a sandbank to east of the marina entrance. Stay 1 cable off-shore until you reach the entrance then turn in. Keep to the breakwater side as that is the deep side.

Facilities

Mid Yell Shop and Post Office (1 mile), leisure centre and swimming pool, taxi service, car hire.

Marina Water, electricity, waste reception, red diesel available by arrangement. Boating Club open Fri and Sat 7pm – 1am.

Basta Voe

On the east coast of Yell 2 miles north of Mid Yell Voe. One mile from the head, the deep water channel is narrowed by a shingle bank off a point on the northeast shore.

Anchorage

Beyond the shingle bank there is good sheltered anchorage off the pier in 5–15m. Good holding in places has been reported.

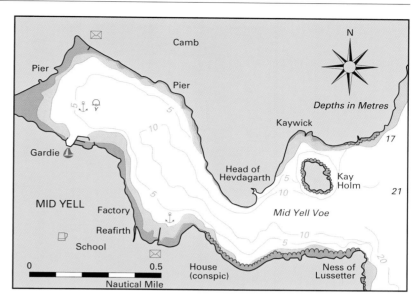

MID YELL VOE

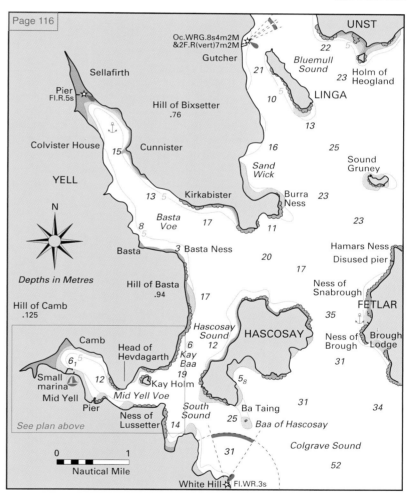

**BASTA VOE AND
MID YELL VOE**

Admiralty Chart
3282, 3292, 3298
Ordnance Survey
1, 2, 3

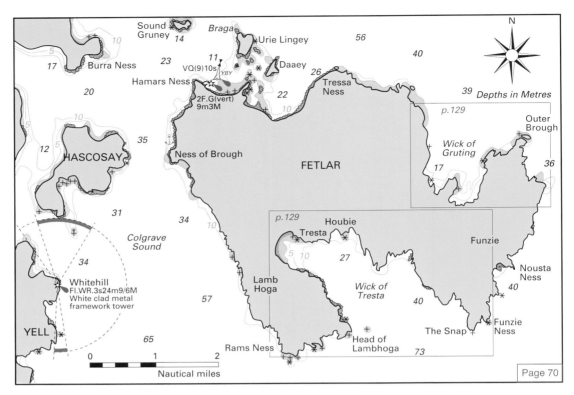

FETLAR

Admiralty Chart
3282, 3292

Ordnance Survey
1, 2

Fetlar

Fetlar lies 7 miles north of the entrance to Yell Sound. There are many magnetic anomalies in the area, particularly in the vicinity of the Wick of Tresta.

Tide

In Colgrave Sound:
South-going stream starts -0400 Lerwick (–0405 Dover)
North-going stream starts +0215 Lerwick (+0210 Dover)
Spring rates in the channels to the east and west of Hascosay are 2kn.

Hamars Ness

Just east of Hamars Ness at the northwest corner of Fetlar is the ferry terminal.

Directions

Approach from north and west is clear. If approaching from the east pass at least 2 cables off Braga, the skerry north of Urie Lingey. Do not pass east or south of Urie Lingey as this is foul ground and encumbered with obstructions.

A west cardinal buoy, Q(9)10s, marks shallows to the east of the terminal. End of breakwater has Iso.G.6s and ferry pier 2FG(vert).

Anchorage

There is an extensive breakwater within which is a 40m quay sheltered from all normal summer weather. Depths from 4–5·5m. Good vertical rubber fendering but a stout fender board is essential. Do not berth on the inside of the RoRo jetty without permission as this is used by the stand-by ferry.

Facilities

Toilets at ferry waiting room. Ferry to Gutcher (Yell) and Belmont (Unst). Water is not available. Easy walk to Brough Lodge but a long hike to Houbie.

Brough Lodge

On the west coast of Fetlar at Ness of Brough.

Directions

It lies in the narrow part of Colgrave Sound opposite Hascosay. It is easily recognised by the prominent buildings and the adjacent tower.

The approaches from north and south are clear of dangers.

Anchorage

Temporary anchorage in favourable winds. Anchor north of Ness of Brough, off the pier, below the tower, in 4–6m. This is out of the tide and the holding is good.

Do not anchor south of Ness of Brough as there are submarine cables.

Wick of Tresta

A large bay on the south shore of Fetlar.

Directions

There is a rock close south of The Snap, the east point of the entrance and a rock 2 cables east of Head of Lambhoga, the point at the west entrance to the bay.

Within the entrance the shores should be given an offing of 1 cable. The head shoals for over 2 cables out from the beach.

Anchorage

If the wind has west or north in it anchoring in the west of the Wick of Tresta offers good shelter. Anchor in 6–8m. Good holding. A temporary anchorage may be had off Houbie. Use a tripping line.

Wick of Gruting

A bay on the northeast of Fetlar sheltered from the south. The shores are foul up to 1 cable off. There is good anchorage in 10m east or west of Ness of Gruting. Landing is difficult in the west arm.

Interest

Ornithology including red-necked phalarope, RSPB Sanctuary and Fetlar Interpretive Centre (May – Sept) on the east side of the island at Funzie.

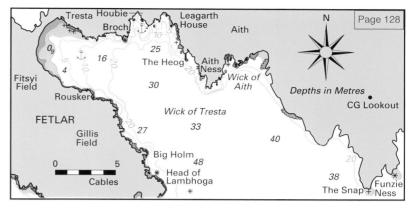

WICK OF TRESTA, FETLAR

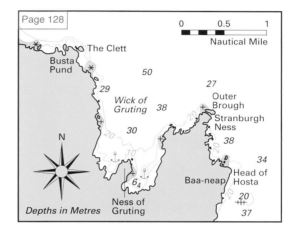

WICK OF GRUTING, FETLAR

The Wick of Tresta

Mike Pennington - Geograph

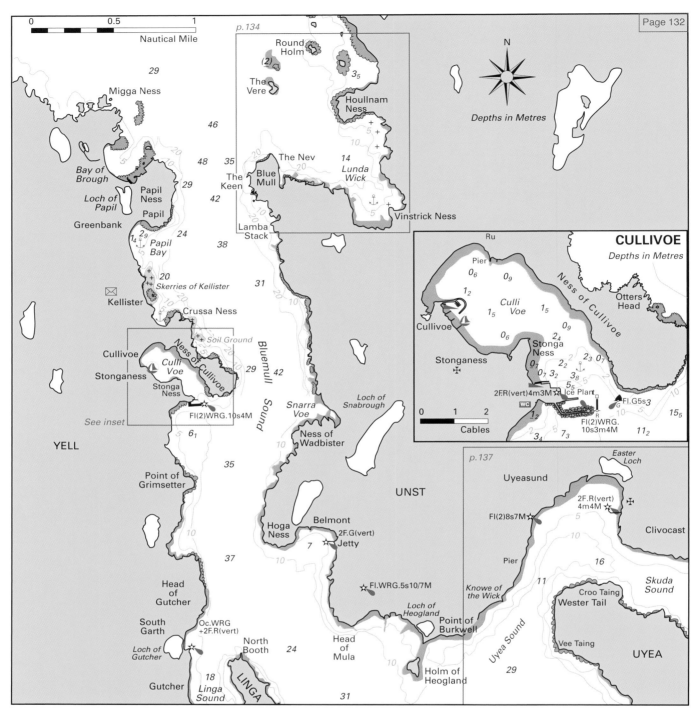

Page 132

CULLIVOE
Depths in Metres

BLUEMULL SOUND

Bluemull Sound

Admiralty Chart
3282, 3292, 3292-1
Ordnance Survey
1

Bluemull Sound is between Yell and Unst. It is reported that there are uncharted rocks off the west coast of Unst in Bluemull Sound north of Snarra Voe.

Tide

In the south entrance to Bluemull Sound:
South-going stream starts +0605 Lerwick (+0600 Dover)
North-going stream starts –0025 Lerwick (–0030 Dover)
Spring rates in the narrower parts 6–7kn

In Bluemull Sound:
South-going stream starts –0425 Lerwick (–0430 Dover)
North-going stream starts +0135 Lerwick (+0130 Dover)
Spring rates in the narrower parts 6–7kn

North of the Ness of Cullivoe large breaking waves can occur in Bluemull Sound when the north-going tidal stream meets an ocean swell. These conditions can be very dangerous for yachts.

During the south-going stream an eddy forms west of a line between Ness of Cullivoe and Point of Grimsetter with turbulence at the stream boundaries.

At springs, races form off salient points on both sides of the sound.

Constant –0140 Lerwick (–0150 Dover)

Heights in metres

MHWS	MHWN	MTL	MLWN	MLWS
2·6	1·9	1·5	1	0·5

Barbara MacLeod

Culli Voe

A shallow voe on the Yell shore (see plan p.130) with a busy fishing harbour at its mouth, 2 miles from the north entrance to Bluemull Sound.

Directions

Tidal eddies can make the approach to Culli Voe tricky but not difficult. With the south-going stream in the sound a north-going eddy can run across the approach requiring careful monitoring of set.

A green starboard hand buoy and a red post off the end of the breakwater mark the channel leading towards the pier and anchorage area beyond. There is a conspicuous ice plant on the west side of the entrance to the voe.

Anchorage

Alongside berths at the pier may be available with depth 6m. Alternatively, anchor as far up the voe as depth permits.

There is a small harbour with marina pontoons for shallow draught boats (1·2m) at the head of the voe (℈ 01957 744262). Visitors' berths are not normally available.

Papil Bay Fair shelter for temporary anchorage in the north and south ends of the bay, out of the tide, but avoid the centre of the bay which is strewn with rocks up to 1 cable off the shore. If entering the south end of the bay approach

from northeast heading for the centre of the bay keeping ½ cable off Crussa Ness.

Facilities

Pier Toilets, fresh water, and engineering services. Waste and waste oil disposal, repairs, chandlery, boat hoist (crane truck for hire).
Village Shop, Post Office, marine diesel, ℈ 01957 744248. Bus and taxi. Car hire.

Cullivoe Marina, North Yell

Culli Voe looking out to Bluemull Sound and Unst

Arthur Houston

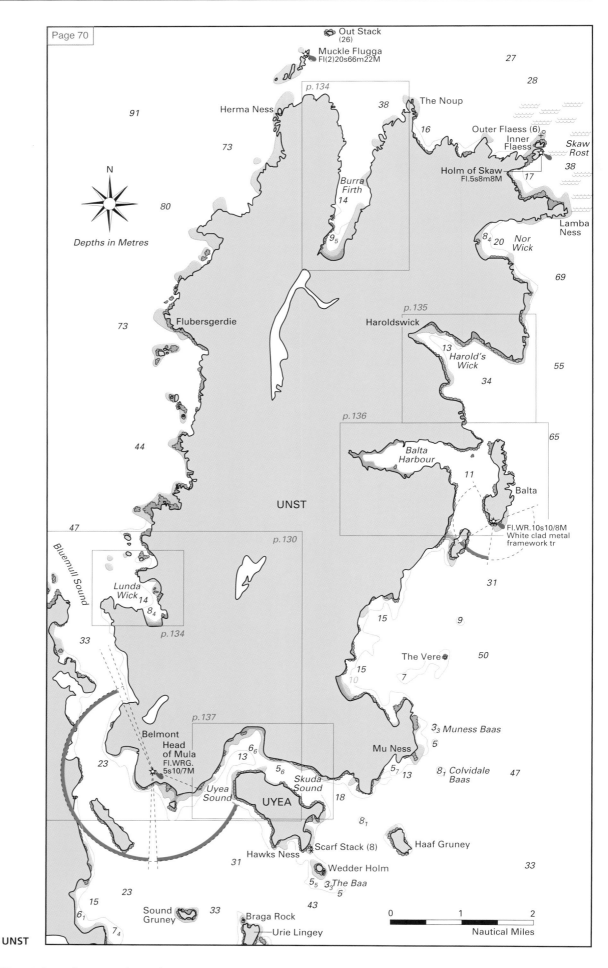

Page 70

Out Stack
(26)

Muckle Flugga
Fl(2)20s66m22M

27

28

91

Herma Ness

38

The Noup

16

Outer Flaess (6)

Inner
Flaess

Skaw
Rost

p.134

Burra
Firth

14

Holm of Skaw
Fl.5s8m8M

17

38

80

N

Lamba
Ness

73

Depths in Metres

9₅

8₄ 20

Nor
Wick

69

73

Flubersgerdie

p.135

Haroldswick

13

Harold's
Wick

55

73

34

p.136

44

Balta
Harbour

65

11

Balta

UNST

Fl.WR.10s10/8M
White clad metal
framework tr

47

p.130

Bluemull Sound

Lunda
Wick 14

31

8₄

15

9

p.134

33

The Vere

50

15

7

23

p.137

3₃ Muness Baas

Belmont
Head
of Mula
Fl.WRG.
5s10/7M

13

6₆

5

Mu Ness

5₆

Skuda
Sound

5₇ 13

8₁ Colvidale
Baas

47

Uyea
Sound

18

UYEA

8₁

Haaf Gruney

Hawks Ness

31

Scarf Stack (8)

Wedder Holm

33

5₅ 3₃ The Baa

23

5

43

15

Sound
Gruney

33

Braga Rock

0   1   2

6₁

Urie Lingey

Nautical Miles

7₄

UNST

Unst

Unst is the most northerly inhabited part of the UK. The are no fully sheltered anchorages on the north and west coasts.

There is a ferry terminus in southwest Unst at Belmont which operates to Gutcher on the east side of Yell and Hamars Ness on Fetlar.

Passage West of Unst

The northwest coast is spectacular with high cliffs and stacks. From Bluemull Sound to Flubersgerdie there are numerous islands, skerries and sunken rocks up to 8 cables offshore. This part of the coast should be given a very wide berth. From Flubersgerdie headland to Herma Ness there are no dangers more than 1 cable offshore.

Passage North of Unst

Muckle Flugga, one of a group of rocky islets, lies northwest of the entrance to Burra Firth and 1 mile north of Herma Ness, the most northerly point of Unst. Out Stack, 5 cables northeast of Muckle Flugga, is the most northerly point of the British Isles. During daylight, the passage may be made between Out Stack and Muckle Flugga. Likewise the passage between Herma Ness and the Muckle Flugga Group may be made during daylight provided that the visible rocks on either hand are given a berth of at least 1½ cables. A clearing line for the reef north of Herma Ness is The Noup open north of the Herma Ness shore.

Passage East of Unst

North of Holm of Skaw are the Inner and Outer Flaess extending 4½ cables north from the Unst shore with a reef extending 2 cables east of Outer Flaess. There is a bank 1½ miles north-northwest of Flaess which, with tide against wind (particularly northwest wind against north-going stream) causes dangerous breaking seas.

Lamba Ness lies on the north side of the entrance to Nor Wick at the northeast of Unst. The Skaw Roost forms between there and Holm of Skaw, one mile north-northwest. Confused seas are experienced most of the time but with the north-going stream the Roost is particularly dangerous.

Even in moderate weather this whole area should be given a berth of at least 3 miles. Fishing boats avoid the Roost by keeping close in to Lamba Ness and Holm of Skaw but this should not be attempted without advice.

For entrance to Balta Sound, see p.136.

2 miles south-southwest of Balta is a dangerous above water reef, The Vere, (0·2m) with banks north and south of it. To clear this, Balta lighthouse must bear not more than 010° until well north of The Vere. At night keep well in the white sector of the light. The coast north and south of Mu Ness (the southeast point of Unst) is foul up to 2 cables off so in bad weather keep well clear.

Colvidale Baas, lying 5 cables southeast of Mu Ness, is no obstacle in summer weather but seas break on Muness Baas (LD 4·4m, 5 cables northeast of Mu Ness) in northeast swell.

Passage South of Unst

Heading southwestwards pass 5 cables south of Wedder Holm to avoid The Baa before passing between the island of Sound Gruney and Braga Rock.

Alternatively make for the passage between Uyea and Wedder Holm holding well to the Uyea side of the channel but taking care to give Scarf Stack (8m), lying 1 cable off the Uyea shore, a good berth to avoid a sunken rock south of the stack. See Chart 3292.

Lights

Muckle Flugga (north end of Unst) Fl(2)20s66m22M
    White tower
Holm of Skaw (northeast point of Unst) Fl.5s8m8M
    White metal framework tower

Muckle Flugga

Admiralty Chart
1233, 3282, 3292
Ordnance Survey
1

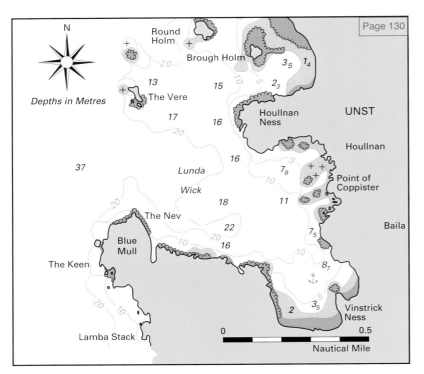

LUNDA WICK, UNST

Lunda Wick

Lunda Wick is on the west side of Unst, immediately to the northeast of the northern entrance to Bluemull Sound. It is convenient anchorage for awaiting a fair tide in Bluemull Sound or the right conditions to round Muckle Flugga

Directions

In the middle of the entrance lies The Vere, a small island with group of drying rocks (2m) 1½ cables north of it. Between these rocks and the shore is foul ground. Enter south of The Vere. The northeast of Lunda Wick is also foul.

Anchorage

At the head of Lunda Wick is the only suitable anchorage on the west coast of Unst. It is sheltered from the south and east but exposed to other directions. Good holding.

Muckle Flugga seen across the entrance to Burra Firth

Mike Balmforth

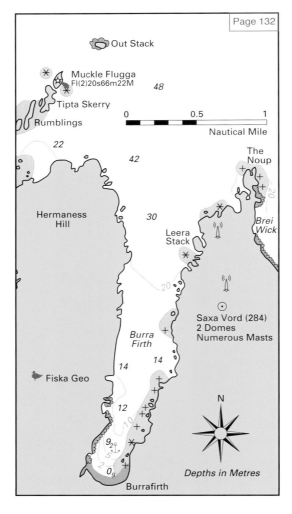

BURRA FIRTH, UNST

Burra Firth

The entrance to this long voe is 1½ miles southeast of Muckle Flugga and 2½ miles west of Holm of Skaw. It has high, steep-to, rocky shores and a wide sandy beach at the head. It is the most northerly anchorage in Britain and a good place to pause before returning south.

Tide

Constant –0110 Lerwick (–0125 Dover)

Heights in metres

MHWS	MHWN	MTL	MLWN	MLWS
2·5	1·9	1·5	0·9	0·5

Anchorage

It is exposed to the north but the holding is good and it may be used as an anchorage in settled conditions.

Interest

Hermaness Visitor Centre and National Nature Reserve. Outstanding bird life.

Nor Wick

The most northerly anchorage on the east coast of Unst, lying immediately south of Lamba Ness and the Skaw Roost.

Anchorage

Nor Wick can be used for temporary anchorage. The holding is good. It is untenable with any east in the wind.

Harold's Wick

This lies midway between Nor Wick and Balta Harbour.

Anchorage

Harold's Wick is exposed to the east and southeast. Keep mid-channel and anchor in the west end of the bay. Temporary anchorage only. Holding variable.

Facilities

Shop adjacent to Boat Haven.

Interest

The Unst Boat Haven, a maritime museum located near the old pier, is outstanding. Unst Heritage Centre. Hermaness Nature Reserve at Burra Firth.

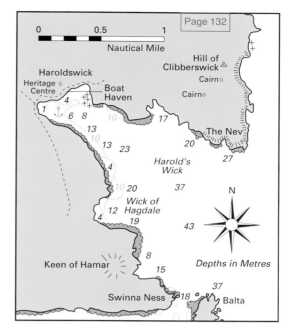

Admiralty Chart
3282
Ordnance Survey
1

HAROLD'S WICK, UNST

The Unst Boat Haven, Haroldswick

Burra Firth

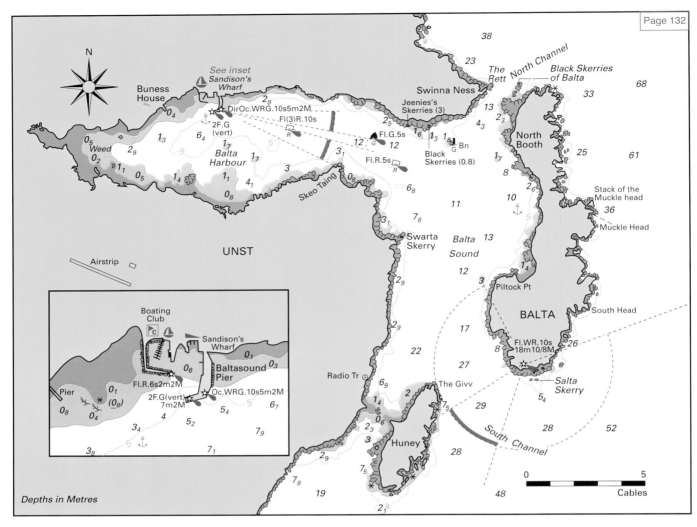

Depths in Metres

BALTA HARBOUR, UNST

Admiralty Chart
3299-1, 3282
Ordnance Survey
1

Balta Sound and Balta Harbour

Balta Sound and the voe which runs 1½ miles inland into Balta Harbour form a large, almost enclosed, area.

Tide

Constant –0055 Lerwick (–0110 Dover)

Heights in metres

MHWS	MHWN	MTL	MLWN	MLWS
2·4	1·9	1·5	1	0·5

Directions

South Channel The main channel into Balta Sound is 3 cables wide and normally provides safe and easy access but in strong southeast winds heavy seas build up in the entrance. Give the southend of Balta Island a wide berth at Salta Skerry where foul ground extends 1½ cables south.

On the east side of the Sound avoid the spit at Piltock Point.

On the west side Swarta Skerry, 6 cables north of Huney Island, also extends 1 cable offshore.

North Channel is less than ½ cable wide abreast of The Rett, the point of Swinna Ness,

but is deep. A rocky patch northeast of the Beacon to the south of Swinna Ness is the shallowest point – just under 5m. The channel is close to the Unst shore which can be approached up to ½ cable. An extended reef lies 1 cable off the Balta Island shore opposite The Rett. At the point on Balta Island east of the Beacon there is a reef extending 1 cable offshore. Pass east of the Beacon before making into the harbour.

Two red can buoys mark shallow patches and can be passed on either hand.

There are shoal stoney patches in the middle of the voe and it is very shoal towards the head. There are two skerries on the south side: one off the house opposite the pier and the other near the head.

Anchorage

Balta Sound and Balta Harbour provide the only shelter from all summer winds in Unst.

Anchor off the north shore, south west of the pier in 4–8m. Good holding in mud but care is needed to avoid patches of kelp. This is exposed to the east when better shelter will be found to the west of Balta Island.

Patrick Roach

Baltasound harbour and marina

Yachts can find a berth at the pier but it is not entirely suitable for small craft. Harbourmaster ☎ 07772 230754.

Baltasound Marina is a small boat marina but it is only suitable for shallow draft boats. Depth 1·5m. ☎ 01957 711444.

Facilities

Village Shop, hotel and pub, leisure centre (2 miles away), swimming pool, taxi, bus service, car hire.

Marina Showers, toilet, water, fuel, waste disposal, engineering services and repairs, boat yard, slip. Boating Club.

Interest

Ornithology, Hermaness Nature Reserve at Burra Firth.

The Unst Boat Haven and Unst Heritage Centre at Haroldswick is a 2½ mile walk.

Uyea Sound and Skuda Sound

Uyea island lies south of Unst. Uyea Sound is the passage between the northwest of Uyea and Unst. Skuda Sound is the passage between the northeast of Uyea and Unst.

Anchorages

Uyea Sound At the north end there is a wide bay, normally with extensive fish farming activities. Reasonable shelter can be had in winds west through north to east. Anchor to suit depth and wind direction.

Good shelter within a substantial 'L' shaped public pier but steel pilings not suited to yachts. 3·5–4m on inside of pier. Busy with commercial craft but berthing may be found alongside (with a fender board) or outside one of the many workboats. Water may be had by arrangement. End of jetty marked by 2FR(vert).

There is a small dock (only accessible at HW), toilets, telephone and a youth hostel.

Skuda Sound Anchor in the bight on the north side of Uyea Island where there is a small pier.

Mike Pennington - Geograph

Skuda Sound with Uyea behind the fish cages. Fetlar in the distance

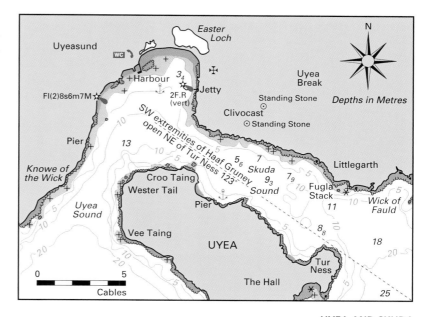

UYEA AND SKUDA SOUNDS, UNST

Appendix

Charts and other publications

Admiralty Charts

It is essential to carry paper copies of Admiralty charts aboard. It is up to the skipper to ensure that these will be adequate in the event of technical problems.

Below is a list of charts for the area. See also the Admiralty Chart Catalogue or the Chart Index opposite

1. Small scale

Number	Title	Scale
2182C	North Sea - Northern Sheet	1:700,000
1239	Orkney and Shetland Islands	1:350,000
1233	Northern Approaches to Shetland Islands	1:200,000
1954	Cape Wrath to Pentland Firth and Orkney Islands	1:200,000
1119	Orkney Islands, Fair Isle Channel	1:200,000
1942	Fair Isle to Wick	1:200,000
0115	Moray Firth	
0223	Dunrobin Point to Buckie	1:75,000
2249	Orkney Islands - Western Sheet	1:75,000
2250	Orkney Islands - Eastern Sheet	1:75,000
3283	Shetland Islands – South Sheet	1:75,000
3281	Shetland Islands – Northwest Sheet	1:75,000
3282	Shetland Islands – Northeast Sheet	1:75,000

2. Medium scale

Number	Title	Scale
2076	Loch Eriboll	1:17,500
1077	Approaches to Cromarty and Inverness Firth	1:20,000
1078	Inverness Firth	1:20,000
2162	Pentland Firth and Approaches	1:50,000
2581	Southern Approach to Scapa Flow	1:26,000
0035	Scapa Flow and Approaches	1:30,000
2584	Approaches to Kirkwall	1:25,000
3284	Moul of Eswick to Lunna Holm including Out Skerries	1:37,500
3294-2	Clift Sound and Approaches to Scalloway	1:25,000
3294-3	Seli, Sansound and Weisdale Voes	1:25,000
3295-1	Swarbucks Minn	1:25,000
3295-2	Vaila Sound and Gruting Voe	1:25,000
3295-3	Ura Firth	1:25,000
3295-4	Ronas Voe	1:25,000
3295-5	Bay of Quendale	1:25,000
3295-6	Dales Voe	1:25,000
3298	Yell Sound	1:30,000
3292	Eastern Approaches to Yell Sound	1:30,000

3. Large scale

Number	Title	Scale
1462	Harbours on the N and E Coasts of Scotland Fraserburgh, Banff, Macduff, Buckie, Nairn, Helmsdale, Wick, Scrabster	1:10,000
1078	Inverness Harbour	1:10,000
1889	Outer Cromarty Firth	various
1890	Inner Cromarty Firth	1:15,000
2568	Stromness and Hoy Sound, Lyness and Flotta Marine, Bay of Houton	various
1553	Kirkwall	1:12,500
2562	Pierowall Road and approaches, Sound of Rapness, Faray, Eday and Sanday	various
3271	Bressay Sound and approaches to Lerwick	1:10,000
3284-1	Symbister	1:7,500
3284-2	Out Skerries	1:7,500
3292-1	Cullivoe	1:7,500
3294-1	Scalloway	1:12,500
3294-4	Sand Wick and Hos Wick	1:12,500
3297	Sullom Voe	1:12,500
3299	Balta Sound, Housa Voe, West Burra Firth, North Haven Fair Isle, Fair Isle	various
1791	Caledonian Canal	various

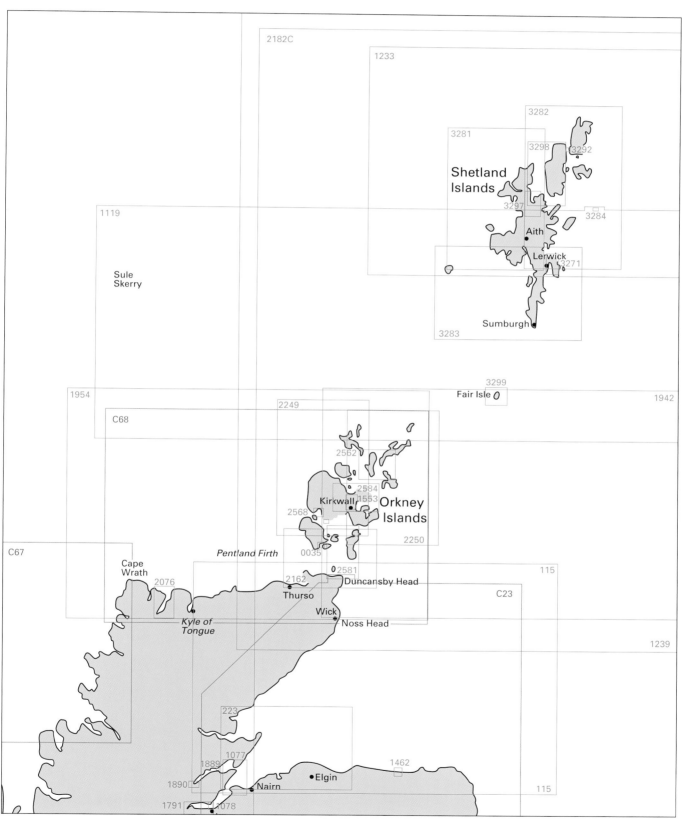

CHART INDEX

Imray charts

The area included in this book is covered by the following Imray C series of charts which are all drawn at around 1:150,000 scale (except where noted), with inset plans, on waterproof material, in folded format and sold in an acetate wallet at approximately A4 size. They can also be obtained flat by special request.

See the Chart Index on p.139 for the area covered by each chart.

C23 Fife Ness to Moray Firth
Includes Duncasnby Head to Inverness
C68 Cape Wrath to Wick & the Orkney Islands
Includes North Coast of Scotland and Orkney

Ordnance Survey Maps

The following 1:50,000 Landranger Maps are relevant to the area covered by these Directions:

OSL 1 Shetland - Yell, Unst & Fetlar
OSL 2 Shetland - Sullom Voe & Whalsay
OSL 3 Shetland - North Mainland
OSL 4 Shetland - South Mainland
OSL 5 Orkney - Northern Isles
OSL 6 Orkney - Mainland
OSL 7 Orkney - Southern Isles
OSL 9 Cape Wrath Durness & Scourie
OSL 10 Strath Naver
OSL 11 Thurso & Dunbeath
OSL 12 Thurso & Wick
OSL 17 Helmsdale & Strath of Kildonan
OSL 21 Doroch & Alness
OSL 26 Inverness & Loch Ness

Availability

Admiralty charts are available from Admiralty Chart Agents, which are established in most major ports and yachting centres in the UK. Imray are Admiralty Chart Agents and can supply Admiralty Charts, publications and products by post as well as, of course, their own publications. They also supply Ordinance Survey maps.

Admiralty Chart Agents in Scotland

ChartCo / Kelvin Hughes, Unit 5 St Luke's Place, Glasgow G5 0TS ✆ 0141 429 6462
Global Navigational Solutions, 27 Crown Terrace, Aberdeen AB11 6HD ✆ 01224 595 045
Caley Marine and Chandlery, Canal Road, Inverness, IV3 8NF ✆ 01463 236539
OBC Hay, 66 Commercial Road, Lerwick, ZE1 0NJ ✆ 01595 692533
The Rope Centre, 24 John Street, Stromness, KW16 3AD ✆ 01856 850646

Some other outlets, mostly larger marinas and yacht centres, will usually supply Admiralty charts, together with most of the Imray publications. They generally stock a good selection of local charts, although others will have to be ordered, sometimes at a premium.

Admiralty Publications

Admiralty Sailing Directions North Coast of Scotland Pilot North and North-east Coasts of Scotland from Cape Wrath to Rattray Head including the Caledonian Canal, Orkney Islands, Shetland Islands and Faroe Islands, 8th Edition, NP52 2012.

Admiralty Supplements for Sailing Directions and Notices to Mariners NP52

Admiralty Tide Tables United Kingdom and Ireland NP201 2015.

Admiralty Tidal Stream Atlas Orkney and Shetland Islands NP209

Admiralty Tidal Stream Atlas for North Sea - NW part, NP252

Admiralty List of Lights Vol. A,   British Isles and N Coast of France NP74

Other publications

Almanacs

The Cruising Almanac, Imray/Cruising Association
Reeds Nautical Almanac Adlard Coles

Sailing Directions for adjacent waters

Ardnamurchan to Cape Wrath, Clyde Cruising Club, Imray
Outer Hebrides, Clyde Cruising Club, Imray
The Yachtsman's Pilot, North and East Scotland, Martin Lawrence, Imray

General books

Orkney

Heart of Neolithic Orkney Miniguide, Charles Tait, Charles Tait Photographic, 2013
Monuments of Orkney, Caroline Wickham-Jones, Historic Scotland, 2012.
A New History of Orkney, W Thomson, Birlinn General, 2008.
Orkney: A Historical Guide, Caroline Wickham-Jones, Birlinn General, 2015 (ebook also)
The Orkney Guide Book, 4th revised edition, Charles Tait, Charles Tait Photographic, 2012.
The Peedie Orkney Guide, 4th edition, Charles Tait, Charles Tait Photographic, 2013. This is a shortened version of the *The Orkney Guide Book*.
The Other Orkney Book: Complete Pocket Guide, Gordon Thompson, Northabout Publishing, 1981.
The Scotttish Islands, Hamish Haswell-Smith, Canongate, revised and updated, 2015.
Orkney Book of Birds, T Dean, The Orcadian.

Shetland

Discover Shetland's Birds, Paul Harvey and Rebecca Nason, Shetland Heritage Publications, 2015.
Mirds o Wirds, A Shetland dialect word book, The Shetland Times, 2015.
Orkney and Shetland Islands Focus Guide. Footprint Travel Guides, 2nd edition, Alan Murphy, 2014.
Portrait of the Northern Isles (Orkney and Shetland). Graham Uney, Halsgrove, 2009.
Shetland from the Sea, Watercolours by Dutch yachtsman Dick Koopmans, The Shetland Times, 2014.
Shetland Islands, James A. Pottinger, The History Press, 2015.
Shetland, Jill Slee Blackadder, Iain Sarjeant (Illustrator), Colin Baxter Photography, 2007.
Shetland's Heritage of Sail, Charlie Simpson, The Shetland Times, 2011.
Small Boats of Shetland, Alison Munro, Centre for Nordic Studies and Unst Heritage Trust, 2012.
The Scotttish Islands, Hamish Haswell-Smith, Canongate, revised and updated, 2015.

The Shetland Bus, David Howarth, The Shetland Times, 1998. Famous world war two story.

The Shetland Guide Book, Charles Tait, Charles Tait Photographic, 2007.

The Sixareen and her Racing Descendants, Charles Sandison, The Shetland Times, 2007. History of this Shetland boat.

Walking the Coastline of Shetland, series of walking guides by Peter Guy, The Shetland Times.

Port Information

Orkney Ports Handbook, published by the Orkney Islands Council Marine Services Harbour Authority, gives useful information on all ports, harbours, moorings and piers in Orkney and the facilities available, together with contact information. It can be obtained direct from the Orkney Harbour Authority, Scapa, Orkney, KW15 1SD, ✆ 01856 873636, email. harbours@orkney.gov.uk

Ports of Scotland Yearbook published by Maritime Publications Ltd

Contact telephone numbers and websites

Imray Charts, Sailing Directions
✆ 01480 462 114
www.imray.com

Clyde Cruising Club
✆ 0141 221 2774
www.clyde.org

Transport

Citylink bus travel enquiries
✆ 0990 505050
www.citylink.co.uk

NetworkRail
✆ 03457 484950
www.networkrail.co.uk

Scotrail
✆ 0344 811 0141
www.scotrail.co.uk

NorthLink Ferries
✆ 0845 600 0449 Holmsgarth Ferry Terminal Lerwick)
www.northlinkferries.co.uk

Pentland Ferries
✆ 0800 688 8998
www.pentlandferries.co.uk

John O'Groats Ferries
✆ 01955 611353
www.jogferry.co.uk

Coastguard

Aberdeen Coastguard
✆ 01224 592334
www.aberdeencoastguardcrt.co.uk

Stornoway Coastguard
✆ 01851 702013
www.stornowaycg.co.uk

Shetland Coastguard
✆ 01595 629976
www.shetlandcoastguard.info
(HM Coastguard in the North of Scotland and the Northern Isles Unofficial Web Site)

Sailing Organisations

Sail Scotland
www.sailscotland.co.uk

RYA Scotland
✆ 0131 317 7388
www.ryascotland.org.uk

Association of Scottish Yacht Charterers
✆ 01852 200258

Orkney

Orkney Islands Council, Marine Services
✆ 01856 873636
www.orkneyharbours.com

Orkney Marinas Ltd
✆ 01856 871313
www.orkneymarinas.co.uk

Orkney Sailing Club's Visiting Yachts Information Brochure
www.orkneymarinas.co.uk/images/files/ OSC-yacht-brochure.pdf

VisitScotland Kirkwall
✆ 01856 872 856
www.visitscotland.com

Shetland

Shetland Islands Council Ports and Harbours
✆ 01595 693535
www.shetland.gov.uk/ports

Shetland Inter Island Ferries
✆ 01805 244200
www.shetland.gov.uk/ferries

Sullom Voe Harbour Authority
✆ 01806 244200

Lerwick Port Authority
✆ 0595 692991
www.lerwick-harbour.co.uk

Sullom Voe VTS
VHF Ch 14
✆ 01806 242344

Shetland Marinas
www.shetland.gov.uk/ports/yachting/
www.shetland.org/plan/marinas has pdf booklet

Shetland Webcams
e.g. Victoria Pier Lerwick Harbour
www.shetland.org/60n/webcams

Shetland Heritage
www.shetland-heritage.co.uk

The Shetland Times Bookshop
www.shetlandtimes.co.uk/shop

Orkney tidal streams

These tidal stream diagrams were prepared following the building of the Churchill Barriers in the early years of the second world war. They are centred on the Westray and Stronsay Firths and the islands and channels bordering them, together with Hoy Sound; these being the areas where the tidal streams were most affected by the barriers. They have never been published but local yachtsmen have found them to be helpful, although no responsibilty can be accepted for their accuracy.

Spring rates only are shown here.

Neap rates approximate to just under one half of the Spring rates where those exceed 2·3 knots, and to nearer one third of the Spring rate where the Spring rate is smaller.

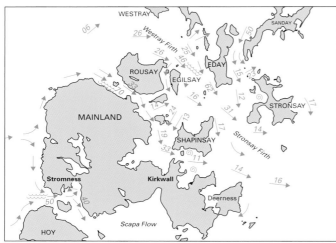

6 HOURS BEFORE HW ABERDEEN
3 HOURS 40 MINS BEFORE HW DOVER

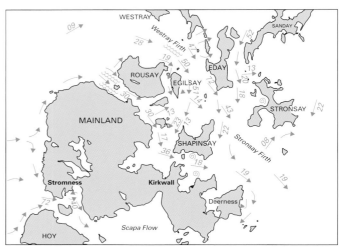

5 HOURS BEFORE HW ABERDEEN
2 HOURS 40 MINS BEFORE HW DOVER

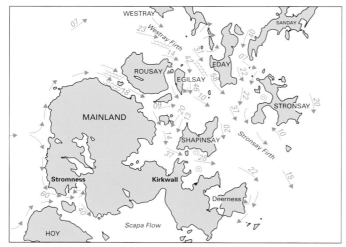

4 HOURS BEFORE HW ABERDEEN
1 HOUR 40 MINS BEFORE HW DOVER

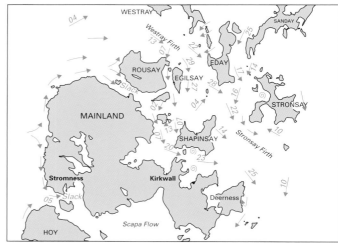

3 HOURS BEFORE HW ABERDEEN
40 MINS BEFORE HW DOVER

Spring rates only are shown here.
Neap rates approximate to just under one half of the Spring rates where those exceed 2·3 knots, and to nearer one third of the Spring rate where the Spring rate is smaller.

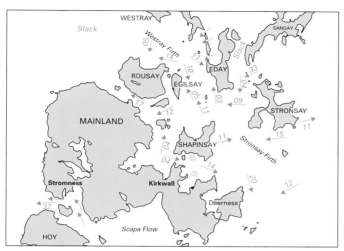

**2 HOURS BEFORE HW ABERDEEN
20 MINS AFTER HW DOVER**

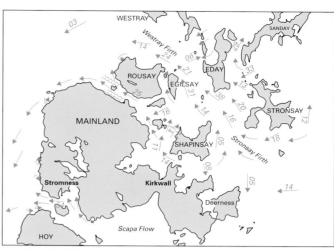

**1 HOUR BEFORE HW ABERDEEN
1 HOUR 20 MINS AFTER HW DOVER**

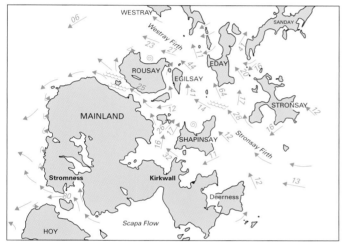

**HW ABERDEEN
2 HOURS 20 MINS AFTER HW DOVER**

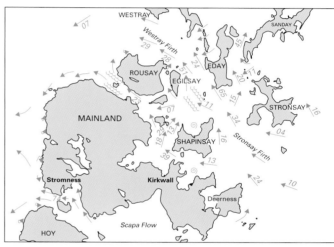

**1 HOUR AFTER HW ABERDEEN
3 HOURS 20 MINS AFTER HW DOVER**

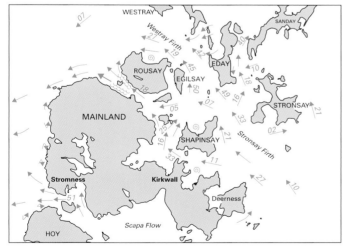

**2 HOURS AFTER HW ABERDEEN
4 HOURS 20 MINS AFTER HW DOVER**

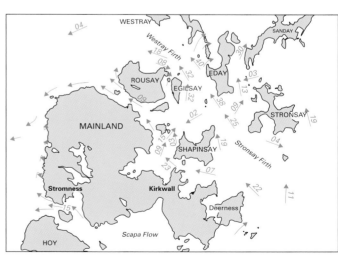

**3 HOURS AFTER HW ABERDEEN
5 HOURS 20 MINS AFTER HW DOVER**

Spring rates only are shown here.
Neap rates approximate to just under one half of the Spring rates where those exceed 2·3 knots, and to nearer one third of the Spring rate where the Spring rate is smaller.

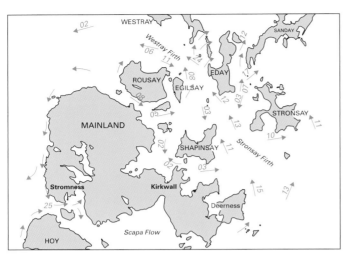

4 HOURS AFTER HW ABERDEEN
5 HOURS 40 MINS BEFORE HW DOVER

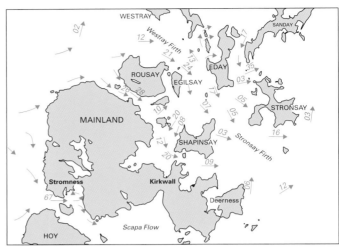

5 HOURS AFTER HW ABERDEEN
4 HOURS 40 MINS BEFORE HW DOVER

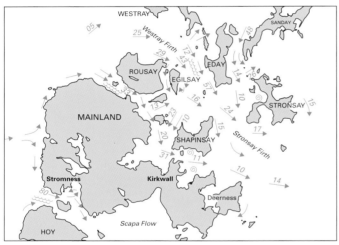

6 HOURS AFTER HW ABERDEEN
3 HOURS 40 MINS BEFORE HW DOVER

Spring rates only are shown here.
Neap rates approximate to just under one half of the Spring rates where those exceed 2·3 knots, and to nearer one third of the Spring rate where the Spring rate is smaller.

Glossary

Topography

Ayre	Sandy or shingly spit, bar or beach
Baa	Sunken rock on which the sea breaks
Broch, Brough	Pre-Norse fortification
Flaes	Above water flat rock
Fugla	Bird
Geo	Cleft in the cliffs; rocky creek into which the sea flows
Gloup	Tunnel or sea cave
Grind	Gate
Grund	Shoal
Haaf	Deep sea
Hamna	Voe of basin-like form
Holm	Islet
Lodberrie	Storehouse at the edge of the sea
Muckle	Large
Noost	Beach shelter for small boat
Noup	Headland
Papa	Priest
Peerie	Small
Roost (Rost)	Tide race
Skerry	Above water rocks
Skroo	Stack of oats built to withstand winter gales
Stack	Detached steep-sided rock in the sea
Sten	Stone
Taing	Rocky point
Ting	Law courts in Norse times
Tombolo	Narrow spit, normally sandy, that connects to an island
Voe	Sea inlet usually long and narrow
Ward (Wart)	Beacon or cairn on hilltop
Wick	Bay

Traditional Shetland craft

Sixern	Six-oar (or sail) fishing vessel of 18th and 19th centuries; of Norwegian design
Fifie Scaffie	Scottish type sail fishing vessels of the mid-19th century
Zulu	Scottish type sail fishing vessel of the late 19th century. Developed at the time of the Zulu War
Yoal	Small open boat of Norwegian design for inshore fishing now used in rowing races
Shetland Model	Double-ended clinker built boat of Viking ancestry used universally throughout Shetland for racing or propelled by oars or outboard engines for inshore fishing or pleasure

Sea birds

Bonxie	Great Skua
Dunter	Eider Duck
Haigrie	Heron
Liri	Manx Shearwater
Skarf	Shag
Tystie	Black Guillemot

Index

The rocks
don't move...

Maybe, but 'new' rocks are discovered and countless other things change. If you see anything, however minor, in these Directions that needs amending or updating please email the editor at:

sailingdirections@clyde.org

Clyde Cruising Club

the active heart of Scottish sailing

CRUISE - under your own steam or in company to musters and social events

RACE - The Scottish Series, The Tobermory Race and a regular programme of racing on the Clyde

TRAIN - learn at our own RYA Approved Training Centre – Bardowie Loch near Glasgow

SOCIALISE - at cruising musters, at the Ball, winter talks, at race events or simply meet fellow members in harbours and anchorages

SUPPORT - the Club in its work of preparing Sailing Directions and upholding the interests of cruising sailors in Scottish waters

WHY NOT JOIN?

THE CLYDE CRUISING CLUB
Suite 101,
Pentagon Business Centre
36 Washington Street.
Glasgow G3 8AZ
0141 221 2774
office@clyde.org
www.clyde.org